Dr. Walter Frostbight

CREOSOPHY

❧

WHY YOU EXIST

Published in 2018 by the Ancient Scottish Order of Creosophists

With the assistance of Lumphanan Press
9 Anderson Terrace, Tarland
Aberdeenshire, AB34 4YH
www.lumphananpress.co.uk

Printed & Bound by ImprintDigital.com, UK

ISBN: 978-1-9999039-7-8

Creosophy is dedicated to men and women, young and old, who have no idea how they came to be here or what the world is about.

"On the right reclined a man ... with a droopy grey moustache, large nose and wearing a silk smoking cap."

Contents

Editor's Foreword

A LIFETIME OF STUDY HAD FAILED TO PROVIDE ME WITH an understanding of the mystery of our existence. We invest so much in life and then die. How can that make sense? Since my search had been fruitless for so long I expected "Creosophy" to be another cul-de-sac. I was suspicious mostly because of its playful context and the humour of the characters – a kind of spoof on the Socratic Dialogue. Nonetheless, I found it had a far-reaching effect on my ideas and my life, and even now I return to it for contemplation. "Creosophy" is unusual in that it makes no claim to be true or reasonable; rather it is an adventure in imaginative thinking, and for all its being unorthodox, it is not only helpful but a pleasure to read. From my own experience, I remember the witticism, "It's not my stinking drinking that's got me thinking, but my stinking thinking that's got me drinking." This book played a significant role in the sorting out of my "stinking thinking".

How did this work come to light? It was thanks to my ancient Uncle Sagacious. Amongst the personal effects he left me in his Will some years ago, I discovered this handwritten manuscript and, pinned to it, the words, "I found this useful. You may too. Author unknown." However, the handwriting was hard to read and I put it aside for a rainy day. As a result, it stayed on my desk, only to become a bed for office paraphernalia, until one of my children came across it while he was visiting. He asked why I had not read it. Suitably chastened, I set to giving the work my consideration.

I found it was the story of a young retired army officer, emotionally and mentally disturbed by the recent War, who loses his way in the Scottish Highlands and comes upon a snowbound castle. He is invited by the owner to join his dinner party, during which he is introduced to Creosophy in a conversation that explores the classic riddles of our existence. The discussion tests the young man's habitual understanding of his self, his life and life after death. Finally his companions press upon him that their ideas are not for tepid intellectuals, but that they need to be acted on if they are to be understood, and the last chapter focuses on how to go about it.

A wise man once said a book is never finished until others read it. However, this work is not for everyone: it depends on what attitude you bring to the table. Those cemented exclusively to academic and Western intellectual disciplines or who depend on well-established source material will surely find it a waste of space; but for others less easily satisfied by convention – and the standard answers – its study should pay dividends.

Does the script fit into an established literary genre? Not really. It is eccentric; part philosophy, part psychology, part religion and part self-help. As for the Creosophists, what can I say? It is not clear how they originated, or whether they really exist. I suspect they do exist, meeting discretely in parts of Scotland, but we cannot know for certain. Who put this work together? Although an "Ewan Evriwun" is said to narrate it, this name was surely a literary conceit, and I rather suspect Dr. Frostbight was responsible, and have therefore given him the credit. While on the subject of credits, I thank my family of co-editors for their help in making the work presentable: my wife, Vicki, my two sons, Edward and Alexander, and Megan, my daughter-in-law, for her sterling work correcting my textual mistakes. As for the illustrations, I admit I added them myself after being piqued into action at von Lottowind's claim that philosophers do not laugh enough.

My hope is that you enjoy it, and like Uncle Sagacious, find the thoughts in this book useful. I encourage myself with the fantasy that one day you, too, will celebrate your imagination.

May 2018   *Robin Chapman Campbell*
                                                           Inverardoch
                                                                Doune
                                                            Perthshire
                                                            FK16 6EA

Aperitif

Part I

❦

Arrival

I PULLED ONTO THE VERGE. A ROADSIDE NOTICE WARNED that the usual route over the mountain was closed on account of the weather, and I could believe it: the sky looked menacing with that slightly yellowish tinge typical of an approaching snowstorm. Other cars passed me by, carrying on regardless, but I had no intention of imitating them – only fools blindly follow the herd. Nor, however, did I want to turn back; I had been travelling all day and longed to be home – preferably before nightfall. Was there an alternative route? I reached into the glove compartment to find my father's old touring map. On unfolding it, a quick scan showed there was indeed a turning ahead – to the left – that was narrower and a longer way round but which would avoid the pass. Although the fuel gauge was low, there was sure to be a petrol station sooner or later. It was worth the risk, and I set off.

The road turned out to be single-track. It wound endlessly up and down, over bogs, rocks, wild tumbling burns and heather. My pre-war Hillman struggled with the inclines and jolted and shook at each pot-hole – the tarmac had not been maintained for years. I shivered. The car had no heater, but I kept a travel rug handy and pulled it over to cover my legs, tightened my scarf and went back to gripping the cold steering wheel – regretting I had come without gloves. Meanwhile the afternoon changed to dusk, and I flicked on my headlamps. As the daylight faded I became aware that the route was gaining height – the last thing I wanted – and rain began lashing the windscreen, swept in by a North wind. I wondered how much further I had to go before I found the main road again, but my car's interior light was broken, so I had no way to check the map. Anyway, I now doubted it was accurate: judging by the distance I had covered, I suspected the cartographers had resorted to guesswork. It was possible this desolate region had never been surveyed.

The Scottish Highlands are said to be Europe's last wilderness, and with good reason. I passed no vehicles, no signs of life, no lights and no houses. Meanwhile the fuel gauge had dropped and the rain was turning to sleet – it could easily become snow. My expecting to get home that night had been over-optimistic, and it was now increasingly obvious I would need to find lodgings. But where? My tireless wipers swept away the wet for mile after mile and my eyes darted back and forth, searching the featureless night and the dark road twisting and turning and rising and falling in front. Then, without warning, rounding another bend and caught suddenly in the headlights, the road forked.

I braked. The Hillman took on a will of its own and swung wildly – the wheels must have locked on black ice. Luckily it came to stop without mishap, and I reversed back to read the sign. My heart sank: the post was missing – probably one of thousands removed as a tactic during the threat of German invasion. I rubbed my eyes. How much further could I go? I tapped the fuel gauge to make the needle jerk up from 'empty', but there was no response. This was not a time for indecision. I gambled and turned left – into the unknown.

Within a minute I was being led directly uphill, an incline so steep that the engine laboured even in first gear. One bend followed another with no chance of turning back. And as soon as I climbed, I faced what I had hoped to avoid: the sleet turned to snow, tossed in the headlights.

The tarmac was rough – possibly not even public – and turning white. Could it be a track taking me to a deserted quarry? Or, maybe, to a forest? Or would it simply peter out? My tyres began slipping. I pulled nervously at my collar. People are known to have died in situations like this. I should have followed the others on that main road after all. Although I had made wrong turns in my life, I had survived the war, and yet now here I was likely facing my end not as a hero on a battlefield, but frozen to death in a

*"And as soon as I climbed, I faced what I had hoped to avoid:
the sleet turned to snow, tossing in the headlights."*

wilderness – the victim of my stupidity. It was a relief when after rounding another corner the ground levelled, but by this time drifts were mounting on the road and the snow so thick it forced me to crawl.

I must have strayed from the road. My heart jumped: a wall was directly in front, and I stamped on the brake with the car coming to a stop only a yard away. Applying the handbrake, I closed my eyes and took deep breaths. It was a close shave. Feeling more composed after a moment, and with the wipers flicking flakes from side to side, I studied the stonework. The structure rose to maybe ten feet – cut stone, well built and too tall for a field boundary. Indeed, not far to the left I thought I made out the shape of an arch, which might have meant there was a courtyard and, with any luck, an abandoned farmhouse. I sat back, turned off the lights and the engine, closed my eyes again, settled my nerves and listened to the wind. Tempting as it was to go to sleep, I resisted – it was conceivable I might never wake up. I checked the time, but my watch had stopped – probably I had forgotten to wind it. It would be a long time until dawn.

Could there enough of this building still standing to provide shelter? There was only one way to find out. I patted the dashboard with my numb fingers, muttering, "Well done old girl," threw the travel rug across the passenger's seat, pressed the lever to my right and thrust my weight hard against the door. Suddenly it flew open, caught by the gale, at which I lost my balance and tumbled into the snow. Getting on my feet and scolding myself for being so clumsy, I brushed down my coat and slammed the door shut.

The blizzard roared amongst the trees. I raised the broad collar of my greatcoat, buttoned it, braced myself and stumbled forward to the wall to guide me to the archway. About ten paces to the left I found my guess had been correct: as far as I could make out, it was a carriage entrance with its gates hooked back. Encouraged, I pushed through the drifts and, once inside the courtyard put out my left hand to other side of the wall to direct me. After pressing on for some twenty yards with my frozen fingers brushing the rough surface, I found a corner turning me right, and on I shuffled. Hoping to find the main door, I was disappointed to come across only a narrow, vertical opening – at shoulder height. When, not long afterwards I discovered another, it became apparent these were arrow slits. I edged further. My idea of a dilapidated farmhouse was way off mark: this construction was no ordinary building, but a bastion of massive walls. Yet there was still no evidence of a way in.

I continued. The next moment I stubbed my foot on something in the drifts. I had stumbled upon the bottom step of a narrow stone staircase which rose in front. Where did it go? I peered into the dark. Impossible to see. Could this place date back to times when front doors were built high up? Unfortunately, even if it were the case, it was hardly likely to be open. Nonetheless, fixed to the stonework on my left was an iron handrail, so I took hold and followed it. It led to a landing, and yes, there, sure enough, low, solid and with snow mounting against it, stood a locked door. My heart sank, but at that moment something caught my eye. Running down the edge gleamed a faint trace of light.

Somebody living here? It was hardly conceivable. What kind of persons would occupy an ancient pile in these mountains – and in mid-winter? My feelings grew mixed. Delighted as I was to come across human habitation, there was no saying what kind of characters they might be or how they would react to a stranger – let alone one arriving at night and in this weather. Nonetheless, whoever they were, I needed to make myself known, and doing nothing but standing there in the cold was not helping. For better or worse, I raised my hand to the brass knocker.

Abruptly I stopped. From the other side there came a thud, the drawing of an iron bolt. And another. The studded oak groaned and inched open, casting a soft light on the swirl of snow. I stepped back. Was someone coming out? Or did someone know I was there?

Nothing happened. "Hello?" I offered, and waited. Still nothing, only the roar of the gale. I raised my voice. "Hello?" Again nothing. A ghost? I took a deep breath, cupped my hands and bellowed, "Hello in there! Is anybody at home?"

Then, barely distinct in the wind, a voice. "Please come in, Sir."

Feeling stupid for asking a silly question – I squeezed through the gap.

The snow tumbled in with me and the doorman wasted no time in forcing shut the heavy door to silence the storm. With the iron bolts back in place and satisfied all was secure, the elderly man, bald and with side-whiskers and in formal black tails turned, held his lantern to my face and peered at me through his specs.

Was he waiting for me to speak? "H ... hello," I stammered. "I mean, good evening."

"Good evening, Sir," he echoed.

"I ... I'm so sorry to disturb you at this time of night. I was wondering whether I might ask for shelter?"

He lowered his lantern. "Are you expected?"

"Expected? Well, no, hardly … I don't know where I am."

"Of course," he replied, showing no surprise and putting his light on a table. "A nasty night to be lost, Sir. May I take your coat?"

"My coat? Why, yes, thank you …" It was difficult to describe the relief at finding a fellow human, however odd. I stamped my wet shoes on the mat; handed him my scarf; pulled down my collar, brushed snow off the coat the best I could and let the old chap help me out of it.

"A fine British Warm," he observed, placing it on the stand.

"Thank you. A hangover from the war."

"I understand, Sir. Your hat?"

"I'm sorry. I don't have one."

"Quite so. Gloves?"

"Gloves?"

"None, Sir? Very good. I shall take you to meet Doctor Frostbight. Would you care to come this way?" at which he retrieved his lantern and turned his back on me.

'Doctor Frostbight'? It must be a joke. However, the doorman said no more and limped across the hallway, evidently expecting me to follow. The setting would have done well for a film, with its gloom, faint smell of damp and the ceiling vaulted in the style of a medieval crypt. They must have had a power cut, for the only lighting was a candelabra hanging from a ceiling rib, and what warmth there was glowed from a stone hearth to my right. Nevertheless, I dared not lose sight of my guide: his tailcoat had disappeared into the entrance of a stair well.

I pursued him and found myself in a narrow, dark spiral. It was steep, and I made sure to keep hold of the rope banister since the steps were uneven. When we came to a landing, his lantern revealed a polished mahogany door and, cautioning me to stay, he knocked and entered. If it were not for a dog barking I could have been back at school, taken to see the headmaster.

Left in the dark, I just made out the doorman's words. "Sir, there is a gentleman here who appears to be lost." I could not hear the reply. In a moment he returned with his light and stood by the door as a sign for me to enter. I swallowed and went in.

The dog – a cross between a terrier and a feather duster – raced across the room and welcomed me as though I were an old friend. I patted its head, and looked about. I was in what must have been a study, furnished with large, comfortable chairs on either side of a fireplace. On the right reclined a man old enough to be my grandfather, with a droopy grey moustache, large nose and wearing a silk smoking cap. On seeing me he put down his pipe on an ashtray, brushed ash from his mustard waistcoat and pulled himself from his chair.

"Down, Snowie, down!" he said in an unconvincing voice as he circumvented the sofa to welcome me with outstretched hand. "Good evening, young man."

"Good evening, Sir," I echoed.

"The name's Frostbight, Dr. Walter Frostbight. My word, your hand's frozen. Come on in. I was wondering when you'd turn up."

"You were?"

"Of course. The weather's bad: that's when people come. Sorry to hear you're lost. Heck of a night, what?" His accent reminded me of my Latin master at prep school. "You took quite a risk coming into the mountains. People have died in weather like this. You all right with dogs? She'll calm down. Travelled far?" and not waiting for an answer he showed me to the fireplace. "Here. Warm yourself up." Speaking to my guide – still beside the door with his lantern – he stated, "Mould, we have a guest for dinner," and turning back to me asked, "you will have something to eat, won't you?" I must have looked surprised. "It's no problem, old chap," he went on, "we're not short – no rationing here."

"In that case," I replied, "yes, please. That would be very kind of you. Thank you."

"And," he added, "you'll obviously be staying the night."

"Gosh," I replied, while rubbing my hands in an attempt to get heat back into them. "Thank you again. My car's completely snowed under."

"I can imagine." He waved his hand. "Mould? We'll need a bed made up."

"Very good," replied the doorman as he remained at attention. "Sir," he said, "Mrs. McWhiteout informs me that she will be serving salmon this evening." It was plain by now that 'Mould' was the butler, arthritic, judging by his gait, and probably deaf as a doorpost – no doubt he had been in service to the Frostbights all his life. Meanwhile I noticed my dishevelled appearance in the over-mantle mirror, brushed the melted snow off my hair and buttoned my tweed jacket to hide the moth hole in my jersey.

The Doctor saw me. "No need to stand upon ceremony, old chap. Partial to salmon?"

"I certainly am." I was famished. This was a welcome turn of events: warmth and a good dinner, and not only that, a bed for the night. "Doctor, I'm sorry I look like a bag of hammers. I haven't even brought a tie."

"Don't give it a thought: we don't dress for dinner. Most people are in a mess by the time they end up here. Settled then. Mould," he said, addressing his butler, "tell Mrs. McWhiteout we'll be one extra would you? Ring the gong as usual."

He waited as the old fellow limped from the room. "Do you know," he started when we were alone, "that salmon hatch in tributaries up here in the mountains? And in due course they descend downstream, following the current, and disappear into the Atlantic?"

"Oh?" I queried, but not sure why he was telling me.

"Yes, and after a number of years they return to where they hatched, swimming against the current – that's when we catch them – returning to where they'd come from. Imagine that?"

"Yes, yes, quite remarkable," I answered politely. It was a peculiar story.

"Anyhow," said my host, "never mind that." He picked up a silver box, opened it and presented it to me. "Cigarette?"

I raised my hand. "Oh, no thank you. I don't."

"No?" He returned the box to the table. "Then how about an aperitif?"

"Yes, please, I'd love one. But would it be all right for me to make a telephone call?"

"Ah! Want to tell your family you're all right? Quite understand, but terribly sorry: there's no line to this place. I'm afraid I can't help. Let's just hope they don't get too worried. Take a pew," and indicated to the chair opposite his own in front of the fire. "Now, about that aperitif: our own liqueur, you know – a speciality of the house. I imagine you could do with a pick-me-up."

Doctor Frostbight went to a table on which there stood a decanter and some goblets while I seated myself, relishing the aromas of burning logs and pipe tobacco – they reminded me of my parents. Meanwhile Snowie, having lost interest in sniffing my legs, settled herself in a cosy spot near the fire. I thought her name was a funny one, seeing she was dark grey. Apart from the fireplace, the only lighting came from a couple of oil lamps. I glanced around. There was a shuttered window behind me, and two tall bookcases on either side of the door to my right. Behind their glass doors I could make out a mixture of leather-bound tomes and modern works and, on the top, a collection of large birds – stuffed, by the look of them, a hundred years ago. On the wall opposite, decorated with dark green wallpaper, old landscapes hung from picture rails.

Doctor Frostbight put a goblet on the small table beside him and handed me another. "Here, this'll help. Your feet must be frozen."

I glanced down. In the circumstances, putting on desert boots this morning had been a stupid idea: they were soaked, and so were the turn-ups on my grey flannels. "Thank you," I said, taking the drink, "I'm sure I'll warm up: it's a terrific fire." I took the cup and held it to admire its colour. I fancied it was made from brass or copper, but was not sure.

"Gold," the Doctor commented casually as he settled in his chair and picked up his own goblet.

I must have looked astonished.

"Yes," he continued, "I had them specially made."

"Really?" I said. "Wow."

Reaching into his top waistcoat pocket, he pulled out a monocle and inserted it into his eye so as to examine his drinking vessel. On turning it in his fingers, he reflected, "Yes, rather fine, don't you think? You see, a while ago, after the war, I wanted to explore for gold."

"Oh? You mean the First War?"

"That's right," he said, pocketing his eyeglass. "When I came back I worked on a Doctorate – on the mining of precious metals."

"A Doctorate on mining?" I responded. "Does that mean you're not a proper doctor?"

He appeared offended. "Not a 'proper' doctor? I'm indeed a 'proper doctor'."

"I'm so sorry, that was rude."

"No, no, not at all, old boy. Lots make that mistake. Originally the term was an honour given by universities – from 'docere', meaning 'to teach', and nothing to do with 'medical practitioner'. Now where was I? Oh, yes, gold. I was determined to find it. For years I travelled the world, sometimes on my own and sometimes employed by others." He smiled. "You know what?"

"No ...?"

"Never found it."

"No ...?"

"Afraid not." Leaning forward, he looked me in the eye and said sub voce, "You see, old chap, I was searching in the wrong place."

"Oh? You were?"

"Yes, yes. It took years to find where the gold really was."

"So you did find it?"

He gestured. "Indeed I did."

"Where was it?"

"Have a guess."

"Me? Not a clue."

"No?" he smiled. "I suppose not. Well, you know what?"

"What?"

"It turned out to be right here."

My mouth dropped.

"Yes," he went on, "fancy that. There was I scouring the world, and what happened? It was under my nose all the time!"

This was another strange story. "Gosh," I replied, "that must have been a surprise – I mean a nice surprise."

"It certainly was." He sat back and raised his goblet. "Well, anyway, let's talk about you. Welcome, young man. Welcome to Chilblane."

"Chilblane?" I repeated. "Is that the name of this place?"

"Quite so. Chilblane Castle."

"Oh? Odd name for a gold mine." I paused. "Is it because it's difficult to keep warm?"

My host laughed. "No, that's not it … although I admit it takes a lot to heat."

"How old is it?"

"Difficult to say. The records only go back to the 12th Century – when the Frostbights came here. We were originally Normans."

"My goodness. So what does 'Chilblane' mean?"

"Well, 'chil' is the ancient word for 'church', or in Scots, 'kil', as in Kilbride. Kilbride means 'the church of St. Bride', so 'Chilblane' means the 'church of St. Blane'."

"Oh. Who was St. Blane?"

"A saintly sort of chap, dating back to the 6th Century: a shadowy figure. Emerged in the earlier days of Creosophy."

I stalled. "I beg your pardon. The what-ophy?"

"Creosophy, old boy." He waved his hand. "Don't worry about that now: we'll come to it. As far as Chilblane goes, tradition has it St. Blane established it as a hospital."

"Really? I didn't know they had hospitals in those days."

"What makes you think that?"

"You know, they're modern things: Florence Nightingale and all that."

"Ah, no. They were around long before that. The word derives from the Latin, 'hospes'."

"Meaning?"

"It means a stranger – or a guest. Hence the word, 'hospitality'. Chilblane was a 'safe' house."

"Oh? Safe for who?"

"For pilgrims."

"Is that so?" I made a face. "I don't suppose there's much demand for that these days."

"Don't you believe it. The tradition goes on."

"Really?" I could not imagine they got any business, but what drew my attention was that while the building itself was unusual, my host was hardly less so himself. Apart from his nose which was as splendid as his grey moustache, the tassel on his smoking cap swung as he turned. He must have dressed with care: the spots on his bow tie matched the handkerchief in his breast pocket. He sported tartan trousers and embroidered carpet slippers.

I hoped he did not think I was staring. I asked, "How do you manage without a telephone?"

"We do the best we can. I might add we don't have electricity either, which can be a nuisance at times. There's a generator for emergencies. Apart from that, we have a septic tank for sewage and our own water from behind the house."

"Drinking water?"

"Certainly. Marvellously pure. It arises high up, you know, runs past us and continues on down."

"That's useful. I mean, to have good water."

"Yes. And you know what's remarkable?"

"No?"

"It's insignificant when it starts up here."

"Well, yes, I'd imagine it is."

"But if you follow it, it grows and takes in other burns. By degrees, when joined by bigger tributaries, it develops into a river and finally joins the ocean."

Another strange ramble, this time a child's geography lesson. So eccentric. "Most interesting," I said politely and, to change the subject, took a sip of the liqueur. "Mmm … delicious."

"Thank you. I hope you enjoy it."

27

"It's different. I mean I've not tasted anything like it."

"Decent of you to say so. We distill it in the dungeon, formulated from highland herbs."

I took a little more, and relished not just the warmth, but also the notion of illicit distillation vessels bubbling somewhere in the dungeon.

"So," started my host, interrupting my thoughts, "how come you lost your way?"

Part II

❧

Why am I Here?

I SIGHED. "I WOULDN'T KNOW WHERE TO START. IT'S A LONG STORY."

"No problem, old chap. We've got all night."

"Oh, it's not that long. Or maybe it is. I don't know any more. The War has screwed me up."

"Yes ... war ... a damnable business. So what brought you here?"

"Nothing did. I got lost."

"Ah, yes, of course. How come?"

"I was driving home when warning signs said they'd closed the road. The strange thing was nobody else paid attention. As for me, I could see no point in following other people just for the sake of it, so I turned off to find another route, but got into trouble anyway. Since my car doesn't have an interior light, I couldn't check the map – not that my father's old map was much help. I've ended up with no idea where I am."

"Uh-huh. You're not the first, even if you could have read the map – we're not on it. You did well to find us."

I grimaced at the memory. "I didn't do well at all. I thought I was going to die."

"You did? Never mind, you're safe now, and I trust you'll enjoy this evening. So tell me: where have you been?"

Feeling awkward, I swilled the liqueur in the goblet and took another sip. Doctor Frostbight waited. "I'm sorry," I said at last. "All I can say is I was travelling."

"Travelling? There's no harm in that."

"There is in my case."

"I'm sorry to hear. What's the problem?"

I hesitated before answering. "The problem, Doctor, is that I don't know where I'm going."

He shrugged. "Not unusual – at least for those who come here."

I looked up. "Really?"

"Yes, really." He arched an eyebrow. "So how are you going to find a destination?"

I took a moment. "You'll think I'm weird."

"Perish the thought." He smiled.

"Well, Doctor, I have this hope."

"First class: I like a man with hope."

I sighed. "Thanks, but it doesn't get me anywhere."

"No? So what're you looking for?"

Again I sighed. "I'm looking for an understanding of life."

"Are you? And if you did come to understand it?"

"I don't know; maybe I'll get an idea what really matters."

"Ah, good, splendid. That's what I like to hear."

"You do?"

"Yes. I hope I can help."

"I'd be surprised if you can. Usually if I talk about these things, I get a belly full of someone's old beliefs."

"Mmm … I sympathise. Let's talk about beliefs later. May I say just now you have an excellent ambition?"

I lowered my eyes. "Thank you, but I'm coming to think no real understanding exists."

"Ah!" he muttered, half to himself. "All that travelling and nowhere to go."

I glanced at him. "You think I'm nuts?"

"Not a bit of it. Most of our guests are in the same boat."

"Are they? So you're not kidding: others do come here?"

"Of course. I told you. We care for pilgrims. Relax." He took a sip from his goblet. "Why don't you tell me about your journey?"

"You mean, tell you about my life?"

"Precisely."

"What, tell you about how I earn a living and about my family and that sort of thing?"

He smiled. "If that's what you'd like to talk about …"

"Actually, no. I'm interested in bigger issues."

"I guessed that. What in particular?"

"I want to know what the world is about and why we were ever born. You see, when the War was on, we obeyed orders and had a common aim. But now it's over, well, what was it all for? I no longer see much purpose to life. And it's worse than that: the truth is, the more I think about it, the more I wonder how I ended up existing in the first place."

"Tip top. Spoken like a man. So what do you think's the solution?"

I was relieved that he did not assume I was a nutter, but the old frustrations rose immediately. "Doctor, I don't know."

"No?"

"I haven't a clue."

"Ah, I understand." He paused. "How about starting from the beginning?"

"From what beginning?"

"From what happened. How did you start?"

Was he joking? It was difficult to make him out, but I took him at his word. "Well, it was like this. I enlisted at the end of my second year at Oxford."

"Oxford? What subjects?"

"Philosophy and Theology. Anyway, the War came along, so I joined up – went for a commission. Like a lot of chaps, I was keen to do my bit."

"Did you?"

"Well, yes, but not the sort I expected. I caught a packet in North Africa, out in the open during an artillery barrage. I was lucky, but so messed up I had to be shipped back. Later, after I'd recovered, I was in France and then Germany. Finally I ended up helping to deal with the mess at Belsen."

"My word. Belsen?" My host coaxed me to go on.

"I'm sorry. I don't like to talk about it."

"I'm not surprised." He reflected for a moment. "I spent four years on the Western Front – but I'm grateful I didn't have to clear up a Nazi concentration camp."

"I doubt your experiences were a lot better than mine. The problem is that life used to make sense, but not any more. I mourn the loss of my innocence." I paused. "I'm in a kind of wilderness."

"Mmm … you're not alone."

"You think so? I often believe I am. Well, anyway," I continued, "that's why I collect petrol coupons. When there's enough I go travelling."

"And you don't know where to go?"

"I know you'll think I'm odd, but yes, that's right. Although the world at large is no longer at war, my private 'war' goes on."

"What a pity. The struggle is …?"

"Just about everything."

"Was it simply," he asked, "that you were disturbed by what you saw?"

"That's an understatement. Why is there so much suffering?"

"Uh-huh. Good existential problem. Do you also ask why there's so much happiness?"

I looked at him. "No?"

"It's a strange thing," he mused. "I don't know why, but people prefer to focus on suffering more than on happiness."

"Oh dear, am I wasting your time?"

"Oh, no, not in the slightest – just thought I'd mention it. Go on."

"The thing is," I grimaced, "we invest so much in this world with its miseries and disasters. Then in the end? We're snuffed out. Dead. Gone."

"No arguing about that! So … your question?"

"The same: 'what am I doing here?'"

"Where? Chilblane?"

"No, Doctor, not Chilblane. Here, in this world."

"OK, just joking." He played with his moustache. "So you don't think you're here for a reason?"

"I can't see how. I'm only around for a number of years before I kick the bucket. My entire existence, like everyone else's, is a total shot in the dark. And not just that: it was both unrequested and unplanned."

"I see." He paused. "But you do make plans, don't you?"

"Yes, I do, from day to day. But my existence: that wasn't planned."

"What do you mean?"

"Well, like you and everyone, I just found myself born."

"Mmm …"

32

"So," I said, "I must be here by mistake."

He chuckled. "That's one way of looking at it!"

I went on, "And you know what, Doctor? The planet would go on quite happily without me."

"Uh-huh, I can see that. What are you suggesting?"

"I'm suggesting I find myself here but I don't belong here and, for that matter, nor does anybody else – you included."

My host took a little more of his drink. "Mmm," he said again, " … let's think about it … So you reckon you're meaningless blob of nature?"

I took a deep breath. "Not a bad description. How could I be anything else? Don't you see? The world has nothing to do with me. Yes, I know you've kindly offered me sanctuary tonight, but apart from that, your life has nothing to do with mine. Nor does this room. Nor Chilblane Castle. Nor the storm outside. The only exceptions are my family and friends. I may mean something to them, but only them, and to nobody and nothing else on Earth." I stopped and gazed at the fire.

My host stroked his moustache. "I suspect," he said slowly, "that by the end of this evening you may find that the world has everything to do with you."

"I beg your pardon?"

"I said you may find that the world has everything to do with you."

I studied his face. He was being serious. "I'm sorry, Doctor, it's out of the question. The whole business is a mystery – always has been, always will."

He shifted position in his chair. "That, my boy, despite what you think, may be not such a bad thing."

"Why not?"

"Because if it were obvious, you wouldn't be asking these questions. Take heart. Despite what you say, I suspect you're much the same as anyone else: you actually like a mystery. Tell me, what do others think about this?"

"As I said, all I've come across are standard beliefs – not insights. But you know what's really surprising? Nobody has any idea what this world is, or how come they're in it, and at the same time hardly anyone gives the matter a thought."

He gestured. "Most people are too docile, and these are heavy duty questions – outside the average comfort zone."

"You're probably right. How come they're not outside yours?"

"Ah! We'll come to that. Chin up, old boy, I'm glad you're here."

"You being serious?"

"I am. There's lots to talk about." He sipped his drink. "What else?"

"What else?" I took a moment to reply. "Well, I keep returning to much the same thing: I never asked to be in this world."

"No?"

"No. And I can tell you," I said with feeling, "I certainly didn't ask for the violence, fear and confusion that goes with it."

My host did not react. "You're sure you didn't ask?"

"Funny question. Of course not."

"Just wondered. Go on …"

I looked at him. His was a strange response, but I went on. "Here's another way of putting it. Say I see myself in the mirror …"

"Uh-huh."

"Well, Doctor, I look at that face – that hair, that nose, those eyes. Who made them?"

He sipped his liqueur. "Pretty good questions. And the answer?"

"One thing's for sure: it certainly wasn't me."

"What's the problem? You think you're ugly?"

"No," I smiled, "I don't. It's just that it wasn't I who designed my own features! And the same goes for my body – and my gender, and my background. And the more I think about it, the more mysterious it becomes. I didn't choose my parents or my family. I didn't choose my country, or the school I went to, or the things I was taught or the pupils I met. The list could go on and on. In the end, I realise there's very little I've chosen in life."

"Huh. So where do you think it's all come from?"

"Doctor, that's what I mean: I've absolutely no idea. I didn't ask to be born, and yet I was. I didn't ask to live, but I do, and I didn't ask to die, but I will."

"Mmm …" he responded. "Well put. I can see we've plenty to chat about. Does anything else trouble you?"

"Yes. You know what? It's not just my body."

He raised an eyebrow. "Oh?"

"Yeah. I realised one day that just the same thing applies to my character and my personality: I've been landed with this particular character – with my interests, my preferences, my aversions, my passions and so on. And …" I paused. "And you know? I'm not even sure about my thoughts.

When I really, really look at them, I'm not sure how many of them I choose. On the one hand they are the building blocks of my life, and on the other I don't plan them – they just arrive out of nowhere. And yet …" I hesitated.

"Go on."

"Here's the mystery: I wouldn't be 'me' without them! I didn't make myself and yet I am myself. Make sense of that if you can."

"Good point." There was a hint of a smile, but he made no reply. Finally he said, "I think you'll enjoy dinner tonight."

I wondered for a moment what I might be getting into. "Anyway," I grunted, "thankfully I'm fit and healthy … touch wood," and tapped the table beside me. "But," I went on," what of those born disfigured or disabled? No one would choose or design that kind of body. And you know what's odd?"

"No?"

"Well, if I look at you, I realise that you didn't choose your body either. And you didn't choose your age – it's just happened. And as for your character, you didn't choose that any more than I did."

"Mmm … not bad. I see you've been thinking."

I shrugged. "So, Doctor, who am I? And who are you? And who is everyone else? I sympathise with Descartes."

"You do?"

"Yes. He questioned whether he really existed." I glanced at my host.

He seemed to be enjoying the exchange and waved his hand. "Courage, my boy, you're observant. Don't stop."

I was flattered he considered me observant rather than a sandwich short of a picnic. "Doctor," I said, "look at us. We're born without directions, a decent road map or user manual, and end up shooting our fellow human beings."

"Well spoken. So what do you think it's all about?"

"Me? You know what? I think we're under a spell of a capricious Wizard who's shoved us into bodies and dumped us on Earth." I stopped. "Gosh, Doctor, do tell me to shut up. I'm talking a load of shit."

He chuckled again. "It's OK. You sound to me like an ancient Gnostic. To be honest, you're on the money."

"I am? With the idea of the evil Wizard?"

"No, no. I'll tell you in a moment. Anything else on your mind?"

"Well, yes. What it boils down to is I have no decent reason for living.

OK, maybe pleasure lightens things up a bit, but that's it. Why don't I just go and 'top' myself? We're all heading that way. I might as well get on with it."

"Well, old boy, we can't have that. Let's toast to the answer."

I studied him. "The answer to what?"

Part III

ఴ

The Answer?

FROSTBIGHT RAISED HIS CHALICE. "TO THE REASON WE'RE
alive. Cheers!"

I knew perfectly well there was no such thing, and anyone
who pretended there was was off his rocker. "You are kidding,
aren't you, Doctor?"

"No," he replied quietly, "I'm not."

He was certainly odd for an old gold miner, and thought it best to
humour him or he might change his mind about giving me dinner. I
raised my goblet. "Cheers! To the reason for life," and took a swig. "I can
tell you," I said, "if you come up with an answer, I'll eat my hat."

" … if you had a hat," he added. "Don't bet on no one knowing the
answer."

"Yeah, but any answer would just be another airy-fairy belief system."

"Who said? I didn't mention beliefs – not yet anyway."

"Well, whatever … from the moment of conception we're doomed.
Our bodies are stalked by accident, bad luck and ill health, and if they fail
to kill us, we self-destruct – with age – and disappear without trace."

He smiled. "You're not exaggerating?"

"All right, I am a bit, but not much." I felt the weight of these endless riddles and fell silent. For a while there was only the crackling fire and the grumble of the storm in the chimney. I watched the flames dance amongst the logs. Were they laughing at me? From time to time one of the wicks in the lamp spluttered.

Frostbight broke into my thoughts. "I agree. It's strange. Nonetheless, death may be more important than you think."

"Yeah, important because it robs life of any chance of finding meaning."

"I wouldn't be so sure – you may find it's the opposite."

"The opposite? I beg your pardon?"

"I see we'll need to come back to this. I'd be interested in whether you've ever been in love?"

"Yes, of course. I am at the moment. Why?"

"Doesn't that have meaning?"

"It does, Doctor, but only while it lasts."

"A bit cynical. OK, what about being of service to others?"

"Yes, helping others generates good feelings, but it's also temporary. Everyone kicks the bucket sooner or later. I tell you, the road ahead's closed."

"So I see." He thought for a moment. "But, look, you're an intelligent young chap: along the road you must have found some solutions?"

I tasted my liqueur before answering. "No, I haven't, and that's not for want of trying."

"I didn't expect it was. Where did you begin?"

I gazed at the fire and reflected. "It started with philosophy."

"A yes, you were studying that at College. Western philosophy I presume? How did you get on?"

"I expected it to be about wisdom – after all, that's the meaning of the word."

"And?"

"I found it was much more about the study of argument."

"Who in particular?"

"German professors."

My host seemed to think that was funny.

"OK," I went on, "not every philosopher's a German professor. The trouble is the giants of modern thinking strike me as being more or less irrelevant to real life. Theories and more theories. Whatever they determine, and whether or not I agree with them, their thinking makes absolutely no difference to my day to day living."

"No?"

"No. They're in a world of their own trying to win intellectual points." I sighed. "Words, words and more words. Verbal diarrhoea."

"I say, old boy!"

"Too extreme? Yes, probably; but for me to become wiser I need ideas I can use. I admire the Indian philosophers in that they expect their students to meditate rather than argue. As for German philosophers, for all their cleverness there are never any conclusions – and nothing changes." I made a face and glanced around.

Frostbight noticed. "No, it's all right, old chap," he grinned, "there isn't one hiding in the cupboard." He paused. "I think," he went on, "the usefulness of philosophy is in the way it identifies logical problems about the nature of the world, knowledge and truth."

" ... and identifies more and more problems as it goes. And yet, Doctor, for all those so-called philosophical 'sages', none address the fundamental question."

"Remind me?"

"How come we exist in the first place."

"Ah yes. I wouldn't disagree with you."

I looked appealingly at my host. "Doctor, what do I do? There's no philosophy which explains who I am or why I'm on this planet."

"I think you're probably right."

"And as I said, I don't want logical theories; I want ideas which make a difference."

Frostbight smiled. "Ah, yes, I can see you definitely need to part company with the academics. That'll mean turning off the main road."

"What do you mean? I did turn off the main road!" I listened for a moment to the deep grumbling of the wind. It seemed to be getting stronger. "Are you," I asked, "suggesting there's an answer?"

"Certainly. We'll give you one tonight."

"I think you're pulling my leg."

"Actually, I'm not."

Who was this old man? "How," I persisted, "can you be so confident?"

He did not answer, but asked instead, "If philosophy didn't help, what about theology? It supplies lots of reasons for our existence." He leant forward to reach for a log to throw into the grate. Snowie looked up sleepily as her master poked more life into the fire.

I waited. What was I to reply? "In my opinion," I began, "theology isn't any more about finding wisdom than is philosophy."

"Oh?"

"No. Who's bothered about how many angels sit on the end of a pin? All right, it's unfair to use such an example, but theology is just another fancy excuse for more intellectual gymnastics, and no better at improving my life. Like with philosophy, I don't end up knowing anything: it's just speculation and more speculation." I ground to a halt. "Lord, I keep banging on. I'm so sorry."

"Relax, old boy, you're doing fine. What about sacred texts? Aren't they helpful?"

"What? You mean the Bible and that sort of thing?"

"Yes, and any of the great texts. Many were written as a result of personal revelations."

"Fair enough," I said. "I can't argue people have been influenced by so-called 'other worldly' experiences. To be honest, I wish I could have one. And I wish I could be certain about God. The thing is, one 'revelation' is not the same as another. No matter how many texts are 'inspired' – whatever that means – there's no consensus. So whether or not a text is 'sacred', it's always open to dispute. Anyway, Doctor, as far as I can see, what religious people love are not just beliefs – whatever they are – but dogma. They want doctrines of certainty rather than knowledge." I stopped: I needed to calm down.

"Maybe," replied my host, "you're a little hasty. Have you read the Book of Job?"

"Yeah ... a while ago."

"Bearing in mind Job was around in something like 500 B.C., you're not exactly the first to question all this."

"Remind me what happened."

"God spoke to him out of a whirlwind."

"And said ...?"

"He said divine knowledge is reserved for God."

"Did He? Whatever ... so Job's not much use." I hesitated. "Or are you telling me that's what you think?"

"I didn't say so."

"Well," I went on, "if I'm going to find meaning in life, it's not much use God knowing what it is without letting me know. What am I supposed to believe: that there's a grand Creator of some kind who rules over us and keeps it a secret as to what it's all about?" I paused. "Huh. I'm simply at the mercy of an unidentifiable 'destiny' – like the Greeks believed."

I couldn't make out what was on the Doctor's mind. He sat, slowly stroking his moustache, first to the left and then the right. "If," he said, "you want to understand life, then maybe you should look at Indian philosophers."

"Yes, I agree they've got a lot to offer, but that doesn't stop them clinging to crackpot beliefs."

"Such as?"

"That stuff about cyclical existence. Am I really supposed to be stuck in rounds of Karmic re-births? Must I really accept that if I stopped desiring the things of life I'd be elevated to 'nirvana'? Anyway, who invented re-births and Karmic laws? For all the Hindus – or Buddhists – there's still no intelligent explanation how I ended up on this planet."

"Huh," he muttered, "and no doubt you would find the same thing with the philosophers in the Far East. You know what?" he asked, his voice rising, "This calls for a top-up!" and rose and fetched the decanter. "Here we are," he grinned, holding it over my goblet. "Keep you going 'til dinner."

"Thank you, Doctor. Just a smidgen: I like to keep a clear head."

"Glad to hear it." My host replenished both of us, returned the decanter to the table and settled into his chair. "All right," he said, "what about psychology? Any joy?"

"You know as well as I it's a huge field of study, but the answer's the same: 'no, not much'. It's just about as dull as philosophy and theology. Ids, Egos, Super-egos, the Collective Unconscious, theories, beliefs and not a single clue as to why I'm here."

"You're a hard one to please. Might I suggest that, if you were abandoned as a child, it's not surprising you grew up seeing the world as a foreign place?"

"Yes, possibly – if I had been abandoned, which I wasn't. I'm not saying there's anything the matter with psychology. It's fine, and maybe childhood experiences can explain why we view life in certain ways, but no psychologist is going to explain why I'm on Earth. A Behaviourist would even maintain it's pointless to ask the question since it has no biological necessity!"

"Ah," my host exclaimed, "he'd be guessing the same as anyone." He reflected a moment. "There are always occult societies. They hold alternative viewpoints."

"And they're closed to non-members. I don't know what they believe. Anyhow, that's just the trouble: even if I did know, I would only end up

41

with more beliefs." I paused. Was I offending my host? Was he a member of a secret Brotherhood?

He casually picked up the pipe he had put down earlier, put it between his teeth, lit a match and applied it to the bowl. Once the smoke billowed he flicked the match into the fire. "Shall we," he suggested, "shed some fresh light on this?"

"Huh? Are you a magician?"

He gave me a meaningful look. "You'd be surprised. We need a different approach."

I let out a long breath. "There isn't one. I've tried them all."

"I'm sorry, but you haven't. There's an avenue you've gone down."

"I don't believe you."

"It's all right, old boy, you don't need to."

"Really? Then what're we waiting for?"

He raised his eyebrows. "I think," he said as he blew smoke, "you'll have a problem with it."

"Me? I don't see why."

"It's single tracked."

"What? Narrow minded?"

He smiled. "No. Too simple."

"What makes you say that?"

"Even a child could understand it."

"So you mean it's simplistic?"

"No. I said, 'simple'."

"Oh, I can assure you," I mocked, "it's impossible for simplicity to be a problem."

"No? Then let's see …"

Part IV

☙☙

The Essential Question

I COULD NOT IMAGINE WHAT HE THOUGHT I WOULD BE 'SUR-prised' about. "Doctor," I said, "these things must be as mysterious to you as they are to me."

"To some extent. Let's whittle it down. What's your main question?"

"Gosh, I hardly know where to start. Let's think." I gave it a moment. "It's nothing very original. In fact it's hackneyed. The overall puzzle must be, 'what's the meaning of life?'"

"Mmm … No need to be embarrassed just because it's hackneyed."

"OK, but do you know what? I don't know what life's all about and I didn't ask to be born, and yet, like you, I have this biological urge to keep myself alive – to the point that I'm frightened of dying. How about that?"

"That's perfectly normal."

"Yes, maybe, but Doctor, I am going to die. So my survival instinct is predetermined for absolute and categorical failure." I threw up a hand in despair. "Try and make sense of that."

He puffed on his pipe while eying me with care. "I think you'll be less fearful by the end of the night. Would you say you're on a quest?"

"A quest? Yes, kind of."

"Good show. Then supposing I told you what life's about?"

"Well," I said, "I'd think you were joking."

"And if I weren't?"

"Then I'd think you were nuts."

He smiled. "How come?"

"Because, Doctor, like Job, nobody's ever found an answer."

He paused, and simply said, "I wouldn't be so sure."

I observed him closely as he idly watched the fire. Was he unhinged?

He went on without looking up. "There's good reason for being alive. What's important is to find the missing link."

"What 'missing link'?"

He turned and pointed the stem of his pipe at me. "This: what causes you to experience the world."

I frowned. "What do you mean? If you read David Hume you'd say that any idea of 'causes' was an illusion."

"So I might. Very well, let's put it another way: who or what makes the world – and you – happen?"

"I'm not with you, Doctor. You mean, 'who created it?'"

"Yes, and who's keeping it going?"

"Nothing keeps it going. It just 'does its own thing'."

"I'm sure it does. Someone or something must be keeping it going."

"Isn't it self-sustaining?"

"If it were," returned my host, "how would you know? And even then, who or what would have made it that way?"

"Ah," I replied, "I suspect you're being a sly old fox and coaxing me to say, 'it's God'." I took a quick sip of my liqueur.

He shrugged. "Actually, I'm not."

"You're not? All right; it was the Big Bang."

"No, that wouldn't solve it either. Even if there were such a thing, the problem would remain: who made the Big Bang happen?"

"Haven't a clue, Doctor. It was random – you know, nature doing its thing."

"How could it be? Who is 'nature'? God? No, I'm sorry, 'nature' doesn't explain who organised it."

I was stumped. "All right then, I give up."

"Please don't give up. If you want a different philosophy you need to ask different questions."

"I thought I had."

"Sadly you've missed the one that matters most."

"No, I haven't. What I want to know is why I'm here, who I am, where I've come from, where I'm going, what's the …"

"Yes, yes, old boy. Sorry to interrupt. That's all very well, but you said you wanted a philosophy that makes a difference."

"That's right, I do."

"So," he continued, "there's something else to ask."

"Oh, yeah, what?"

"As you know, an answer is only as good as the question. There's one particular thing you need to be clear about."

I was out of my depth. "So what is it?"

He shifted position again and studied me. "The key to understanding existence is …"

"Yes?" I bent forward.

He puffed at his pipe. "Relax."

"I am relaxed. What's the question?"

"You sure you're relaxed?" He blew some smoke.

"Yes, yes, I just said so. Please tell me the question."

He raised one eyebrow. "Very well. The primary one that gets the ball rolling is this: what is life? In other words, you need to go right back to the beginning. You need to understand how come there's such a thing as existence in the first place."

I sat back again. "Is that it? It's as bad as asking, 'what is existence?'"

"Yes, pretty much. It's the essential question."

"Yeah, well, that's another question without an answer."

"How do you mean?"

"It just is. Life is life."

"That tells me nothing." He could see I had no inkling of what he was getting at. "Here," he said, "is the bottom line. If you don't know what life is, how're you going to understand who you are or why the world exists?"

"But, Doctor, nobody can say what life is – or why the world exists."

"That's your belief," he frowned, "and therein lies your problem."

"Does it?" I took a deep breath. "But look, nobody's answered it since the dawn of history – at least not sensibly."

"We don't know that. What matters is for you to answer the question."

"Well, I can't," I said emphatically. "And if you think you can, how about spilling the beans?"

"You'd like me to tell you what life is?"

"Of course, if you really think you've cracked it."

Doctor Frostbight took a moment to re-light his pipe. "I can tell you," he said as he threw the spent match into the grate, "in one sentence."

I laughed. "I knew it. You're pulling my leg."

"One sentence," he persisted with a wave of his hand.

"Well," I replied, "don't hold back the horses."

"The thing is, old boy, if I told you, you'd say I were crazy."

"Me? I wouldn't say you were crazy." I lied.

He grinned. "I think you would. And anyway, as I said, you'd reject it for being too simple."

"No, I wouldn't."

"Pleased to hear it. So you want to learn what life is?"

"Yes. How many times do I have to say?"

"And you won't dismiss it as nonsense?"

My frustration was building. "Doctor, of course not."

He took another sip of liqueur. "I've got an idea you like arguing."

"Me? Oh, no, not me. And I swear, I'm fine with 'simple'."

"All right then …"

The clock chimed the hour. He stopped, and as he did so a low booming came from somewhere in the castle. "Ah," he exclaimed, "the gong." He tapped the ash out of his pipe into the ashtray and, reaching for the rack next to the mantelpiece, placed the briar with others on the wall. Snowie meanwhile had perked up her ears, abandoned her bed and made for the door, evidently knowing a routine.

Without reference to our conversation, my host stood. "Feeling warmer?"

"Oh, yes, thanks, Doctor, much better."

"Good, good; come along then. Dinner's up. Polish off your drink and we'll go down. There're a couple of friends I'd like you to meet." Depositing his goblet on the table, he put the guard in front of the fire, picked up an oil lamp and waited. "You want," he said, "to know what life is?" I caught the glimpse of a smile.

"Only if you promise it's not a shaggy dog story."

His smile broadened without commenting. "Follow me," he said and strode to the door.

I had no option but to gather myself, finish the last of my liqueur, leave the cup next to his and allow him to show me out. I squeezed my eyes tight for a second. Was I dreaming? No, this was for real. Who might be his 'friends'? He had not mentioned them. So we made our way – with Snowie in the lead – down the spiral stairs to the hallway, which we crossed, and where our steps on the flagstones sounded disproportionately loud in the hush of the ancient building. As we turned and passed along a vaulted passageway with shadows from the Doctor's lamp dancing on the carved stonework, I imagined the days long gone when cowled monks shuffled along here in contemplative silence. To our left, I caught a glimpse of a woman in jodhpurs with a wee willie winkie light hurrying down a passage. I glanced again. She was gone.

My host did not notice.

"Doctor," I whispered.

"Yes, old boy?"

"Who was that?"

"Who was what?"

"That woman with a candle."

"Oh? You saw someone?"

"Yes, didn't you? She came out of the door back there."

"She did? Ah! I know. That'll be my late wife. She often appears when we have a guest."

I was too surprised to reply. The dog distracted my attention by scratching at a door.

Frostbight stopped outside it, turned and said, "I'm terribly sorry, old boy. Jolly rude of me: I didn't catch your name."

"My name? Oh, that's all right, Doctor, it's Ewan. Ewan Evriwun."

"Ewan Evriwun, eh? Good man. Then let's go in." He turned the handle and bade me enter. It was strange: I felt butterflies in my stomach.

"Oh? You saw someone?"

Appetiser

Part I

❧

The Search for Purpose

W E CAME OUT OF THE DARKNESS INTO THE LIGHT
of what must have been the original refectory, with the
ceiling built in the now familiar rib vaulting. Copper
candle sconces hung on oak-panelled walls between
pictures – probably of ancestors. To the right were three full-length
recesses barred with shutters, and these, I assumed, obscured French
windows. In the middle, a white cloth covered a rectangular table set for
dinner, while set against the wall to my left was a mahogany sideboard,
and there stood the butler, in white gloves, waiting. Beyond blazed a log
fire, and next to it, keeping warm, two middle-aged men. Had I joined
a theatre production? So much for Doctor Frostbight's saying there was
no dressing-up for dinner: one fellow was decked in full clerical costume
with dog collar, biretta, tails, breeches, silk stockings and buckled shoes,
and the other sported a wing collar, bow tie and a black velvet frock coat.
On our entering they ceased their conversation, and Snowie, wagging her
feather duster, made a beeline to greet them like old friends.

Doctor Frostbight placed his lamp on the sideboard and led me down
the room. "Gentlemen," he said, "may I introduce you to Mr. Evriwun?
He's joining us for dinner. Snowie, that's enough." He pointed to a basket

beside the fire. "Bed!" Snowie paid no attention. "Such a naughty girl," he said to me. "Anyhow, I'd like you meet our resident Rector, the Reverend Father Foggie, Order of Creosophist Clerics."

I was not expecting to come across a cleric, let alone one dressed in retro clothing and belonging to a dubious 'Order'. Talk about High Church! But I think I managed to avoid a show of surprise and said politely, "How d'you do, Father. Ewan Evriwun."

"Good evening, my son," he smiled and shook my hand.

"And," continued my host, "I would also like you to meet Gusty von Lottowind, an old friend from Germany."

Von Lottowind? A curious name. I held out my hand. "How d'you do?"

Instead of following suit, the man stood to attention, snapped his heels and made an impeccable bow. "Gustav von Lottowind, Professor of Philosophy, Winterbad University. Gooden abend Herr."

Was this a comedy? And did he expect me to reply in German? Evidently this time I failed to hide my surprise.

"You were not," he asked with a pronounced accent, "anticipating a Professor from Prussia?"

"Well, no," I replied. "And nor, I confess, have I heard of Winterbad."

"Nein? It was situated in the Black Forest."

Was he making it up? I could not tell. Why did he say, 'Winterbad *was* situated'? Where was it now? But whatever, it was surely bad luck to find myself at dinner with both a theologian *and* a German philosopher. As for von Lottowind, I did not know whether I was astonished more by his name or by his mat of curly ginger hair and well-groomed beard. "No, I wasn't expecting a Prussian Professor," I responded, bringing my hand to my mouth in pretence of clearing my throat, "but then I wasn't expecting to be here in the first place."

"You were not expecting to be here in the first place?" echoed the German. "Das is unfortunate. Where did you expect to be?"

"Actually, to be honest, I've no idea. I was driving around in the dark and nearly crashed into the courtyard."

"Ah so? You may find you are not here by mistake."

"I'm sorry?"

"So ..." he said, ignoring my question, "you say you are lost?"

"Well, yes, Professor. You see, I don't have an interior light. I couldn't read the map."

"No interior light? Das is most certainly a problem."

"My son," the theologian said quietly. "It's not just the light. The map wouldn't have helped either."

Why did he say that? He was like Doctor Frostbight: a map certainly *would* have helped – if it had been a decent one. To my surprise, he turned to the butler. "Mould?" he asked. "Can you remember how Melville described Queequeg's village?"

"Queequeg's village? In Moby Dick, Sir? Let me think. I believe he said, 'it is not down in any map; true places never are'."

While I wondered at this unusual exchange, Doctor Frostbight spoke. "Come along, no time to chatter. I can hear supper coming. Gusty old boy, would you care to sit beside me? And you, young man," he said to me, "can be next to the Padre on that side. Snowie! Bed!"

Snowie at last settled into her basket. Out of the corner of my eye I caught Mould raising his hand to pull a lever in the wall. One of the oak panels creaked open. It was too good to be true: this *had* to be a stage set. Through the secret door shuffled in a well-proportioned and ruddy-faced woman, her hands clasped to a trolley rattling with crockery.

"Ah, Mrs. McWhiteout," said our host. "Very good. We were just taking our seats. Great smells coming from the kitchen. What've you put together?"

She halted her cart, wiped her hands on her apron and grinned. "Good evening, Sir. Tonight, for starters, you're having borsch."

"Borsch? Splendid! My favourite. What about you," he said, addressing me, "fond of borsch?"

"Sounds great, Doctor. What is it?"

"Soup, old chap. Eastern European thing. Beetroot. Delicious."

"Oh? I'm hungry enough to eat a horse."

"That's the stuff. No wartime rationing here."

I was pleased to hear, and took my seat where he had indicated, to the right of the Rector, opposite my host and the Professor. I admired the spread on the tablecloth: assortments of dishes, condiments, crystal, gold, silver, glasses and plates variously reflecting the two magnificent candelabras in the centre. As I regarded this display, I became aware that the others had remained standing.

"Grace," murmured Father Foggie bending to my ear.

"Gosh, I'm so sorry Father," and, pushing back my chair, I followed the others, standing with my head bowed.

The Rector, touching his head and shoulders in the sign of the cross, intoned, "Cirrus lenticularis altostratus cumulonimbus virga precipitatio …"

After more Latin, "Amen," was chorused. I wished I had paid more attention at school and maybe I would have understood it. Anyway, who *were* these three? Schoolmasters or actors? I could not make them out; but right now I was famished and looking forward to dinner.

This time, taking my cue from the others, I sat, lifted the linen napkin from my tablemat and, laying it on my lap, waited while Mould put warm bowls in front of us. The Professor tucked his napkin into his collar. A moment later, Mrs. McWhiteout, with a tureen of steaming soup, was standing on my left.

"Help yourself dear," she said in a Highland lilt. "There's plenty for everyone. The beetroot's from the walled garden."

"Thank you," I replied, "it looks very good." I ladled two large helpings into my bowl and let her proceed to the others. Mould came to my side with a silver sauceboat.

"Yoghurt Sir?"

"Tuck into the yoghurt," said Frostbight across the table.

"Yoghurt?" I queried.

"Yes. Scandinavian stuff. Mrs. McWhiteout makes it. Milk from our cow."

I looked at the cook.

"Yes, dear," she said to me. "Very good for you. You'll enjoy it."

"I'm sure I will," I returned and landed a couple of dollops into the midst of the crimson. Locally grown vegetables? Their own milk? These people were certainly 'Digging for Victory'. I picked up my spoon and stirred white circles in the deep red, idly musing that the mess was a good analogy for my life.

The Rector was the first to speak. "So, your life's a mess?"

I left my daydream with a jolt. How did he know? On looking around, I realised the others hadn't started. "Oh, dear," I said, and let go of my spoon. With discreet skill, Mould rescued me from embarrassment by offering a basket of crusty bread rolls. I thanked him and took one. Here was I, an impromptu stranger welcomed in during a storm, and I was not showing good manners. Fortunately Doctor Frostbight lifted his spoon signalling us to begin, while to my left Mrs. McWhiteout rumbled the trolley back to the kitchen.

"Do tuck in," said our host. "I hope you find it tasty. You know," he went on, reaching into his pocket and extracting an eye-glass to look closely at the soup, "strange isn't it? Beetroot grows underground, never seen the light of day and yet, when it's dug up, here it is: this splendid crimson. Odd, don't you think, Gusty?"

"Exceptionally odd, Watty."

The Doctor returned the monocle to his waistcoat, and as I couldn't think why there was a fuss about the colour of beetroot, I started a conversation with the Reverend Foggie. "Father, why does Dr. Frostbight call you 'Padre'?"

He smiled. "He's called all clerics 'Padre' since he was in the trenches."

"Were you involved in the war?"

"Yes. In Italy – regimental chaplain."

"Italy? I don't suppose that was a laughing matter."

"No indeed. I wish we could see an end to wars."

"Don't we all. So how come the Doctor said you were a member of the 'Order of Creosophist Sages'?"

"Creosophist *Clerics*," he corrected.

"I'm so sorry. It's the first I've heard of them."

"That's all right. The Order keeps a low profile."

"You're not joking. So it really exists?"

"Of course."

"What does it do?"

"Our job's mostly teaching."

"Theology?"

"Yes," he replied, "that and other things."

I wondered what he meant by 'other things'. "Is it connected to Winterbad?"

"Winterbad? Yes, or rather, it used to be." He looked opposite him. "Professor? Do you expect the University will reopen?"

"Unfortunately, Herr Pastor," replied the Prussian, "it is too early to know. So much was lost."

"I'm sorry to say," commented the Cleric to me, "that the University was razed to the ground by the Third Reich."

"Lord, that's rotten. Sounds like the same thing as happened to Steiner's Goetheanum."

"Indeed. The Nazis pretended it was an accident. The Professor escaped and finally ended up here."

"The story of our times." I turned to von Lottowind. "Professor, I'd hate to think what you've been through, but I'm sure you're a credit to Chilblane." That was my way of being polite – what with his being a German philosopher.

"Danke," he replied, thanking me. "So, Herr Evriwun, you say your life is a mess?"

I was hesitant to reply.

The Prussian began sipping his borsch. "In a mess?" he repeated.

I picked up my spoon. "Well, yes, in a manner of speaking, it is; although it'd be more accurate saying it's my *understanding* of life that's a mess. I was talking about it to the Doctor before dinner."

"Ah, so? You have difficulties?"

"Difficulties? That's one way of putting it!"

"Such as?"

"*Loads* of unanswered questions."

"You say you have many unanswered questions? What questions?"

"For starters," I replied, "the sort you Professors avoid."

"Ah, so?"

"Yes. Such as why we have come to exist."

He showed no surprise. "Existence is a problem for you?"

"Well, no, Professor, *existence* isn't a problem – at least I don't think it is. Where I come unstuck is in the *making sense* of it."

"I regret to hear it. What is your explanation?"

"Don't ask me: *I don't have one.* That's the trouble."

"Nein? Ah, then I anticipate you will find tonight beneficial. What troubles you in particular?"

"What I said to the Doctor earlier: life does nothing but lead us to oblivion at the end of it. And that's it. All over: a waste of time. Does anyone receive a reward for a decent life? No! They get the grave instead." My outburst seemed to amuse him, but I persisted. "Even if I were to become famous for something, so what? That fame, too, will one day disappear. Whatever I do, it's doomed – doomed to insignificance."

Father Foggie joined in. "My child, there's nothing wrong with insignificance. It's not, you know, an 'evil'."

"Oh no? Well I think it is."

"I recommend you make friends with it. Trying to be significant is chasing after wind."

"You think so? People like Nietzsche and Tolstoy said you're supposed to do something exceptional if you want to make life meaningful."

"My child, leave those men behind: they had their own problems." He sipped his soup. "What do you think is *your* purpose for existing?"

"Absolutely none except to feed worms at the end of it – unless I get cremated."

The Rector smiled. "Oh, dear."

"What's the matter?"

"Nothing." He put down his spoon and looked at me. "Do you absolutely *know* that you have no purpose beyond that?"

"Well, Father, if I did have one, I'm certainly not aware of it."

"Is it possible," asked the Cleric, "that you *do* have a purpose but don't know what it is?"

"I don't see how."

"I take it that you like to think?"

"Well, yes, of course I like to think, otherwise I wouldn't be asking these questions."

"And you're passionate about it?"

I was taken aback. "Yeah, I suppose I do it a lot."

"Could *that* be your purpose?"

"What? Just thinking?"

"Yes."

"But ..." my voice faded.

"What's the matter?"

"Well I can't spend *all* my time thinking. I can't have *that* as a '*purpose*'."

"Why not?" He broke a piece of bread and spread it with butter. "It doesn't stop you doing other things."

"You reckon?"

"I don't know. What do you think?"

"Lord! Are you trying to contort my brain?"

"My child," he persisted, "what are you going to do if you *don't* think?"

"But Father, I can't spend *all* my life thinking."

"Ah! You'd make a fine Calvinist. Leave it to the Protestants to focus on production and achievement. In days long ago, a contemplative life was a good life."

"Really? Does that mean you're a Catholic?"

He shrugged. "Maybe, maybe not."

No one else spoke, and glancing across the table I wondered what the other two were thinking. I could not decide what to make of the 'Padre'. "You know," I said to him, "I once read – although I can't think where

– 'We live and we don't know how. We love and we don't know why. We die and we don't know when'."

"Mmm," Foggie commented, "well put."

Behind me Mould cleared his throat. He was doing another 'round', this time with a jug. "A little water, Sir?"

"Yes, please," I replied, and pushed my tumbler so he could reach it.

"Sir?" he asked.

"Yes?"

"May I be so bold?"

Such old fashioned formality. "Of course," I replied. "What about?"

"I believe those were the words of Olga, in Anna-Elizabeth Weirauch's 'Der Skorpion'."

"Gosh. *Really?*"

"When Olga was eloping with Myra."

"Oh, yeah, I know. You're quite right, so it was."

"A rather saucy novel, if my memory serves me correctly."

I hardly knew what to say. "Which translation did you read?"

"None Sir. I was practising my German."

"Wow, I'm impressed."

"Thank you, Sir."

"Mould," exclaimed Frostbight. "Enough. Bring the water round here."

"Very good, Sir."

"And you, old chap," he said to me, "how're you finding the borsch?"

"Tasty," I answered, taking a sip. "Very tasty."

"Splendid. It's good for the heart. Drink up or it'll get cold."

Part II

✌

Two Schools of Thought

WHILE I WAS CONSIDERING WHY MY HEART MIGHT need beetroot soup, the Reverend Foggie returned to our conversation. "How would you know," he asked, breaking off another piece of his roll, "if your life *weren't* a mess?"

I wasn't sure why he was asking it, but it was a good question, and I needed to ponder. "Well," I replied, "it's the same old thing again. It would be less of a mess if I understood why I'm alive."

"Enjoying your life isn't enough?"

"Well, no, not really. It's not that I have anything against pleasure, but it doesn't tell me why I exist."

"Ah! In that case, we need to turn to religion."

"We do?" I stopped to take some soup. We were bound to get to religion sooner or later. Was the Reverend going to try and convert me? I had better tread carefully. "Father," I said as I sipped, "people only take up religion because they're looking for certainty in an uncertain world."

"You're too hasty, my son, too hasty. Yes, they may be hooked on certainty, but *atheists* are hooked on the same kind of certainty with their *dis*belief in God."

The 'my son' and 'my child' was quaint. I started again. "All right. Maybe what I should have asked was, 'what *is* religion?'"

"Good question," asserted Frostbight from across the table. "The Padre's the right man to ask."

"Thank you, Doctor," replied the clergyman. "Although I don't claim to be an expert." He returned to me. "My son, humanity can be divided into two schools of thought."

"Oh? I can assure you there are a *many* more than that."

"I'm aware of it, but in this case there's two I want to focus on."

"All right. Which two?"

"Firstly, the one that declares life's ultimately meaningless; that the world's mysteries will one day be solved by scientific scrutiny and that, I might add, we humans are simply animals with big brains."

"I'm right with you on that."

"I thought so."

"Anything else is hocus-pocus."

"Ah, you'd make a fine Humanist. I expect you believe the secrets of life will one day be revealed by physics."

"It couldn't be otherwise, Father. The material world is the only thing we can measure. Anything you can't measure is airy fairy."

"Oh?" he queried, turning slightly towards me. "Does 'airy fairy' include your emotions?"

"Well," I replied cautiously, "of course I've got emotions ..."

"Are they 'airy fairy'? I think not. Can you *measure* them?"

I cast my eyes down.

He went on. "And beliefs? What about beliefs? Or philosophy and questions about the meaning of life? Are there such things?"

"Er, no, I mean, yes."

"Yes, of course, whatever they are they're an essential part of life. But how are you going to measure them?"

"Er, well, I can't."

"That's right," he continued. "And what about intelligence? And even better, what about your *imagination?*"

"Imagination?" I replied lamely. "It's a by-product of the brain."

"Or so you *imagine.*"

"Huh. Very funny, Father."

He slowed and smiled. "But does it exist?"

An expression came to mind, 'caught by the short and curlies'. How can something exist that doesn't exist? I thought it best to go back to where we were. "You were going to say something about religion and the two schools of thought."

"Ah, yes." He looked to von Lottowind. "Professor, you taught about the two schools. What did you tell your students?"

The German addressed me. "You wish, mein Freund, to know about the second school?"

"That's the general idea, Professor. I've just been shot down in flames on the first one."

"Ah so, the other one: *that* school is made up of those who do not assume, like you, that the Universe is a closed system."

"Huh. What's that supposed to mean?"

"You, Herr Evriwun treat the Universe as if it were some kind of grand machine."

"Do I? Yes, I suppose I do. That's what it is, isn't it? Anyway, carry on."

"You believe that the universe is an end in itself? And you think that it can be completely knowable?"

"Right enough, Professor."

"But, Herr Evriwun, there is a particular problem."

"Yeah? What?"

He lowered his eyebrows and gave me a stern look. "How, mein Freund, can you possibly *know* it is completely knowable?"

I faltered. "Isn't it reasonable to think so? There are plenty of scientists and physicists who do."

"Reasonable?" He sniffed loudly. "It is not '*reasonable*'. Nein. It is a *belief*, and it is as dogmatic as any religion."

I grimaced. "I wouldn't know. Still, I say believing in '*spiritual*' realms is merely wishful thinking."

"You are too rash. The second school of thought admits that what we know is much less than what we do *not* know."

"Phew. Does it?" I gave it a moment to sink in. "So what am I supposed to do? Believe in hocus-pocus?"

He grinned. "Ah! You and your hocus-pocus. You do not understand?"

"No, actually."

"Physics," he said gravely, "is simply a visual exercise – a visual exercise along with a lot of calculations."

"Oh?"

"Ja. It is so. It handles only a fraction of your life experiences."

"I beg you pardon?"

"Without vision there would be no weighing machines, no rulers, no thermometers, gauges, monitors, microscopes or telescopes – and nor, for that matter, charts, graphs or geometry. Physics depends on good eyesight!"

"Well, all right, but what are you saying?"

"I am saying that physics is, to use an English expression, a 'dead duck' when it comes to the rest of your life. It is a 'dead duck' when it comes to the Arts, to music, rhetoric, story-telling, falling in love, joy and sorrow and so much more, including the things we're talking about tonight. Physics, mein Freund, is very, very limited."

I was not for giving in. "Professor, you can only *hope* there's more to existence than what the senses register. As far as I'm concerned, the laws of physics are something we can rely upon."

"Ach, so? You believe you can rely on nothing except the physical world?"

I hesitated.

"My child," cut in the Cleric from my left, "you're so old fashioned. Don't you know that people have been making claims that there's nothing more than the material world practically for ever?"

"Have they? Well, if they have, it's for good reason."

He stopped and looked across the table. "Doctor, do you want to say anything?"

Our host had been quietly observing us. Having finished his borsch, he was breaking apart morsels of bread. He waved a hand at the Cleric. "Not at all, Padre. Keep going. You're good at this stuff."

"I don't know about that, but thank you." The clergyman turned again to me. "Where were we? Oh, yes. Do you remember the Wisdom of Solomon?"

"No, not really."

"A pity: it's interesting. The author wrote that in his day the Greek philosophers believed thoughts were sparks emitted from the lungs – the sort of thing Demetrius upheld, remember?"

"Er, to be honest, no."

"Not to worry. Of course," he went on, "nowadays neuroscientists explain thoughts as 'sparks', not in the lungs, but in the brain." He took another sip of soup and said, "You see, modern thinking hasn't advanced very far."

"Maybe Classical times were more enlightened than we give them credit."

"Don't you believe it. Can you *see* 'sparks' in anyone's brain?"

"Well, no, of course not, unless I hook you up to a monitor."

"That's right. So right now how do you know I'm thinking?"

"Um. Because you're speaking?"

"Naturally. And you're trying to tell me my brain somehow fires into life, somehow creates my thoughts, and then, somehow, turns them into words via my larynx and lips?"

"Yeah, something like that."

He sighed. "My child, Demetrius wasn't as bright as you imagine. It's a totally circular argument: he didn't notice that the *theory itself* – that thoughts are 'sparks in the lungs' – is *also* made from the very same 'sparks'. Are the '*sparks*' somehow intelligent and self-conscious? How could that be?" He paused and said with a faint smile, "If Demetrius had had a few *more* sparks he would have realised he was talking nonsense!" Father Foggie lowered his specs. "Look here," he said as he regarded me, "the crucial question is this: *who* or *what* is firing the brain?"

"Who?" I repeated. "Well, me, obviously."

"Oh?" he returned. "And where does the 'me' come from? Another bunch of sparks?"

It was a tough question. "Search me. *I* don't know."

"No? Well, you need to know. Is the brain working randomly? Does it just do, as you call it, it's 'own thing'? You tell me."

I puckered my lips.

"The answer's not difficult," he continued. "As you've just said, you know perfectly well it's *you* who are creating your thoughts. *The* key question remains: *who is this invisible 'you' who's doing it?*"

I had no reply.

"Actually," he said, "I'd be astonished if you had given me an answer. We'll be coming back to this in due course. In the meantime …" He stopped. "Oh, dear, I've lost my train of thought. Professor?" he asked. "Where were we?"

"We were questioning, Herr Pastor, whether physics is something we can rely upon."

"Ah, yes, thanks." Turning again to me, the Rector said, "Here's another key thing: you, like everyone, *can't say what the world is:* you can only describe *what it seems* like – what it seems like to *you.*"

"Huh? What's that? Double Dutch?"

"If it sounds like Double Dutch, I'm sorry, but we'll talk more about it shortly. For now what I'm saying is important. Your believing there's nothing more to existence than what's physical is *not an observation.*"

"No? Well, I think it's a jolly good observation."

"Oh dear. As the Professor's just said: it's dogma." He leant towards me and said quietly, "My son, scientists rarely make good philosophers."

I sipped my borsch. It was getting cold.

He went on. "You see, scientific theories depend on beliefs just as much as do the sightings of garden fairies."

"Oh, come on, Father," I replied briskly. "You can hardly say garden fairies are predictable and repeatable."

"No, I wouldn't. Nevertheless, science is ruled by beliefs."

I mulled it over. "Is this your roundabout way of telling me that the second school of thought believes religion gives us *real* explanations?"

"I didn't say that. The value of religion, my son, is that it's a way of raising the proverbial glass ceiling – something we'll be doing tonight."

"What 'glass ceiling'?"

"The prejudice that there's nothing beyond what's physical."

"But it's *not* a prejudice."

"Of course it is."

I sighed. "Well, whatever, it's no use turning to *religion* for help: it tells us nothing about the important question of how we landed on Earth." I quickly raised my hand. "No, no, please: I don't want one of those old Creation Myths."

He shrugged and tore a piece of his bread and buttered it. "So you don't think God created you?"

"Well, Father, if, *if* He created me, *how* did he 'create' me?"

"You don't think he had the power to do so?"

"I have no idea. What is He? A magician or something, pulling a rabbit out of a hat?" I took a breath. "You see, Father, loads of religions talk of God or gods creating the world, creating mankind, creating other gods, creating angels or whatever, but they avoid the vital question: *how* do they manage it?"

"Mmm ..." He nodded slowly. "That's good thinking. Well done. You've raised a matter which most people miss. That's another thing we'll return to later. Right now, I'm sorry you don't find religion helpful."

"Are you being serious? How could I? It's simply a hotbed of myths, doctrines, rules and taboos." I finished my soup and put down my spoon. I was worried I was being too confrontational. "I'm sorry, Father. As you gather, I'm hardly convinced about God."

"Don't give up on religion."

"And why not?"

"As I say, my child, it respects that there's a lot we don't know."

"Humph!" I mumbled, "so it may, but it's not much good at it."

"I beg your pardon?"

I spoke up. "It may address things unknown, Father, but it hasn't come up trumps with any answers – at least no *real* answers."

He smiled. "But it provides the rational for an organised universe."

I couldn't make out whether he really meant what he said. "All right," I asked, "so what *should* I believe? I want to know the *Truth*."

"Ah," he replied. "It's easy."

"No it's not."

"It is." He grinned. "The *truth* is you're wasting your time looking for it."

"Crikey. How cynical can you be?"

"My child, I'm not being cynical. Nothing can be true unless you *believe* it's true. Truth isn't a 'thing' in itself. But for now, don't worry: we'll come to it."

Part III

❧

The Importance of Religion

THE RECTOR TOOK A DRINK OF WATER. "SO," HE ASKED, "what do you believe about God?"

"God? Huh. I believe religious people are in love with an imaginary Person or persons ruling over a visible earth and an imaginary heaven – to say nothing of hell."

"Oh, so you've no shortage of beliefs?"

"I don't," I replied, missing the irony, "believe anything except that it's a pious fraud."

"Dear me. You're sure?"

"Yes, it's fiction."

He raised his eyebrows. "Oh? Don't you read novels?"

I hesitated. "Yes, of course."

"They're fiction."

"I know. So what?"

"It doesn't stop you reading them, does it?"

That caught me with my pants down. "No," I replied quietly, "I suppose it doesn't. But the trouble with religious adherents is they pretend it's *real*."

"Ah, very good," he responded. "Nevertheless, where religion comes into its own is where it gets you to do what you do so little."

I looked at him. "I expect, Father, you want me to ask 'what's that?'"

He smiled. "Of course. You see, whether or not it's fiction, religion is a view of life that coaxes your imagination to expand beyond the mundane – what we'll be doing tonight."

I did not respond for a minute. "All right," I said. "I can't say what you hope to do tonight, but do you think I *should* believe in God?"

He shrugged. "Maybe, maybe not. 'Should', as they say, is 'shit'."

"Father, did I hear you say '*shit*'?"

He smiled again.

"But look," I went on, "religion doesn't help: it stops us using our intelligence. God was somebody *else's* idea – neither yours nor mine – a very long time ago."

"So what do you suggest?"

"*I* don't know. *You're* the chaplain, not me!"

He buttered some more bread. "Patience my child," he said. "You're conducting an exercise in logic. Religion, remember, is an exercise in imagination."

I wasn't feeling in the least bit patient. I persisted. "Father, you may think that God is a good thing, but you're asking me to pin myself to a *belief* that someone, *unknown to me*, created me – and created me in an equally unknown manner. Do you understand what I'm saying?"

"Of course," he replied.

It was both a frustration that Father Foggie was giving away so little, and yet a relief he was not trying to get me to join some secret sect. If this chap was anything to go by, Creosophists were a strange lot. "OK, Father, so what do you *really* think is so important about religion?"

"I've just said," he replied. "Expanding your imagination." He glanced across the table to von Lottowind. "Professor, you're quiet. What're your thoughts?"

I had noticed the German toying with his beard as he listened. "Mein Freund," he said to me, "you are exceptional."

"I am? Well, thank you, Professor, except I don't know what you're talking about."

"You are exceptional because you ask questions."

"So what? *Everyone* asks questions."

"But *you* ask ... Ah! Danken sie, Mould." The butler was reaching over and removing von Lottowind's bowl. "A most excellent soup."

"Thank you, Sir. I shall tell Mrs. McWhiteout."

As Mould went from place to place lifting the bowls, I said, "Professor, I'm still not with you."

"Nein? I refer to your question, 'why do I exist?' Tell me: why is that exceptional?"

"*I* don't know. It seems a pretty obvious thing to ask."

"It is because of your time frame."

"Oh?"

"That is the difference. Most time frames for most people are limited – they stretch to about a week."

"Yeah, don't I know!"

"Das is so. *You*, however, ask about the *whole of life* – and beyond."

"And?"

"It shows you are ready to expand your imagination."

"Huh. So you're also into 'imagination'?"

"Indeed. And you must be aware," he added, "that if you ask unusual questions you invite unusual answers."

"No problem with that, Professor. I'm fine with unusual answers."

"You are? Good. I trust you are prepared ..."

I did not imagine I needed any 'preparation'. In the meantime, the butler was reaching over my right hand side to pick up my bowl.

"Thank you," I said politely.

"Would you care for some butter with your bread roll, Sir?"

It was evident Mould was an old hand at looking after guests. I had forgotten about my bread. "Yes, please." He passed me the silver dish, and moments later I was scooping lashings of soft, yellow butter onto my side plate. It was so good to be here, free of rationing – one of the perks of country living.

I looked left as I tore the roll in my fingers. "Father Foggie," I started, "despite what you lot are saying, you've *got* to remove God from the picture."

"But then what?" he asked.

"Well, nothing. It's *obvious* I tell you: the world's meaningless. It's a random bundle of atoms."

Dr. Frostbight intervened. "I love those words 'obvious' and 'random'." He wiped the napkin over his moustache and gestured discretely to Mould, who lifted an ornate gold jug from the sideboard. "A little wine, everyone?" Without waiting for an answer, he went back to me. "Yes," he said, "that word 'obvious'. Obvious to whom? The cat?"

"No, not the cat. *Everyone.*"

"Well, I can tell you, old boy, it's certainly not obvious to everyone. And as for 'random', it's just a posh way of saying, 'I haven't a clue'."

"My son," said the Rector, "you have to face the all important question."

"Das is so," agreed von Lottowind. "Or we make no progress."

I looked at each of them. "Another one? *What* question?"

Part IV

☙

Metaphors for Life

"COME ON, OLD CHAP," CAME IN FROSTBIGHT. "I TOLD YOU."

"Told me what?"

"The key thing you need to ask."

"What 'key thing'?"

"The question we discussed before dinner."

"Oh? You mean '*what is life*?'"

"Exactly. Or, as we've been saying, 'what is the universe?'"

I was unimpressed. "Doctor, I really don't see why you make such a fuss. The question's not going to get us anywhere. I keep telling you, *nobody knows*."

While saying that, I was distracted by the claret jug as Mould filled our glasses. It was magnificent: embossed with exquisite designs of exotic faces and oak leaves. If it were really gold, it must have been priceless.

Our host noticed my gaze and winked. "Not bad, eh?"

"I should say so, Doctor."

"My favourite piece."

"I'm not surprised. How did you come by it?"

"Simple. We supply the gold. Others change it into a work of art."

"Oh?"

I had the queer sense that Doctor Frostbight's comment was more than what it seemed. Nonetheless I was frustrated. "Doctor, you ask me what life is, but you know it's a philosophical chestnut no one's explained."

"Mein Freund," interposed the German, "it is most wise to find the answer. If you know *what life is*, you know what the world is, and if you know what the world is, you might find the answer to why you are here on Earth."

"Gosh, that's steep. All right then, *if* you reckon you can answer the impossible, what is it?"

The clergyman intervened. "Let's go back to what we were talking about a short while ago. Phrase the question differently. Try this: what does life *seem to be* to you?"

"Father, that's the same thing."

"Maybe, maybe not."

I wished he would stop saying that. Nonetheless, I could see I was not going to be let off the hook. What to reply? It was no use stating 'life is life' as I had before dinner. So I grunted, half seriously, "Well, all right then, I'll tell you what life is. *It's a sausage-making machine.*"

There was a brief lull. Von Lottowind fiddled with his beard, and murmured, "Aha, a *sausage*-making machine?" He thought about it and began to chuckle and then laugh, which increased the more he considered it. And the more he considered it, the more he laughed, and the more he laughed the funnier he thought it was, until he ended up holding his stomach and sobbing and repeating, "*A sausage-making machine!*" The effects of these antics took hold of the Rector. He, too, was soon doubled up in stitches. Finally the contagion spread to Doctor Frostbight until all three were gasping for air and wiping their eyes.

I could not see the big joke. "It's wasn't *that* funny," I said weakly against the hullabaloo – but that only doubled their convulsions.

It was some time before the Professor settled down, dabbed his eyes again and stopped muttering 'sausages'.

I waited.

"Ah, mein Freund," he began when composed enough to take a deep breath, "philosophers do not laugh enough." He took another breath and gently let it out. "Can you tell me what life is when it is *not* a sausage making machine?"

"Search me!" I exclaimed briskly.

That reply was enough to spark off more laughter. The Doctor was the first to calm down. "OK, OK," he said as he also took a breath to steady himself. "Sorry about the hilarity. I know: let's try putting the question another way." He hiccupped. "'How do you *describe* your life?' Or could we ask, 'how do you describe your *world*?'"

"My child," said the Reverend Foggie, blinking and using his handkerchief to clear his specs. "You really are most amusing. Nonetheless, your noticing how you describe your life is essential. You see, everyone has their individual description, and we experience life according to how we imagine it."

"Oh? I'm not with you."

"Well, for example …" He pondered. "For example, I'm sure you've heard of people calling life a 'rat race'?"

"Yes. It's pretty common."

"It is. And what else? What about, 'life's a party'? Or, it's 'a bowl of cherries'? Or a 'game'?"

"All right …"

"Whatever *they* call it, it will lead to a different experience of life from that of the man who says it's a 'rat-race'."

"Das is so," agreed the German, still drying his eyes. "We describe life in metaphors."

"Exactly, Gusty," came in Frostbight. He looked at me. "Got the hang of it old chap?"

"Sorry, Doctor. I can't say I have."

"No? OK. How about this? Some people describe life as a 'nightmare'. Others call it an 'adventure'. Again, for others it's a 'journey' – that's a common one."

"So?"

"Each one answers the question."

I felt stupid. "What question?"

He sighed. "The question of *what life is*."

"Oh." I thought for a moment. "Well, as far as I'm concerned, life's a bitch and then you die."

This sent them into further rounds of hysterics. Von Lottowind found it so funny I thought he might haemorrhage. And there I had been thinking German professors had no sense of humour.

"All right," I resumed once they'd got over their amusements, "I can tell you lot one thing for sure: *whatever* life is, it's a struggle."

"Ah, good," mused the Professor as he relaxed. "Very good: a battle metaphor."

I frowned. "A what?"

"A battle metaphor, mein Freund."

"What've battles got to do with it?"

"You speak of 'struggles'."

"I know. So?"

"A 'struggle' is what *you* think life is – a metaphorical war."

"A what?"

"You are at 'war'."

"No, I didn't say that."

"But life, for you, is a fight or a battle? No?"

"I didn't say it was a 'battle'. I said it was a 'struggle'."

"But a 'struggle' is a fight, and a fight is part of a battle."

I stopped to think about it. "Yeah," I muttered, "I suppose."

"Good. And a battle is part of a war. No?"

I shrugged. "All right. So?"

"For you in particular, whether or not the struggles of the World War are over, your own personal, invisible war carries on."

I raised my hands in submission. "All right. I agree."

"Ach! Another battle metaphor."

"What, my agreeing with you?"

"Nein. Your submission. Surrendering is part of a battle."

I found myself rubbing my face.

"But," continued the Professor, "you must also understand it is also poetry."

"What? My 'surrender'?"

"That too. I was thinking more of your idea that life is a 'struggle'."

"Humph," I said, mulling it over. "I can't see how it's poetry. Life *is* a struggle, and there's nothing 'poetical' about it."

"It is indeed poetical," he said. "The 'struggle' is a metaphor, and metaphors are poetry."

"Is that so? Well, *I* don't think it's poetry. Maybe *you're* not struggling, but *I* am and so are a lot of people. If you ask me, your 'metaphors' are a refuge for scoundrels who don't know what they're talking about."

Across the table, Frostbight chuckled. "Ah!" he said. "A sentence loaded with metaphors."

"Oh? Where? *I* don't see any."

"Trust me young chap, I'm a Doctor."

There was a twinkle in his eye. He knew I was finding it hard.

Part V

❧

A Different Description

"BUT, DOCTOR," I ASKED, "WHY DOES THIS ALL MATTER?"
He focused on me. "Because your *description* of your life
will impact *your whole world*."

"It will? Yeah, sure."

He did not rise to my scepticism. "Tonight," he carried on, "we're aiming to teach you the distinction between what you experience and how you *describe* what you experience."

"Oh? I didn't know there was a problem."

"I can see that."

I did not understand what he was talking about. "But," I asked, "do we *have* to call life *anything*?"

"Absolutely. Whether you like it or not, you can't escape calling it *something.*" He was emphatic. "Everyone has a description for their life, even if they haven't verbalised it."

"You're sure about that? I don't think I have one."

"Of course you have. You've called your life a 'struggle'."

"Oh, yes, so I have."

"And that makes sense to you."

"Well, yes, it does, Doctor. What's wrong with that?"

"Nothing – except you're miserable and you wonder why."

I fiddled with some crumbs on my side plate. "So now what?"

"You need is a better 'picture', that's what."

"All right," I said slowly. "Which picture?"

The Doctor used his napkin to mop his moustache, first to the left and then the right. "We'll come to it."

"We will? When?"

"Soon."

"Huh. So you say. What am I supposed to do in the meantime?"

"Look at how you portray your experiences. Up until now you've portrayed life as a matter of winning and losing 'fights', whether it's with your career, your health, your finances, your family or your love-life." He looked to see if I were following him.

"Carry on," I said, waiting to see where this might lead.

"Well," Frostbight went on, "what we're going to suggest is a description of life which can change how you experience the world."

"Goodness me," I muttered. As I said this, the butler was to my right, pouring me wine. I wondered if it were the 'done thing' to engage him. He wasn't as deaf as I thought – and nor as short sighted. I liked hearing the opinion of ordinary people. "May I call you 'Mould'?" I asked.

"Of course, Sir."

"Thank you. What do you think about all this?"

The old fellow cleared his throat. "About metaphors?"

"Yup. Ever heard of them?"

"If, sir, you are talking of life as a struggle, may I draw your attention to Professor Einstein?"

"Albert Einstein?"

"Quite so. He states we need to ask ourselves, 'is the universe friendly or hostile?'"

"Gosh, really? I thought he was a scientist. Whatever, it's a good question. If you ask me, the world's often hostile."

"That is not an unusual opinion, Sir." He moved placidly on.

"Das is so," nodded the Professor. "As Mould indicates, many see life as a struggle because they believe the world is hostile, and if you also think life is a struggle, you too will assume it's hostile. On the other hand, if you describe it as a 'bowl of cherries', you will find people – how shall we say? – genial. So it goes on. If you think of life as a journey, you might expect an adventure, but as a 'battlefield'? You expect a fight."

"So?"

"Adolph Hitler adopted your belief – he even wrote about it. You have heard of his book, 'Mein Kampf': 'My Struggle'?"

"You bet."

"Good. We all know what *his* 'struggle' led to – especially when the German nation adopted his idea."

"But Professor, you're German and you didn't adopt his idea."

"That is because, as a Creosophist, my description of life is not that of a 'struggle'."

"Oh." I gave it some thought. "I don't know about your 'Creosophist' stuff, but everyone *else* seems to struggle. Look at the millions of Islamists."

"What of them?"

"Their religion says everyone should 'struggle' – you know, 'jihad': finding someone to fight."

Father Foggie came in. "That's a good observation, though I suspect 'jihad' also refers to the 'struggle' for self-improvement. Either way, you've made your point."

"So?"

"You're fortunate. You live in a culture where you're free to see life exactly how you wish to see it – independently of any religion or dictator."

"Whatever …" I responded without enthusiasm. "But whether you like it or not, a description is still just a description."

"You are underestimating – grossly underestimating – its power, but bear with us."

This was too much. I raised both hands again. "OK, I'm not surrendering this time, but stop right there." It was obvious the Rector did not understand. "What *I'm* saying is you can't explain what 'Life' – as a whole – *really* is."

"Why so?"

"Because it's impossible. *Nobody knows.*"

The Rector adjusted his specs. "I can't say what others do or don't know. However I *am* suggesting you're here tonight for a reason: we'd like to show you something different."

"Really? What?"

"We'll come to it."

"You're no better than the Doctor. When?"

"As he said: soon."

"Huh. And it's a big deal?"

"It is. It's pivotal."

I snorted. "I still don't know what you're talking about."

The Reverend continued. "As the Doctor said, if you adopt a different description, it will alter your life."

I sighed. "For the better?"

"Naturally. It goes without saying." He took a sip of his wine. "Maybe an analogy will help."

"Ugh. I hope so."

He shrugged. "We can only try. Imagine, for a moment, you'd received a head injury, lost your memory and recognised no one."

"Hard to imagine, but OK."

"Fine. Now say a man enters your room. Is he a friend or a relative? Or is he your doctor? Or maybe he's your lawyer to discuss your insurance? Or could it be the cleaner who's there to empty your waste paper basket?"

"Or," Professor Lottowind interjected, "is he a thief?"

"Exactly," said the Cleric. "Your response to your visitor will be very different according to how you describe him and how you understand who he is."

"So what?"

"It's just the same with your life."

"Is it?"

"Ja," returned the Professor. "If you think he is a thief when really he is your doctor, your response will be, how shall we say ... not exactly appropriate."

"I suppose it wouldn't."

"Now do you see the importance of how you describe someone – and, by extension, life itself?"

Part VI

✧

Agent or Patient?

"**Y**EAH, MAYBE." I PAUSED AND TOOK A SIP OF WINE while I thought it over. "All right, Professor," I said, "where's this leading? Maybe, *in theory*, if I described my life in a new way, it *might* make a change …"

"It would most certainly."

"But what do I do? If life for me *is* a struggle, it's no use my *pretending* it isn't. If I *don't believe* that life's a 'bowl of cherries', what happens? 'Fake it until I make it'?"

That raised a smile from the Rector. "No, my son," he interjected, "you don't have to fake it – in fact you don't even need to believe it."

"Humph. And I'm supposed to believe that?"

"You'll see. As I say, *it'll effect every experience you ever have.*" He returned the napkin to his lap and his specs to his nose as though he had said nothing of consequence.

"Hang about, Father," I objected, "that's a huge claim."

"Yes," he replied calmly. "And I think you might find it helpful."

"What we're saying," came in Frostbight, "is that it puts you in the position of agent rather than patient."

I gave him a blank look.

"You don't remember? You did grammar at school?"

"Grammar? Well yes. For years. What's that got to do with it?"

"Maybe you didn't cover the topic: in any one sentence, if the 'actor' performs something deliberately, that person's called an 'agent'."

"So?"

"So in the following sentence, 'Mould pours you a glass of wine', he is an 'agent'."

"He is? OK. So what does it make me?"

"It makes you a 'patient'."

"Huh."

"You're the 'patient' because you're the one receiving the effects."

"Oh, and not an actor?"

"Yes, you're an actor, but not an agent."

"Lord!" I exclaimed.

"And if," Frostbight continued, "you found this conversation so boring you fell asleep, you would be an actor – and yet not an agent."

"Because I didn't fall asleep deliberately?"

"Well, let's hope you didn't. Yes, you'd be a 'patient'. The action needs to be on purpose for you to be an 'agent'."

"So what happens when, say, I have an appointment to see my G.P.? I'm *his* patient, aren't I?"

He nodded. "A good point. That's a case where you're not just your doctor's patient, but also a patient with regard to your own health: you've handed it over to your doctor. He then becomes the agent – the one who prescribes you the drugs."

The Rector raised a hand. "May I make a comment, Doctor? I wish to point out that regarding your health, you *can* be the agent."

"Oh?"

"Yes. If you compromise your health through reckless living, you'd be the *agent* of its breakdown. And visa versa a propos good health." He paused. "I'd also add another thing."

"What?"

"This: any position of patient is passive and, therefore, vulnerable."

"So being a 'patient' is a bad thing?"

Frostbight answered. "No, old chap, that's not the idea. What's important is to be the 'patient' at the right time, such as being silent when listening to another, or when someone you love gives you a gift. It'd be rotten to refuse it."

"OK, I get that. So when shouldn't I be a 'patient'?"

"When you claim you're the *recipient of life* rather than its agent."

I frowned. "What do you mean?"

"When, for example, you think you're being criticised – or when you feel frightened or depressed."

"Well, Doctor," I commented, "it's all very interesting, but you've gone off the subject."

"It's relevant, old boy. You see, whatever's happening in your life, you'll be either the patient or the agent; and it's solely your description which will determine that."

I took time to chew over it. "But that means if someone thinks he's 'God's creation' he's playing the role of 'patient'."

"Exactly. And the same applies in your case when you think you're the victim of your 'struggles'."

"Oh." I pursed my lips. His point was clear. "I think you're telling me I'm mostly passive."

"Just so. And vulnerable. And unhappy. But it doesn't have to be that way."

"What makes you so sure?"

"Trust me."

I smiled. "Of course."

"You know, old chap, it only takes one sentence to turn you into the 'agent'. One sentence … and, of course, a bit of practice."

"Is that so? I like the sound of it. One sentence? OK. Come on: let's have it."

"Whoa, tiger. We haven't got there."

"Are you going to make me wait all night?"

He ignored my impatience. "Mind you, you're still going to have to make the journey yourself."

"I've no doubt I do. Where do you suggest I start?"

Frostbight leaned forward, scrutinised me and answered, "You need to listen more and argue less."

"Me? Argue?"

"You've got *two* eyes and *two* ears – but only *one* mouth."

"What's that supposed to mean?"

"It means that you'll need to keep that trap shut if you're to 'get' what we're talking about."

"Ouch!"

"That was a bit strong. Sorry. The thing is, we could talk all night, but what's crucial is *do you really want to know?*"

I was taken aback. "*Of course I do.*"

"We're not wasting our time?"

He was getting me worried. "No, Doctor, I'm not. What's the fuss?"

"Because unless you really want to know, you won't apply what we tell you, and you'll remain a typical philosopher playing intellectual games."

"Is that wrong?"

"No, it's not wrong – if that's what you want. But we might as well gossip or talk about the weather."

"All right. I promise I really want to know, but I wish you'd stop playing cat and mouse. If it's true you could change my life, what's with the secrecy?"

"We're not hiding anything. I want to be sure you're more interested to listen than to play around." He paused and looked at me carefully. "Very well, then. Here's the key. This is what'll take your life to a new level ..."

I leaned forward.

He stopped and turned to the kitchen door. "Uh-oh, what's that? Sounds like grub's on the way."

The rumble of the approaching trolley competed with the sound of the wind in the chimney. Conversation ceased. Mould sprung the hidden lever; the door opened and in walked the cook, wheeling our dinner.

How could this be? It was exasperating. Both times when he was going to reveal his great 'disclosure' we were interrupted. Was I *ever* going to hear it?

Doctor Frostbight admired the trolley. "Champion," he exclaimed, "the main course! Mrs. McWhiteout, it looks splendid. What've you got?"

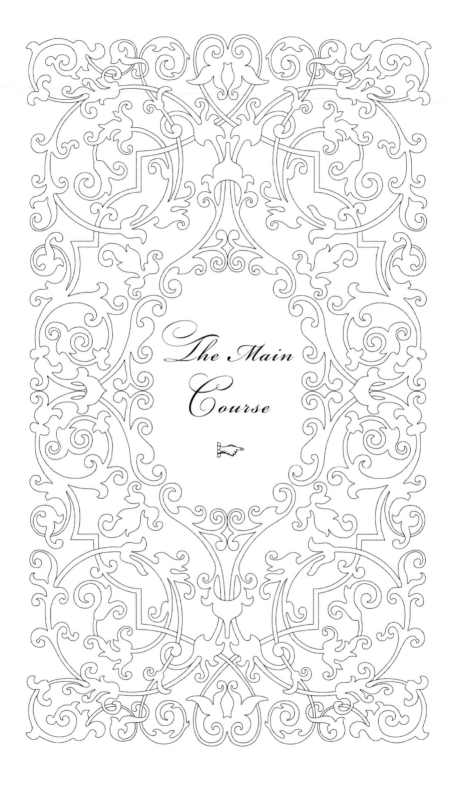

The Main
Course

Part I

e/o

Grand Revelation

S HE BROUGHT THE TROLLEY TO A HALT NEXT TO THE
sideboard and off-loaded a platter holding the salmon. Our cook
looked flushed and healthy, no doubt on account of standing
over a kitchen range. "I am pleased, Doctor," she said, in reply to
his question, "that the fish has turned out well: steamed with capers and
garlic and served with a dill sauce." Lifting another dish from the trolley,
she said, "here are buttered brusselsprouts picked this morning in the
frost, and here," she went on, "are roasted salsify and Jerusalem artichokes.
I thought they would make a nice change from potatoes. Finally," she
uttered proudly, "especially for the Professor: sauerkraut." In the corner
of my eye I caught sight of Doctor Frostbight turning up his nose, and
in so doing he set up a round of jocular quips and comments from the
others. Meanwhile, Mould set about the salmon with the fish slice, and
Mrs. McWhiteout placed warm plates in front of us.

While I was looking forward to dinner with relish, it was frustrating
having to wait for the discussion to resume. What *was* their 'Grand
Revelation'? It was as if the Doctor had orchestrated the delay. Maybe they
needed to egg me on in preparation for some 'mystical' experience? Still,
there was nothing to do but bide my time and be grateful for this feast. I
must say, I could not wait to tuck in.

"Finally," she uttered proudly, "especially for the Professor: sauerkraut."

It took some time for Mould and Mrs. McWhiteout to finish seeing to us, placing before us the salmon followed by the sauce and offerings of vegetables. Finally, with the serving dishes left on the hot plate, Mrs. McWhiteout wheeled her empty cart back to the kitchens; Mould went round with the claret jug and Doctor Frostbight and his friends made light conversation. I sat there with my hands on my lap until I saw my host lift his knife and fork.

"Pass me the salt would you old boy?" said the Doctor.

I pushed the silver saltcellar toward him to where he could reach it.

"Thank you." He spooned some granules onto the side of his plate. Without looking up he said, casually, "So?"

About to take a mouthful, I returned my fork to the plate. "I'm sorry?"

"The essential question remains, old chap. What is life?"

I waved my hand about. "Doctor, I give up. I've no idea."

"Then put it another way: what sentence, or even one word, could change your world?"

"Now you *are* pushing your luck. Down to only *one word*?"

"Yes, one would do it."

"Impossible. It's nonsense." What else could I answer? On looking around I caught von Lottowind's eye. "Professor?" I asked, looking for guidance.

The German mopped his beard. "Ah! So you wish to know the description that makes the difference?"

I groaned. "I wish *someone* would come up with the goods."

"Herr Foggie," said the Professor, "do you wish to tell him?"

The Cleric shrugged.

"Good idea," seconded Frostbight. "Come on, Padre."

Father Foggie took a moment to finish his mouthful and dabbed his mouth with his napkin. "My child," he responded quietly, "what we're referring to is this ..." He turned to me. "Life is many things ..."

"Thank you, I've got that." I waited. "And ...?"

"There's one especially ..."

"OK ... does it mean you're going to tell me?"

He smiled. "Yes, it does. It's this." He fixed his brown eyes on me over the rim of his specs. "Life, my child, *is a creation.*"

As he said this, the gaps in the shutters lit with a sudden brilliance. Instantly the table trembled with an explosion of thunder that shook the room. My heart missed a beat. No sooner did it pass than the storm, roaring like no other, burst open the shutters and with a crash blew apart the French windows. It was extraordinary the glass did not shatter. Snowie barked and scuttled for cover; cold air flooded in and snow swirled about. The candle lights danced in all directions and sparks from the fire flurried up the chimney. This was better than Hollywood. Where was the spectre of the Doctor's late wife?

The others paid little attention. "Such pesky windows," commented Frostbight. "Ah, thank you, Mould." The old butler was already limping to sort out the problem. Before long order was restored and the shutters back in place, this time with the locking bars properly secured.

"That's better," stated our host. "Peace, perfect peace. My goodness me, thunder snow. A lively night, eh what, Gusty? Most unusual."

"Most certainly, Watty," agreed his friend. "Das is no ordinary storm."

No, indeed, I thought, and no ordinary stage set either.

"I say," asked our host, looking at me. "You all right, old boy?"

I was wiping my forehead. "I'm sorry, Doctor. It's the war. Loud noises: they set me off."

"Shell shock, eh what? Jolly bad luck. Let us know if we can do anything."

"Thank you," I replied, "I'll be fine in a minute," embarrassed for being so neurotic. Near the fireplace, Snowie gingerly slunk to her bed, and the rest of us resumed our dinner. For a time the company was silent, save for scraping cutlery, the crackling of the fire and the background hooting of the wind. I had to admit those windows blowing open like that was pretty spooky. Still, no ghost walked in. Was it just a fluke it happened when the Rector said 'life's a creation'? And now that I had a chance to think about it, why the hype about '*creation*'? What was *that* for a Revelation? Was that it? Talk about anti-climax. I put down my fork, looked at everyone and exclaimed, "You mean that's that? All over?"

Frostbight wiped his moustache. "What's over old boy?"

"Well ... the *Grand Revelation?*"

"What Grand Revelation?"

"You know: the Great Secret you were going to reveal?"

"Is there a problem?"

"Yes, there is. Where're the fireworks? What about a Voice from Heaven?"

He grinned. "You wanted pyrotechnics?"

"I don't know what I wanted, but I thought there would be *something* with at least a bit of *oomph*."

"'Oomph', eh?" He looked at me with mock seriousness. "Those windows getting burst open wasn't bad, was it?"

I could not decide how seriously to take him. "Yeah, all right, it did take me by surprise. But what about your 'Revelation'? Are you saying that's all it is? Life's a creation? That's your 'Great Secret'?" It was hard to hide my disappointment.

Frostbight looked at me. "What's the matter?"

"Just one word? A creation? End of?"

"Yes," he replied. "One word. You see? Simple. Even child's play."

"Yeah," I snorted. "A bit *too* simple for my liking. Is that the end of the discussion?"

"Ah!" he replied. "You've not yet grasped the implications."

"Implications? I can't see any. What's so 'exciting'? That the world's a creation? It's *obvious*."

"Good. Glad to hear it."

"What do you mean, 'glad to hear it'? *Everyone* knows that *something* created the world *somehow*."

"So who do you think it was?"

"*I* don't know. We've already been through that. Maybe God? Or some sort of invisible Intelligence? The Big Bang? Don't ask me, I'm not the expert."

He took a moment to answer. "If," he said, "Father Foggie thought the world was created by God or the Big Bang he would have said so. He simply said 'life is a creation'."

"Doctor, that doesn't help. If the world *wasn't* created either by God, Big Bang or whatever, it shows it's random."

"You're sure?" He looked at the Rector. "Come on, Padre, help me out here."

Father Foggie spoke. "You see, my son, even if it *were* serendipity, you'd still be left with the question: 'who did it – who made it like that?'"

"Who made it like what?"

"Serendipitous."

I didn't seem to be getting anywhere. "Maybe," I suggested in desperation, "*nobody* created it: it just happens spontaneously."

There was silence. Von Lottowind cleared his throat, smoothed his ginger beard and studied me. Finally he stated, "Sie, mein Freund, stellten die Welt her."

Was he really Prussian, or just pretending? My only German was, 'Achtung! Spitfire!'

Dr. Frostbight came to my rescue. "Not up on German? What he just said was that it's *you* who created the world."

I stopped. "Huh. He did, did he? Well, if he really said that, tell him if it's not a joke, he's a Prussian nutcase."

"My goodness, old chap. What's the upset?"

"Doctor, I'm not a total idiot, you know. *I* didn't create *any* world."

Our host laughed. "So you think he needs his head tested?"

"I should say so. He's talking rubbish." My response was blunter than I meant it to be. But telling me *I created the world?* That was it – confirmed – these men? Off their rockers.

"Too dull to be a grand Revelation?" asked Frostbight with a quizzical expression.

"Dull?" I replied. "No, not at all. Just bonkers." Remembering what he had said, I smiled. "Yeah, Doctor, and *far* too simple!"

He returned my smile. "I told you. A grand Revelation isn't necessarily a blockbuster. Think about it: the greatest river starts in the hills as a spring that's so insignificant you'd hardly notice it."

"What's that got to do with it?"

"The idea takes time to grow. As I said, you don't yet realise the implications embedded in the simple sentence."

I piled salmon onto my fork and took a mouthful. He was right. I could not see any 'implications'.

It was the Rector's turn again. "My son, it'll take you a while. We're not telling you your life is *any* creation. We're telling you it's *yours*, not somebody else's. It's yours – at all times."

I put down my knife and fork, ran my napkin over my mouth and straightened up. "Oh, I realise what you're getting at, and you know what?"

"No?"

"It's not new."

"Is it not?"

"No – anything but! Any clever dick could tell me the same thing. How does it go? 'You're the architect of your life'; 'life's what you make it'; 'you're responsible for what happens'; 'for the world to change, *you*'ve got to change'; 'it's you who designs your future'. There's loads of them. *I've heard it all before.*"

The Rector sipped a little water. "Take your time. Those sayings have their merit, but there's more."

"Oh, yeah? For me there isn't."

He turned to look at me directly. "My son," he said slowly, "listen. The *whole* of your life is your creation, every jot and tittle. We're talking of not just your actions, thoughts, feelings and memories, but the *whole world* and everything you've ever experienced."

"Whoa! Extreme!"

"Patience, my child, patience. What we're saying is that there has never, ever been *anything* in your field of consciousness that you haven't created yourself … no exceptions." He resumed eating. "How's that?"

"How's what?" I grumbled.

"What I've just said."

"It's totally crackpot, that's what."

"Oh, dear, you don't mince your words."

"Well, really, Father: I had no more to do with my coming into existence than you or anyone else."

"You're sure?"

"Oh, I wish you lot would stop asking me that. My life simply *happens*. Or, rather, it happened because of my parents, just like yours."

"And that," he answered, "is what you imagine."

"Well, of course it is! It's *true*."

"Ah, it's 'true', eh?" came in Frostbight. "To whom? You talking to your cat again?"

"No, I'm talking to *you*."

"Look, old boy, when you said life 'just happens', you're not telling us anything."

"Maybe, but at least it's not lunatic."

Frostbight played with his wine glass while he thought. "What the Padre is saying," he explained, "is you don't 'happen' *because* of the universe, but that the universe 'happens' *because of you*."

"Whoa. Steady on, Doctor. That's too clever by half."

"Is it?"

"Yeah, it's nothing of the sort."

"How do you know?"

"Ask anyone."

"Really? 'Ask anyone'?" Frostbight sniffed his wine and took a little. "What do you think?"

"Me? You don't have to ask. I think you've got bats in your belfry."

He chuckled. "You're right about the bats! No, actually I was asking about the wine."

I calmed down and realised I was getting too excited to pay attention. I tasted it. "Very good, Doctor. Quite distinctive, in fact."

"As long as you enjoy it."

"Do you really grow grapes up here?"

"Yes. Under glass."

"Wow! I wouldn't expect it."

"Yes, surprising, isn't it? Now," he said, "back to where we were. Look. What you're talking about are simply beliefs."

"I know. What's the matter?"

"Because, as my late wife used to say, 'a thousand beliefs don't make a truth'."

It was not the first time I had heard that. "Oh, all right," I replied, "fair enough: your late wife was probably right and a thousand beliefs *don't* make a truth. But you can't escape the fact that the world *is* just a 'happening thing' going on out there more or less randomly."

"I'm sorry, old boy, but you're simply making a stab in the dark."

"Huh. So what do you expect me to do? Take on some loony belief?"

Out of the corner of my eye I saw the Reverend Foggie put down his knife and fork and wipe his mouth. I wondered what was coming. "A loony belief?" he said. "We're not talking about beliefs."

"No, Father?" I said, turning to him. "Sounds awfully like it to me. How can you possibly know life's my creation?"

"Neither," he quipped, "are we talking about knowledge."

"Uh …"

"Yes, most students ask that question. We'll come to what we do or don't know later. For now, what we're doing is drawing your attention to an *idea* – one you can't escape from."

"Oh yeah? Try me."

"All right. *Describing* the world as a creation is *itself* a creative act, and believing it's 'random' is equally a creative act. So is denying it. Making a stab in the dark is a creative act. You can never not be creative."

I gave it a moment's thought. "What if I didn't believe you?"

"It makes no difference. I've just said: it's not about beliefs. You can see it for yourself. *However* you react to these words – no matter what – it will be a creative engagement. Full stop. That's it, in a nutshell."

Part II

❦

Two Imaginations

H IS WORDS KEPT ME QUIET FOR A BIT. OFTEN FRIENDS had told me that I was rather 'creative' in my thinking, but this stuff took the biscuit. Definitely time for a break. I tackled Mrs. McWhiteout's alternative to potato. I had not come across salsify before.

Von Lottowind spoke up, seemingly none the worse for my calling him a Prussian nutcase. "I wish to emphasise," he started, "that, as Pastor Foggie said, the kind of 'creating' we're talking about is more than simply what you say or do."

"I'm sorry, I'm not with you," I mumbled through a mouthful.

"As he stated, *all of your life* is your creation – your whole world, 'hook line and sinker', as you have it in English. It includes your beliefs and the beliefs of others; the people you have met; your family; the places you have been; the books you have read; your self; your country; your past; your present; your future. All of it."

"Steady on," I replied.

"Maybe I should be more precise?"

"Have a go."

"It is this. Your life is not just one creation."

"Goodness. It isn't? Well, you had me fooled."

The Chaplain smiled and explained. "The Professor's saying you're running two simultaneously."

"Two, Father? What? Two at the same time?"

"All the time."

"Humph," I grunted. "One's plenty, thank you."

"I make it clear," said von Lottowind, taking over, "and I expect we will return to this from time to time."

"OK," I sighed, "let's have it."

"Good. You operate by means of two kinds of creation. We will call the first your 'Instant imagination' and the second we will call your 'Dependent imagination'."

"Phew. What's this? Some 'Creosophist' doctrine?"

"We are not talking of 'doctrine'. We are talking of creative *observation*."

"You are? Whose?"

"Yours – if you wish."

"Who says?"

"We do."

"Well, I can assure you it's not *my* observation, and nor anyone else's. It sounds like something you've just cooked up."

"Is that a problem?"

"What? You think you can go about making up any crazy ideas you want?"

"Ach! I ask you a question. Which do you prefer to trust: someone else's authority or your own intelligence?"

"God, I don't know. All I can tell you is I can't go round making up anything I want."

"Nein? Then how are you going to discover new ideas?"

I took another mouthful and chewed for a moment. "Haven't the foggiest," I replied. "You'd have to give me evidence. But whatever, I've never heard of your 'two imaginations'."

"So they are not familiar to you?"

"No, of course they aren't. Anyway, go on."

"Good. I will. Firstly, your 'Instant' is what you call 'reality'."

"It is? Well, reality's certainly not *my* imagination!"

"I did not say the distinction is between reality and imagination."

"Excuse me, but you did." I stuffed in a brusselsprout.

"Nein. It is between one *kind* of imagination and another."

"Oh, is it?" I frowned. "But you're making out reality's *imaginary*. You can bet your bottom dollar reality's a good deal more than that: that's why it's called 'real'."

The Prussian was not persuaded. "Reality is *only* real," he emphasised, "*because that is how you have made it.*"

"What? Impossible!"

"Ah so? Then tell me how it could be real if *someone else* invented it."

"Don't know. It just ... well ..."

His eyebrows knitted. "You would dismiss it."

"No I wouldn't."

"You most certainly would – or," he persisted, "you would at least question it. Your problem is you fail to value your *own* imagination."

"Hey, I do nothing of the sort."

"We will talk more of this. For now I wish to move on."

"Fair enough," I huffed. "You can move on if you want, but you're barking up the wrong tree."

"I am sorry? Barking ... up ...?"

"An expression, Professor. Keep going. What about that so-called 'Dependent' imagination?"

"Ah, your Dependent imagination. It is your daily thoughts – sometimes called your 'Shadow' or 'Reflective' imagination."

"And what's the surprise about *that?*"

"There is nothing surprising about it. It is what you would normally call your imagination. Maybe Watty talked to you about this before dinner?"

"I don't remember."

"Das is a pity. So ... what is reality?"

"Lord! 'Reality'? *You've* just said it's my imagination. For all normal people it's the physical world."

"Let me explain. Reality is your Instant imagination creating the world around you, which you *imagine* goes on independently of you."

"Humph," I said again, "sounds like a Creed."

"Ah, so? A Creed?"

"Nothing. Anyway, what's with this 'Instant' imagination? Imagination or no imagination, any physical experiences *are* independent of me."

"Nein. 'Reality' is a creative construct, but right now you cannot see that."

"You're telling me!"

"Ach, you see? You have such a poor opinion of your creative imagination."

"Have I?" I pouted. "I'm sorry, I still don't know what you're talking about."

"Maybe that will change. For now, I wish to look at your *Dependent* imagination."

"Oh? All right. I can't exactly stop you."

"Good. You must understand the Dependent imagination deals with your explanations *about* life."

"What explanations? I haven't got any."

He shook his head. "You have more than you could number. You may not be aware of your explanation for life as a whole, but you are never without daily explanations. They are endless: your commentaries, judgements, justifications, beliefs, stories and so on."

"They're OK aren't they?"

"In some ways they are, and in some ways they are not."

I chewed on some artichoke. "Well, I don't think I know what you're saying, but there's nothing wrong with my judgments – or my stories."

"Herr Evriwun, you have much to learn. At this moment, you need to be clear that you create the world with your two Imaginations."

"Huh. Sounds to me like a load of mumbo jumbo."

"I would understand you do not think much of this idea?"

"Want me to be brutally honest?"

He gave a knowing smile.

"Then, no," I went on. "I *don't* think much of it – at all."

"Why so?"

"Because, Professor, you're making out I'm hallucinating."

"Ach. You are hallucinating?"

"No, I'm not. I didn't mean that. Haven't you heard of the *reality* of 'reality'? You know …" I tapped the table, " … the thing everyone else calls 'the physical world'?"

Von Lottowind frowned and turned to Frostbight. "Watty," he said, "you are better at explaining these things."

The Doctor finished his mouthful. "Thank you, Gusty," he replied, "I don't think I'm any better than you. It's not easy." He looked over to me. "You want to know the reality of the reality of reality?"

I swallowed. "Doctor, that's an awful lot of realities."

"It is, old boy, and all of it's your own invention."

"Huh. Beginning to sound like a broken record."

"That's because we'll need to keep drumming it into you."

"Drumming or no drumming, I have no intention of thinking everything's my invention."

"That's OK. You're not the first person."

"Whoa! You're as bad as the Professor. I'm sorry: you're talking baloney. You're making out reality's 'in the mind'. It's not. It's *out there*. I keep saying, *that's* what makes it *'real'*."

"Positive about that?"

"Naturally. If a brick drops on my head, it jolly well hurts. Reality is objective by *definition*."

"You're sure?"

"Of course I am! What do you think science is all about? If the external world weren't *objective*, science couldn't exist."

"So you think the world has nothing to do with you?"

"I *know* it doesn't: the universe runs with or without me – and the same goes for you. Ask any scientist."

"What would be the point of asking a 'scientist'?"

"He might put some sense into you."

Frostbight put in a mouthful. "You think so?" After a moment's chewing, he said, "Look, a training in science, old boy, makes a scientist: it doesn't make a *philosopher*."

"So?"

"*So no objective scientific analysis is going to tell you the meaning of life.*"

"Oh, all right, all right." He had a point.

The Chaplain interrupted. "Remember the words in the Gospel? 'Render unto scientists what is measurable, and unto philosophers what is wise'."

"Is that so? An unusual translation. Well, never mind." I returned to Frostbight. "Whatever this philosophy, it's whacky. External existence was around before I was born, and I can tell you: it'll be around a long time after I'm pushing up daisies."

The German interjected. "Pushing up the daisies? Was ist?"

"Nothing, Professor. Colloquial. It means 'dead as a doornail'."

"Ach. A doornail is dead?"

I shook my head. "Ignore it. Were you about to say something?"

"Ja. I wished to say that *your belief* that the world is 'separate' from you is just that: *a belief*."

"I know. So?"

"Ach. We have much ground to cover. Respect your imagination."

"But I do respect it!"

"Nein. You have a great deal to learn. We have already said, *if* you were *not* creating the world with your imagination – if it were the creation of someone else – it would not and could not be 'real'."

This needed thought. I pushed some salmon around my plate. "Oh," I said, *"I* know what you're up to. You're saying reality's my illusion – a sort of Buddhist thing."

"Please understand," he resumed, "your reality is not an illusion."

"Then what is it?"

"It is real – otherwise it would not be *called* 'real'. As for illusions, you are perfectly able to create them whenever you wish."

"Am I missing something?"

"What you are 'missing' is that reality is, as you say, 'separate' from you only *because that is how you configure it."*

I took a little wine. I needed help.

"Can you not see?" he said. "Reality – what is created by your Instant imagination – and what *you believe* about it – in your Dependent imagination – are not the same."

"Phew! I wouldn't know which is which. I still say the *real* world *is* independent of me."

"That is a philosophical *belief* about your Instant imagination, and that belief is created in your Dependent mind."

I stopped eating and rubbed my hand over the back of my neck. I was in deep water. "But," I moaned, "the world *is* independent of me."

The Rector came to my defence. "My child, we know that on first hearing this stuff it sounds nonsense."

"I should say. Anyway, why are you making such a big deal about it?"

Part III

℘

Maya

"I T MATTERS A GREAT DEAL," RESPONDED THE CLERGYMAN, "because if you don't see *reality's* your creation you'll never see *life's* your creation." He paused. "Maybe there's a way I can help."

"There is? Oh, good."

"Have you heard of the Indian idea of Maya?"

"Yeah … sort of." I had read some of that Indian philosophy. "Isn't it that thing: 'all form is emptiness'?"

"Uh oh," he smiled, "no, that's Buddhist."

"Oh, yeah, I suppose you're right."

He turned to Frostbight. "Doctor, how do you describe Maya?"

"Good question, Padre. Let's see …" He looked to Mould decanting wine at the sideboard, and asked, "Mould? Help us out. When you spent time in India what did you learn about Maya?"

Mould straightened up. "I confess, very little indeed, Sir."

"Now look here, you wouldn't expect us to believe that would you?"

"Very well, Sir. Maybe there was one story which impressed me as being especially educational in nature."

"There was, was there? Well come on, let's hear it."

"I am afraid, Sir, I recall few of the details."

"Never mind that. Tell us what you *do* recall."

This exchange had my attention. It never occurred to me that Mould might have been to India. I put down my knife and fork.

The butler began. "To my recollection Sir, the tale goes that a young disciple was accompanying Krishna on a long journey ..."

"Oh?" said Frostbight. "Really? Where to?"

"Watty," reprimanded von Lottowind, "you are interrupting."

"Was I Gusty? Oh dear, so sorry. Righty-ho, Mould, carry on."

"Thank you Sir." Evidently Mould was used to the ways of his employer. "I regret, Sir, that I did not ascertain where they were going. Nevertheless, while they were walking, the young disciple kept pestering the God to show him Maya. Krishna was wise and discouraged the lad, and however much the boy persisted, the God refused. In due course they came to a river. The only way to cross was by swimming; so they agreed to dive in and meet again on the far side.

The current was strong and the boy had to swim so hard he was exhausted by the time he pulled himself onto the opposite bank. There he dried off and recovered while waiting for Krishna. To his dismay, although he stayed all day and into the next, Krishna never showed. The local villagers were kind to him and, in his grief, brought food and water. Finally, after several days, he gave up and went to the village to find work. He was welcomed, settled into a new life and, in due course, married a local girl and bore a number of children. Decades later, blessed with many grandchildren, he had become a much-loved village elder, and when he came to his end he was surrounded by friends and family. As he lay dying he bade farewell, and took his last breath. All at once he found himself, a young disciple again, his clothes wet, sitting on the riverbank, with Krishna holding his hand. 'Well,' said the God, 'what did you think of Maya?'"

The butler finished his story. There was silence but for the crackling fire and the wind's whistle in the chimney. Finally Doctor Frostbight spoke. "Jolly good show, Mould. Excellent!"

"Thank you, Sir." He returned to his affairs.

Our host addressed me. "There you have it, old boy. What d'you think?"

"Well ..." I answered, not really knowing what to say. "It's a good story, but I think it illustrates that reality's an illusion."

"Oh? A *real* illusion?"

"Well of course. You can't have a *fake* illusion."

"All right, I'm teasing. Isn't this business of what's 'real' a tricky thing? Of course Maya's got to be a *real* illusion or it'd be nonsense." The Doctor went on. "No, the point is this: we're suggesting that reality's not an illusion, but 'magic'."

"Magic? I thought magic was all about illusion."

"Not in this case. I'm talking about proper magic. It arises out of nothing. Nonetheless, one thing's missing."

"Oh?"

Frostbight picked up his napkin and wiped his moustache. "In fact, there are two things missing."

"Two?"

"Yes, two."

"What?"

"For a start, the listener is left to guess for himself where Maya comes from."

"Where does it come from?"

"From the disciple's own creative abilities. He was the one who conjured it up."

"But the story doesn't say that."

"It didn't need to. And the same goes for Krishna. That's the other bit missing. The God was *also* a product of the boy's creativity."

"I'm not so sure," I remarked on weighing it up. "It sounds like another of your clever ideas. It's speculation. What Mould has told us is just a story. It doesn't make Maya *true,* does it?"

"My son," observed the clergyman to my left, "it's no good asking whether or not it's true. As we keep saying, *something* or *somebody* must be creating the world for it to exist."

"So?"

"It's the same thing: if *you're* not responsible for it, then *who is?*"

I had no answer.

"Look, old bean," said Frostbight. "The real reason you won't agree you're creating the universe is because, until now, the idea's never occurred to you. Simple as that."

"Doctor, it's not as 'simple as that'. It's crazy."

He had that twinkle in his eye. "I agree, it *does* seem crazy. What did I tell you? You see, one of the reasons you claim the world's independent of you is because *other people* say so. You didn't work it out yourself: you copied the idea."

"No, I didn't."

"The Doctor's right," Father Foggie cut in. "You copied it … and copying something doesn't make it *true*."

I was being outsmarted, but was not giving up. "What I am trying to put over," I said, "is that there's no way you can *prove* my life's some kind of self-created 'Maya'."

"Ach, proof!" the German Professor exclaimed. "You think 'proofs` are going to give you the answer."

"I couldn't say, but at least they'll stop me talking rubbish."

"Nein. You want proofs because you do not wish to think for yourself."

I was taken aback. "Whoa," I protested. "I certainly *do* wish to think for myself, and I want proofs because they're backed by *evidence*; then I can *choose* what to believe – and be objective. Without evidence, you lot can brew up any crack-pot idea."

"Mein Freund, 'proofs' are intellectual fashion accessories."

"Hey! That's rubbish."

"It is rubbish?"

"Yes. Rubbish. Some things *are* true."

"Ach, 'truth' comes and goes, like your Scottish weather."

"For goodness sake, you can't say that."

He looked at me intently. "Think of the Flat Earth Society."

"What about it?"

"Those people say it is '*true*' that the earth is flat."

"Yeah, but they're loonies. I wasn't thinking about them. I was thinking about, what's his name? Parmenides. Yes, Parmenides."

"What of Parmenides?"

"He said truths are those cases which remain so, independently of what anybody believes about them."

"Ah so? At Winterbad, we taught that there is no such thing. Any understanding of the world depends on belief. The only 'truth' is that there is no 'truth'."

This was exasperating. "Professor, I don't know what went on at Winterbad, but if nothing's *true*, then there's nothing we can be sure about. And that goes for trying to tell me the world's my creation." I put down my fork and took a swig of wine.

Father Foggie spoke. "Calm, my child. You're as bad as St. Augustine."

"Oh yeah? Why?"

"Because he also obsessed about 'truth'."

"What's the matter with it?"

"As long as you go looking for it, you'll lock yourself into pointless arguments."

"No, I won't."

"You will. Don't you know how people work? They *decide* what they want to believe, and then drum up the evidence that fits their 'truth', and discount anything that doesn't."

"What do you mean?"

"Well, people *first* decide say, the earth's flat, *then* they argue the case tooth and nail for its 'truth'. You'll find people doing the same thing with loads of subjects, such as claiming that God exists, or that science can explain everything or that there's no life after death."

I remained silent. His ideas sounded dodgy to me. I could not say what they normally talked about in this place, but they were unhinged to think truth did not exist. Meanwhile, I needed to get on. Leaving the sauerkraut for later, I forked up some more salsify. It was better than I had expected. A bit like parsnips? Not really. They tasted more like oysters. I was sorry there were no roast potatoes. My mind buzzed with thoughts. How could the world possibly be my creation? I had an idea. Without addressing anyone in particular, I announced, "I get it. I realise what you lot are: Creationists!"

"Creationists?" queried my neighbour.

"Yes, Father. Fundamentalists. You've got that Bible belief that God brought the universe into existence in a day or two – you know the sort of thing."

He cocked his head. "Mmm … let's see …" He turned to the butler. "Mould," he said, "when was the world made?"

The butler was stoking the fire. Putting aside the poker, he stood and closed his eyes for a moment. "If my recollection serves me correctly, Sir, Archbishop Ussher worked it out – a fine scholar. The start of Creation was 4002 B.C., the 23rd of October at 6.00 a.m. on the Monday morning."

"It was?" responded Frostbight. "Tch, tch! Ussher was using the wrong calendar."

"I beg your pardon, Sir, the Archbishop was certainly correct."

"Huh. Definitely not 23rd. Oct."

"Ach," commented von Lottowind, "I agree with Mould, except it was 6.00 p.m. *in the evening*."

"What, Gusty? Not on your Nelly. It was first thing on Monday morning."

"Maybe," suggested the clergyman meekly, "it was midday?"

The words 'taking the Mickey' sprung to mind. "OK, OK," I interrupted when I saw the fun they were having, "I get the picture: you're not Creationists."

"No," replied Frostbight with a grin, "at the least not the ones you're talking about. Why d'you mention it?"

"Because, Doctor, if I showed a dinosaur fossil or a multi-million year old rock strata to a Creationist, he would say, 'this was made at the same time as everything else: God can create multi-million-year-old things in an instant.' So there, you *are* kind of Creationists if you claim *I'm* creating reality moment by moment. Am I making sense?"

The Cleric answered softly. "Yes, my son, you're making sense. And you *are* creating reality moment by moment: all of it, as you speak."

"Then you *are* Creationists."

"Calm yourself, my child," he replied. "You'll understand better as we go along."

"Humph! Well, I don't know what'll happen when we 'go along.' The next thing you'll be telling me you believe in miracles."

"Ah!" he replied. "Miracles? Thank you." He turned and looked at me with a gleam and put down his utensils. "Indeed I do."

I sighed. "By your expression, Father, I'm in for a sermon."

"You're close. Let's have a look at 'miracles'. Where I probably differ from you is that I don't think they're rare."

"Well, they certainly *are* rare in my books, that's for sure."

"Perhaps I can change your mind. Miracles are daily events. In fact, there's nothing on earth which *isn't* one."

I frowned.

He went on. "Hear me out. Uncommon events do occur, such as the spontaneous healing of sickness, but its *rarity* is simply a rarity. Infrequency doesn't make a miracle."

"Humph. Is that the best example? Miracles are what someone makes happen which can't be explained in normal terms."

"You mean," he said, "something like levitation or walking on water?"

"Yeah, that would do – defying the laws of physics."

He shook his head. "I tell you, *obeying* the 'laws of physics' is as miraculous as defying them."

"Now come on …"

"I'm not kidding. Standing on land is as much a marvel as walking on water."

"No it's not. Standing on *land* isn't a miracle. It's normal."

"Ah, that's the point, my child. Being 'normal' doesn't *stop* it being a marvel. You see, for you, if everyone walked on water, you would no longer call it miraculous."

"But walking on water's impossible."

"Maybe, maybe not. 'Miracle' is from the Latin, 'mirari', to 'be amazed'. Over the years your familiarity with your creation has killed your sense of wonder."

"Has it?"

"Yes, and you don't realise you've lost it. Now, what about illness? How do you regard that?"

"I don't know. Illness is a misfortune."

"I can't say whether or not it's a misfortune, but I can say it's as 'astonishing' as strength and vigour. And ageing is as wonderful as the birth and growth of a child. And death? That's equally amazing."

"I say, Father, that's stretching it."

"And that's because your sense of astonishment has degraded. When you come to realise that the world's the creation of your imagination, you'll appreciate it's an ongoing miracle – stamped, as you might say, with your initials."

Part IV

℘

The Threshold

THERE WAS SILENCE. WHILE I WAS RELIEVED THEY WERE not Creationists, I could not agree with Father Foggie and his 'miracles'. Nonetheless, I found myself landed with a riddle. These men were bonkers to call the world some kind of magical event, but if it *was not*, then what *was* it? I had no proper answer. I took a forkful of sauerkraut while I pondered. I had to admit Dr. Frostbight was right that 'random' was a pompous way of saying 'I don't know', and yet I had no better explanation.

I pushed some of the Jerusalem artichoke onto my fork. It was quite chewy – a bit like this discussion – but was tasty. The problem was that, on the one hand, it was obvious that I do create *some* things. I was happy with that. If I were to paint a picture or compose music, it was clear that I was inventing it and, if I were honest, the same applied to my private thoughts. On the other hand, calling *everything* my creation? That was out of the question: codswallop to be honest. I laughed to myself to think that if these fellows went on like this, they would be telling me I made the sun rise every morning!

Dr. Frostbight interrupted my thoughts. "How's dinner, old chap?"

"Dinner's really delicious, thank you: a feast. And now I've got used to the salsify I'm rather enjoying it."

"Splendid." Then he leaned forward and, in a conspiratorial tone said, "Fancy my sauerkraut?"

I was caught unawares, but happily did not have to answer. The Professor intervened. "Watty, you must consume your sauerkraut. It is most beneficial to your intestinal flora."

Frostbight pulled a face. "Gusty, there's nothing the matter with my intestinal flora." The two thought this was funny. The Reverend Foggie, however, returned to our conversation. "So you think it's a load of codswallop?"

How did he guess? "Well, Father," I confessed, "maybe not codswallop, but what you're talking about is out of the question. Look, I agree I'm responsible for my thoughts. After all, I can hardly accuse anybody else of making me think what I think. And yes, I admit that I am, for the most part, responsible for creating *some* of my own behaviour. But more than that? It's ludicrous. I can't be responsible for what *others* think or do."

"My son," said the Rector as he toyed with his wine glass, "you're at a threshold."

"O Lord, am I? What threshold?"

"Alice's in front of the Looking Glass."

"Mmm ..." I smiled, "this gets curiouser and curiouser.".

"Very witty my child."

"Sorry, Father, I couldn't resist. So what's Alice in Wonderland got to do with it?"

"We're presenting you with a choice to enter a different world."

"Really? A nice one – less bizarre than Alice's?"

"I hope you'll find it less bizarre."

"Oh good. So what do I do?"

"Easy. Step – or leap – over the threshold."

I raised my hand. "Father, you're deliberately being obscure."

"All right, maybe I am. Let me explain. Try this. Think of a pink elephant."

"Really?"

"Yes. D'you have one in mind?"

"Yeah, now I have."

"Good. Let it jump about. Make it take off and fly."

"OK, if you must. What's the problem?"

"There isn't one. It's about beliefs. I suggested conjuring the picture of a pink elephant because the same thing applies to beliefs – you invent them."

"Maybe. Sometimes. So?"

"It means that you can adopt or discard any belief at any time."

I shrugged. "Possibly."

"Do you see? You believe the world has little to do with you, and yet you are free to drop it at any time. What about adopting a miraculous view of life?"

"Oh? We're back to miracles?"

"Yes. This is the crux. Listen." He paused and played with his cutlery. "Whether you opt for a scientific *or* a theistic explanation of the universe, either way you are obliged to submit to a belief system."

"Oh … that's what you're getting at."

"Yes. And what *we're* pointing you towards is a different approach altogether."

I rubbed my face in my hands. "You mean the business of seeing *all* my experience as my creation?"

"Exactly. *See* it rather than believe it."

Von Lottowind spoke. "Pastor Foggie, may I interrupt?"

"Of course, Professor. On you go."

"Mein Freund," he said to me, "to help you understand that you generate your universe, I give an example."

"Oh, good. Don't hold back the horses."

"I am sorry?"

"Just joking. What were you about to say?"

"I was about to say, have you ever bought a national lottery ticket?"

"A lottery ticket? Well, yes, I have. Why?"

"Did you win?"

"Me, Professor? No."

"Do you know why not?"

"What kind of question's that? It's obvious. The odds are millions to one against it. You only win if you're seriously lucky."

He shook his head. "Nein. Das is not why you did not win."

"Oh yeah? Then you give me a better reason."

His eyes narrowed. "I want to show you," he said, "that you are thinking in a linear manner. Crossing the threshold requires a different approach. Ja, the statistics *are* against your winning, but *really* there was only one reason you did not win."

"Oh yeah?"

"You had no intention of winning."

"What? That's nonsense. Of course I intended to win."

He persisted. "For whatever reason, you did not want to win. If you had *fully* intended to win, you would have."

"You think? I reckon you're away with the fairies."

"I am sorry: 'away with the fairies'?"

"Oh, just a turn of speech. What I'm saying is your theory's got a button missing."

Von Lottowind looked puzzled. "A button missing …? Ach. No matter. I wish to say the lottery is like all of your life: under your direction."

I rubbed my face again. "I hardly think so, Professor."

"You see," went on the German, "you did not just invent the lottery: you also invented the statistics. That is what Pastor Foggie meant about crossing the threshold. You must wake up and suspend the habitual way you see the world."

"Huh. Who says I'm asleep?"

"Crossing the threshold is a wake up call."

"Huh. A nice idea, but I don't know what you're talking about."

"It is like any new habit. At first it is hard."

"You're telling me!"

"And why? Because you are in love with what you can rationally prove – or disprove. You use those as crutches."

"What crutches?"

"Crutches for explaining life."

"But … but …"

He ignored me and continued. "Throw away your crutches. You have now the chance to arouse your imagination – and leap the threshold."

"Hey. There's nothing *wrong* with my imagination."

"Das is good."

"Look, Professor: we all know that paying attention to what we can prove has changed our world."

"Proving what in particular?"

"Well, various natural laws, for a start."

"Ah, so?"

"Yes. You can *prove* the laws of physics and chemistry. You can *prove* that water boils at 100C … at least," I added, remembering we were in the mountains, "you can at sea level."

"Ah, another metaphor!"

I looked at him. "Metaphor? What metaphor? 'Sea level'?"

"Nein. I refer to 'natural laws'."

I grimaced. "I see no metaphor."

"You must understand. 'Natural laws': they are metaphors."

"Oh, for heaven's sake, you know perfectly well that natural laws are scientific observations."

"Mein Freund, the laws are *invisible.*"

"I know. So what?"

"They do not exist."

"Now, come on. Of course they exist. The world couldn't happen without them – every schoolboy knows that."

"You think they exist?"

"Without doubt."

"Even though no one has seen one?"

"You don't *need* to see them. They just *are.*"

He raised his palm. "Quiet. I will explain."

"Fine. Have a go."

He composed himself. "You must understand," he said slowly, "that laws in *this* world are made by parliaments."

"I know, Professor. What's that got to do with it?"

He pointed upwards. "Look. Can you see a parliament up there, in the sky, making 'laws'?"

I resisted following his gaze.

"Of course not," he continued. "Laws in this world are made by *people.*"

"So?"

"What we call '*natural*' laws is *poetry.*"

I was bewildered. "Huh. *I* don't see anything 'poetic' about natural laws."

Von Lottowind looked despairingly at Frostbight to his left. The Doctor took over. "What the Professor is saying, old chap, is that a scientist observes sequences, shapes and patterns – and calculates his predictions accordingly."

"Uh-huh ... so ...?"

"What happens is he observes a repeatable event, such as the boiling of water at a constant temperature, and calls it the action of a 'law'."

"And that's what it is."

"No, it's not. It's a *metaphor.*"

"It *can't* be."

"It can be. While you *can* see patterns, you *cannot* see 'natural laws'."

"All right, all right, I heard you. So they're invisible."

"Excellent!" He drank a little water and continued. "You see, natural 'laws', old boy, are modern inventions that've replaced God."

"Whoops. Say that again? Done *what?*"

"They've replaced God."

I made a face. "That's mad."

"No it's not. Scientific 'laws' have displaced Divine laws. As I say, they're the new supernatural 'agency'."

"What's that supposed to mean?"

"It means that people use invisible 'laws' instead of invisible 'Gods' to explain how the world works."

"Huh." This needed some thought. "Well," I said, "I don't know about replacing God, but by observing 'laws' we can make proper predictions – instead of flights of fancy."

"That is correct but not the point. Tonight we attempt to wean you from believing that sequences and patterns arise from inexplicable 'laws of nature' or, indeed, that they're the invention of an unseen Divine Being."

"So how do you think they *do* arise?"

"They are the action of the imagination."

"Whose imagination?"

"Yours."

I sighed.

The German interjected. "Your problem is you still want to prove that you can prove the reality of reality."

"Of course I do, Professor. We'd be in a mess if we *couldn't* prove things." This talk was enough to make my head hurt. Maybe having more wine would not be a good idea. But laws or no laws, if nobody could *prove* that life was my creation, there was no point in discussing it. Still, it was time to scoop up the last of my sauerkraut. Maybe this German food was all right – albeit an acquired taste.

"So," continued von Lottowind, "whether you are proving or disproving that life is a creation, you are engaging in a creative act."

"So?"

"Unfortunately, *you* are hoping logic will tell you whether it is 'true'." He paused.

"Oh, so now you're saying there's a problem with logic?"

"Please understand I am not asking for a leap of logic."

"No? So what're you asking for?"

"I am asking for a leap of imagination."

"Wow. A leap of imagination?" I hesitated. It reminded me of my philosophy lectures. "Oh, yes," I exclaimed, "I know! Kierkegaard. A 'leap of faith'."

"Ach so?"

"Yeah, you're expecting me to have *faith* that the world's my creation."

"Nein," said the German patiently, "I'm *not* talking about Kierkegaard."

"Oh? Then what *are* you talking about?"

"I am saying that you must stop deciding whether the concept 'life is my creation' is *true* or not."

"And just have faith …?"

"Ach. How many times must I repeat? It is a matter for your *imagination*."

I sighed. "Well, Professor, you know what? I reckon you've got a problem."

"While you, mein Freund," he shot back, "argue too much."

"No, I don't."

My response seemed to amuse him.

The Rector spoke. "Arguing, debating and disagreeing are creative acts as much as anything else you do … but not very helpful. It's a heck of a job shifting a lifetime of bad habits."

"What 'bad habits', Father? What do you think I am? A doormat that's supposed to agree with everything you say?"

"I'm sure you're not a doormat, but how about *listening* to what we're saying instead of mismatching it?"

"Mismatching? What? Wearing odd socks?"

"No," he smiled. "*Not* your socks. I'm talking about how you mismatch what we tell you."

"I don't mismatch."

"Oh no?" He took a breath. "Remember the old saying, 'There's a time for keeping, and there's a time for casting away; a time for arguing and a time for listening'?" He glanced at me from over his specs. "Ecclesiastes. Chapter 3, verse 6."

"Huh? No, I don't remember it. Sounds like another funny translation."

The Professor spoke again. "You recall that Pastor Foggie was saying that crossing over the threshold is like your Alice stepping into Wonderland?"

"Yeah …"

"We invite you to convert to a new mindset."

"So I gather."

"Please understand: the whole universe is an act of your imagination."

"So you keep saying," I mumbled. " ... *So* far fetched."

The German waited for me.

"Well," I resumed, "imagination or not, it still doesn't make it true. And Alice's Wonderland was fiction. I'm not going to abandon truth for make-believe."

"Ach so," said the Professor, "you are still hooked on 'truth'. The truth about truth is that it, too, is an act of imagination." He took a sip of his wine and left me to ponder.

In the meantime we had all polished off our salmon and vegetables, and there was silence but for the wind. After a few minutes our host spoke. "Food for thought, eh, old chap? Quite a testing session. Now ... how' s everyone getting on? Who's for seconds? Anyone for any more?"

"I wouldn't say 'no' to a little more, Doctor," replied my neighbour. "Absolutely yummy, don't you think Professor?"

"It is delicious, Pastor Foggie," agreed von Lottowind. "Watty, I would find some more sauerkraut most agreeable."

"And I'd love a bit more of that salmon," I added, "if there is any. It's a treat."

"Of course," grinned Frostbight. "I like a man with an appetite. And you'll need to build up your strength for what's coming. Where's Mould?" He reached for a small brass bell.

Second
Helpings

Part I

☙

The Self that Never Was

OMENTS LATER THE HIDDEN PANEL CREAKED AND opened. The butler stood to attention. "Sir?"

"Mould? Ah, good man, there you are. Hungry fellows here. Second helpings all round."

"Very good, Sir." He set to, lifting the dishes from the hot plates and, by making his way round the table, allowed each of us to help ourselves.

Was it the effects of the wine, or of the conversation? Ideas spun in my head. While Mould held the platter and I topped up with some vegetables, I spoke to our Cleric. "Father, that stuff about my being responsible for what other people do ... you don't really think that, do you?"

"I do."

"But how could you? You and I know everyone exists in his or her own time and space. They do exactly as they please. It's simply not open to question."

"There you are again," declared Frostbight. "Not listening."

"Doctor," I said, turning my attention to him, "I *am* listening, but you don't have to be a brain surgeon to realise it's madness. *Nobody*'s under my control."

"My son," the Rector said to me quietly, "the whole universe is under your control."

"Now hold on, Father ..." I waited while Mould allowed the clergyman to spoon sprouts onto his plate. "You're not seriously talking, are you, about the 'universe' as in '*Universe*'?"

"I'm not being funny: yes, we do mean 'universe' as in 'Universe'. Maybe you don't yet dare entertain the thought."

"Huh. Not surprising."

"Yes," he said, taking the cellar and spooning a little salt onto the edge of his plate, "it takes courage at first."

"I should say so!"

"Your universe is self-created."

I rolled my eyes.

"You don't have to roll your eyes. You'll find out for yourself."

"You reckon? When?"

"When you give up looking for the answer 'out there' in the world."

"Well, there's nowhere *else* to find it."

"There is."

"Oh yes? Where? I suppose you're going to say, 'within'."

"To some extent. More accurately, in your imagination."

I grimaced. "Yeah, well, it's not the kind of imagination I'm used to."

"No, maybe not." He picked up his knife and fork. "I agree it's tough to stretch your imagination in a new way."

"You're telling me." I, too, picked up my utensils and started eating. "But here," I said after a minute, "what about this? I'm sitting in this chair. I can choose to eat, talk, walk, lift, pull and push things around. And the rest of the world?"

"What about it?"

"You *know* I have nothing to do with it."

"You're sure?"

"Yes, I am. You're just as aware as I am that it goes on without me."

The clergyman finished a mouthful before he mopped his mouth and replied. "In some ways it does, and in some it doesn't. You see, it's 'separate' and 'independent' because of the genius of your imagination."

Before I could say anything more, Doctor Frostbight returned to the fray. He pointed to me with his fork. "I've a question for you."

I took a breath. "OK, Doctor, sounds like trouble. Do you worst."

"Relax, old bean. The question is, 'who are you?' That might make things clearer."

I was taken aback. "Who? Me? What've I got to do with it?"

"Everything. You could also ask, *what* are you?"

"What do you mean? I'm an ordinary human being – just like you. Why?"

"Here's another one. *Where* are you?"

"You feeling all right? I'm here in front of you."

"Ah, yes, your *body* is in front of me, but where are *you*? I ask, old chap, because as long as you keep hold of your limited vision of who you are, you'll never 'get' this creation stuff."

"Limited vision?" I remonstrated. "How could you say, 'limited vision'?" Then it twigged. "Oh, I know what you're up to," I said brightly. "You think I'm not in touch with my 'true self'."

"Actually, no. *If* you had a true self, it would be every bit as true or false as you imagined it."

"Huh? What's *that* supposed to mean?"

The clergyman stepped in. "It means the 'true self' is a spoof."

"A spoof? Lord, what now? Now come on, Father. OK, supposing I call it my 'real' self instead?"

"True self or real self, if you go looking for it you're wasting your time."

"But I've got to have a true self *somewhere*. You know – my *authentic* self."

"True or authentic, where do you think it is?"

I shrugged. "I don't know. Somewhere. OK, I agree I don't know where it is."

The Reverend smiled. "Forget about a true self. Your self is never the same from one moment to the next."

"I think you're splitting hairs."

"You do? Even since the start of dinner you've had minute physical changes and your body's not quite the same – and you've had new experiences, so your mind's not quite the same either. And that's only in the last hour. What about in a year or two? Or a decade or two?"

"But the point is that the 'true' self *doesn't* change."

"That's right, exactly. And that's why there's no such thing."

"Er …" I replied cautiously, "I'm not sure. You're sounding kind of Buddhist."

"Maybe, maybe not. What I'm driving at is you need to realise where the world's coming from."

"Well, *you're* telling me it comes from me. So where does my ordinary 'self' come from?"

"Your ordinary 'self' is *one part* of your creation."

"It exists," butted in Frostbight, "because of you."

"Wooh!" I exclaimed in the best ironic tone I could muster, "now *I* exist because of *me*. Tell me another."

Frostbight smiled. "'Another' is that the rest of the world *also* exists because of you."

"Oh, dear." I let out a hearty sigh and said no more.

"Patience, my child," encouraged the Rector. "It'll become clearer." He rounded up a sprout and pushed it onto his fork. "Here's the key question: yes, you are doing the creating, *but who is the 'you' who's doing it?*"

Part II

☙

The Non True Self

"WHAT DO YOU MEAN?" I REPLIED. "IT'S *ME*. YOU just said so."

"Yes, but who is 'me'?"

"My true self? No, you'll say there's no such thing. OK. I give up. Haven't a clue."

He smiled. "Well observed. *Nobody* has a clue. And that's because 'You', as the Original Being who's doing the creating, are incomprehensible."

"What's new, pussy cat? Half of what you're telling me's incomprehensible."

Across from me, Doctor Frostbight grinned. "You'll soon get the hang of it. All you need to know is how grossly you underestimate the Original Being who is behind the façade of your self."

Now doubting whether I ever had a self, I also chased a brusselsprout round the plate, and grunted, "Doctor, I'm just who I am. How confusing can this get? How do you know I've got some sort of 'Original Being' floating about?"

"Because," he answered, "once you realise the world's your creation, you'll also realise the 'You' who's doing the creating is miles beyond your ordinary self."

I stabbed the sprout. "Huh. A bit of an understatement? Sounds like God."

"To some extent. We'll discuss God in due course. At the moment what I'm getting at is *You are* the 'Original Being'. The 'You' I'm talking about is 'pre-existent', or anything you want to call it, but – without wanting to sound obscure – this 'You' doesn't exist."

I groaned. "I exist, I don't exist. I do exist, I don't exist. And now I've got an Original Being."

"Yes," he smiled, "it's tricky. You exist as far as you're a body which can be measured; but you don't exist as someone who's generating thoughts."

"Thanks for clearing *that* up."

The Doctor ignored my grumbles. "The point is, old chap, you don't *have* an Original Being. You *do have* – and do 'possess' so to speak – a body, and *that's* your 'property'."

Von Lottowind cleared his throat, brought up his napkin to wipe his moustache and turned to his neighbour. "Watty, we do *not possess* our body. We possess money and the things we can buy, but we do not *possess* a body: we *operate* a body."

"Sorry, Gusty. Slip of the tongue." The Doctor put his hand by his mouth as though it stopped the German hearing. "Gusty – so pedantic. It's all right if you say you 'possess' a body: keep it simple." He put down his hand. "Still, where was I? Yes: you do *not 'possess'* an Original Being – *that* would make it an object."

"Excuse me, Doctor, but you just said I *did* have an Original Being."

"No I didn't. What I said was, 'You *are* the Original Being'."

"But there's no difference."

"There is. As a *possession* it would be *separate* from you."

"So?"

"It begs the question."

"What question?"

"W*ho is it* who '*has*' it?"

I was lost. "Has what?"

"You – or, rather, your body."

The German intervened again. "The Original You," he said to me, "has created your self, but your 'self' has *not* created the Original You."

"Excellent, Gusty," said the Doctor. "So, young man, now do you see?"

"Uh-huh … clear as a bell."

"Don't worry if it's confusing just now. We'll talk more about it. What matters is that if you think you can go looking for your 'True Self' you're going to have an awfully hard time – and *that*, in case you wondered, is an understatement."

"Then what is this 'Original Being' you're talking about?"

"First of all, it's not a 'self'." He addressed Father Foggie. "Padre, how do you describe something that can't be described?"

"I wouldn't try, Doctor," smiled the Rector before turning to me and saying, "What's more important is that you avoid muddling up 'You' with your 'self'."

"But, Father, they're the same."

"They're *not* the same."

"They must be."

The Professor butted in. "They are not the same. Think about it. You cannot experience this world without a 'self'. But if you wish to understand *life as your creation*, you must think of it from the point of view of You – who does not exist – and *not* from the point of view of your self, which does exist. Does that make sense?"

"Does it make sense?" I repeated. "You must be joking. You're doing my head in." Or was it the booze? I pushed the last of the salmon around my otherwise empty plate and admired the designs. 'FB' was monogrammed in the centre in gold.

Doctor Frostbight looked to the end of the room. "Mould?"

"Yes, Sir?"

"When you were in China, how did those chaps there tackle this stuff?"

His words caught my attention. What? Mould? First India and now, China?

The old man cleared his throat. "It is indeed perplexing. I recall that the Tao-te Ching began, 'the Tao that can be *told* of is not the *eternal* Tao, and the name that can be *named* is not the *eternal* name.' And Chapter Thirty-seven says, 'all things come from being, and being comes from non-being.' And in Chapter 43 …"

"All right, all right," interrupted the Doctor. "We don't want the whole book. And while you're at it," he said, pointing to me, "this young man could do with some more sauce."

I did not expect our host to notice. The butler was by my side in no time. As he coated my salmon with sauce, I took the chance to ask, "Mould, is that true?"

"I beg your pardon, Sir?"

"You. In China?"

"Yes indeed."

"Doing what?"

"Researching Taoist philosophy."

"Gosh! How did you get on?"

"Difficult."

"I bet. Tricky language?"

"Mandarin was not the problem, Sir. It was the Japanese. They were advancing."

"Wow!"

"Indeed. I nearly did not come back."

"Oh? Tempted to go native?"

"No, Sir. I received a bullet in the leg."

"You're not kidding?"

"I am not, Sir. I was fortunate. The local militia smuggled me out – over the mountains."

So that was why Mould limped! I could only mutter, "That's plenty of sauce, thanks."

"You're welcome. Would you like me to retrieve your napkin?"

"What?" I felt my lap. Blow! I had dropped it. "Thanks, Mould, but it's all right, I'll see to it – I don't want you straining that dicky leg of yours." I bent down and grabbed the napkin from the floor.

On regaining my seat, the German addressed me. "Perhaps you did not find those passages from the Tao-te Ching helpful?"

"That Tao stuff? Hardly, Professor."

"Nein?" I was sure the German knew perfectly well I was having a rotten time with this 'self' business. "I shall," he announced, "make it easier."

"Oh good! Don't let me hold you back."

With a slight smile, he said, "When you say that 'the light shines', does that mean that the light is separate from the 'shining'?"

"No, Professor, I suppose it doesn't."

"Das is correct. The 'shining' *is* the light. Likewise, if I say the 'odour is smelly', or the 'sound is noisy' or the 'thunder rumbles', am I talking in each case of separate things?"

"No ..."

"Of course not. The thunder *is* the rumbling, and the rumbling is the thunder."

The German addressed me. "Perhaps you did not find those passages from the Tao-te Ching helpful?"

"All right. So …?"

"So when you say, 'I think', is the thinking separate from the 'I'?"

"Um …"

"Good. You see? There is no distinction."

I made a face.

"So it goes," he went on, "for 'I feel', 'I believe', 'I hope', 'I speak', 'I live', etcetera. Therefore, when it comes to discussing the 'I' who generates your experiences, where is it?"

"Search me."

"Good. It does not exist."

I took a deep breath and let it out. "If you say so … I'm beginning to wonder what *does* exist."

"You're not the first to find it muddling," interjected the Reverend. "It's the problem of language. Here's another way of looking at it. The *invisible* can describe the *visible*, but there are no words for the visible to describe the '*in*visible'."

"Huh," I grumbled. "I bet there aren't. But how do you know there's any such thing? *I*'m not aware of it."

"Oh dear, so sorry, I'm sounding like the Professor. What you're not aware of tells you nothing. When you look at a beautiful sunset, you're not aware of your method of seeing it. Would you then be surprised to find you had eyes?"

"The eyes," Frostbight added, "generate the picture – along with the brain – but are not themselves the picture. Or are they? Maybe they are. I'll leave you to chew it over. Ticklish old business, eh, what? However I think we'd better move on. If we call 'You' the 'Original Being', it'll have to do. Or we could call 'You' the 'No-self'."

"We can't call it that," I remonstrated. "If it *were* a No-self, it wouldn't exist."

"And that, old chap, is the paradox."

"What paradox?"

"That it doesn't exist."

"What? Then how can we talk about it?"

"As you'll come to see, just because it doesn't exist doesn't mean we can't talk about it."

At this point I felt I was sinking fast. "Doctor," I asked, "what *does* exist?"

"Good question. Actually, it doesn't matter. It's just that *if* you told someone you invented the world, he'd assume you were referring to your 'self' and think you barking mad."

"Yeah, and he'd be right."

He nodded. "Then be sure not to make that mistake. *Of course* your self doesn't invent the world. The No-self does. I repeat what we've been saying: it's important that *you* understand that your 'self' is *just a part* of Your – the No-self's – creation."

By now I wished I had not started this talk about the self. "Well," I stated, "I'm not sure I'm making much headway. Would it be all right to change the subject?"

"Of course. Finding it testing?"

I faked a smile and remained silent.

Part III

❧

Eternal Life

"Take it easy," Frostbight resumed. "These ideas take getting used to."

"Yeah, maybe," I replied, "but how do you know this stuff in the first place?"

"What stuff?"

"The stuff you're talking about. I mean, how do you *know* that life's my creation, or that reality's my imagination or that I'm really an Invisible Me?"

"You want to know where these ideas come from? They don't come from anywhere."

I blinked. "Then ..."

"Don't you get it? No idea ever comes from anywhere."

"Humph. Sounds like more of your mumbo-jumbo."

"I'm sure it does. Well, the good news is it gradually gets obvious."

I made a face. "Is that a promise? Anyway, who cares?" I wanted to change the subject. "For all your philosophy and 'creation' stuff, whatever you say the only thing *I* know is that, Original Being or not, at the end of my life I snuff it. Puff! It's all been for nothing."

He straightened the cutlery on his plate. "Is that so?"

"Yup, sure about it."

"How come?"

"Because it's science. You can't argue. The lights go out and I'm a gonner. That's it."

"Really?"

"Yup. Really. No Original Being. No No-self. No Invisible Me. It's over."

"I say old boy!"

I scowled. "And I expect, Doctor, you're one of those people who're going to tell me there *is* life after death."

"Without a doubt," he returned.

"Huh. I thought you might, but I can tell you, you'll have a hard time persuading me."

"I see you've already made up your mind, and we're not here to persuade you otherwise. But look, old boy, don't you know? Your belief that consciousness is wiped out at death is *not* science."

"Uh-oh, here we go: more wishful thinking."

"Don't be fooled: a scientist can be a brilliant scientist, but a rotten philosopher."

"That's what you said before, but *philosophy* can't prove there's life after death."

"Proof? You're off again on a wild goose chase. Have you ever asked yourself how many times you've died?"

"What, and resuscitated?"

"No. *Died.*"

I shook my head. "I'm sorry, I don't understand."

Frostbight gave me a stern look. "It's this. If you *haven't* died, how can you be so jolly sure what happens when you *do* die? Is that 'scientific'?"

It was hard to answer, but I was not going to admit it. "So, you think I'll go to heaven – or maybe hell?"

He pointed to the Reverend Foggie. "Come on, Padre, this is your field."

The Cleric put down his cutlery and dabbed his lips with the napkin. "Doctor, you can guess what I'm going to say."

Frostbight grinned. "I know, but I like hearing it."

The Rector took a sip of his wine and turned to me. "The belief in going to 'heaven' when you die? That's an ancient belief, probably first introduced by Zoroaster thousands of years ago."

"Who?"

"Never mind. What the Doctor is referring to, my son, is that you do not *go* to heaven after you die."

"I know. That's what I'm telling you."

"Oh dear, I'm not explaining myself very well. There *is* such a 'thing'. It's *here*. I mean you're *in* 'heaven' – in the afterlife – right now."

I grimaced and took a moment to answer. "What? Right now? How absurd is *that?*" I realised I was waving my fork about, and put it on my plate. "I beg your pardon, Father, but you're off your head. What? Are you trying to make out I've died and don't realise it?"

"Calm, my son, calm. No, you're not dead: you're alive. What I'm saying is you're stuck in this idea that you *go* somewhere – or not – at the end of the road."

"I'm not stuck in anything. *If,* as you say, I continue being 'alive', I've got to go *somewhere.*"

"You don't 'go' anywhere."

"Father, you've just contradicted yourself."

He raised his hand. "Slow down. As I said, you're already in the after-life – as you speak."

"With respect, that's nonsense."

"It's not nonsense. You, like everyone else, are *always* in the 'afterlife', only you don't see it that way. This world is an expression of the 'afterlife' – or, if you prefer, a distortion of it."

"Yeah, but everyone on Earth *dies* – sooner or later."

"Naturally we die." He paused to collect his thoughts. "I'm not pretending your *body* is eternal – obviously not. In due course you'll dispense with your body, at which point you'll create something else."

"You mean we're etheric entities floating about in space-suits?"

That made him laugh. "I suppose that's one way of looking at it!"

"Sorry, Father, you've lost me."

"My child", he remarked quietly, "your 'self', along with your life and your death are, as we said, your creation – and your story."

"Oh? Now it's a story? What story?"

"Life is your story."

"Oh? Is this another of your 'revelations'?"

"No. It's obvious. The Original You, the No-self, is the storyteller."

"Is that so? I didn't know I was a storyteller."

"Well, you do now."

"Huh, I don't, actually. What kind of a storyteller?"

"We'll come to that in a minute. In the meantime the 'No-self' is the one telling the stories, and your physical self is an actor in your story."

"Well, I don't think my life's a 'story'. And anyway, even if it were, sooner or later it'd come to an end."

"Yes, it will, but You, the *storyteller*, don't come to an end."

"No? So what happens to the storyteller?"

"He can do whatever he wishes – start another tale."

I chewed over it. "So you're talking about reincarnation?"

"Yes, you could get reincarnated if you wanted to. Or not."

"Does that mean I *do* get reincarnated?"

"Yes, but only if you want to. You could do whatever. You could repeat exactly the same story as your present one – if you liked it that much."

"Oh," I said, "I'm not sure *that'd* be a good idea!"

He smiled. "Or you could make up a new story about a totally different world. It'll be up to you."

While I was wondering about it, von Lottowind spoke. "Permit me to explain. Where were you before you were born?"

"Before I was born? I wasn't anywhere."

"So you think you were not alive?"

"Before I was born? Of course not."

"How do you know?"

"Obvious. I'd remember it."

"But you cannot even remember your dream from last night."

"So?"

"That does not mean you did not dream."

I shrugged.

"And," he continued, "you cannot remember your birth into this world. That does not mean you were not born."

"Well, Professor," I said, "if I *did* exist before I was born, where was I?"

"Nowhere. Think of your dream. When you awoke from it this morning, did you arrive '*from*' anywhere?"

"Well, no."

"Ja. You simply woke up. You changed a sleep experience for a waking experience – and without moving."

"And you're saying …?"

"I am saying that when you were born you did not arrive from anywhere, and when you die you do not 'go' anywhere."

"So what happens?"

"As Pastor Foggie said, you are always in 'heaven'."

"My child," explained the Reverend, "there is *only* life, albeit disguised now as a physical body. Your dying is simply part of it."

We were quiet for a while until Frostbight spoke. "That reminds me of something." Raising his voice, he said, "Mould? Who was it who wrote, 'if the doors of perception were cleansed, everything would appear as it is, infinite'?"

"I would presume, Sir," replied the butler from the end of the room, "you are referring to Professor Huxley?"

"Huxley? Yes, that's the chap."

"I understand that his idea was that the brain is a reducing valve for restricting consciousness."

"Huh? A reducing valve, eh? I thought so."

"'The Doors of Perception'. 1954. Originally William Blake, 'The Marriage of Heaven and Hell'. 1793."

"I say, Mould, firing on all cylinders tonight, what?"

"Thank you, Sir. A little more wine?" He picked up the decanter.

"Good plan. Do the rounds." Our host turned to me. "So there you have it, old chap. Think of the brain as a horse with blinkers. That's why you can't see you're in 'heaven'."

I was too startled to reply – not because of the horse with blinkers, but because 1954 was years away. I pinched myself. Was this real?

Von Lottowind spoke up. "As I said, when you came to be born, you did not 'leave' some astral realm to 'arrive' on earth."

"Huh? *I* don't know. You tell me, Professor."

"Nein," he said, "you have *always* been 'here'. You simply started a new story – a theatre – in three dimensions."

A three dimensional story? That was a new one on me. "But," I replied, "why do I have to die?"

"Because," answered the German, "every narrative *has* to have an end."

"And *that*," added Frostbight, "is where you make your mistake."

I was taken aback. "What mistake?"

"You told us your life is meaningless."

"Yes I know. It is."

"Don't you see?" he said, regarding me carefully. "You've got it back to front. You think death makes your life meaningless? No. It's the other way round. The ending of a story *gives it* its meaning."

"I beg your pardon?"

"If a tale goes on and on without ending, it's meaningless, and if your life went on forever and ever it, too, would become meaningless."

"I'm still not with you."

"All activities need to stop for them to be meaningful. Think, say, of a football match. If the referee never blew the whistle to finish it, the match becomes pointless: it must have a time limit. If you were to eat this dinner forever, it would stop being a pleasant experience. The same would apply even to sex. If you could make love forever you would end up hating it. In just the same way you need to die to stop yourself hating your life." He regarded me carefully. "Here's another way to explain it ..."

"Phew. Have a go."

"If," he began, "I were to tell you a fairy story about a good kingdom being invaded by an evil knight ..."

"Yes?"

"So far that tells you nothing."

"I know. You've hardly started."

"Yes, but that's the point. It must have an end for it to be a story."

"So?"

"Remember what you said before dinner: your instinct to stay alive is doomed to failure?"

"Yeah ..."

"Don't you see? Death's *not* a failure. It's the final act that wraps up your tale. In short, for your life to have meaning, it *depends* on your dying."

Part IV

❧

The Mystery of Dying

THIS WAS HEADY STUFF. I STOPPED TO TAKE A SIP OF WINE and think. Finally I said to Frostbight. "Whatever our ideas, they still don't really explain what *happens* when I die."

"No?"

"No. It's one thing for Father Foggie to say that I, as my 'Original Being'– or whatever you call me – am here in 'heaven' all the time, but that doesn't tell me much."

He paused to consider. "Look, old boy, don't get too hung up on death."

"Oh, yeah? How could I not? It's coming my way: I don't get out of this world alive."

"You're sure?"

"Why do ask? Whether or not this world *is* a kind of heaven, you know perfectly well my *body's* going to fall off the conveyor belt."

"That's correct, but you haven't noticed you've been through it already."

"Through what already?"

"Through death."

I looked to the other two, but they said nothing. "Doctor, are you being serious? I thought we'd agreed I *hadn't* died before."

He went on. "I'm not pulling your leg. What do you think you were before you were born?"

130

"I've already said: I didn't exist before I was born."

"No, that's right. You were 'dead' of course. You'd been 'dead' a long, long time before you became aware of this world. It's nothing new. You're an expert at it."

"Er ... you mean death? I may be an expert in some things, but certainly not death."

"Not thought of it that way?"

"Doctor," I snorted, "you know perfectly well!"

"Just testing. Look. First you start off being 'dead' – if we can call it that – but of course you're not, you're simply in another state of consciousness. Then at your 'birth' you activate your Instant imagination in a fresh way to make a physical world, followed by the development of your Dependent as you get older. In the end, you return to how you were before you started – and you reactivate your imagination in ways you had done before you were born."

I took a good swig of water. "All very imaginative stuff," I replied, "but it doesn't *prove* that when I die, I – along with my 'Original Being' – don't go 'kaput', as the Professor would call it."

Von Lottowind smacked his forehead. "Ach! 'Proof!'"

I looked to the German. "What's the *matter* with proof?"

"We have been over this before. It is a smokescreen – and this time it comes with a metaphor of possession."

I groaned – again.

"Don't mind Gusty, old chap," said Frostbight. "He's very particular. You were talking of your 'Original Being' just now as though it were a handbag. No. We've already said, you don't '*have*' an Original Being. Your Original Being – the No-self – just *is*. This 'You' – which can't be described – invents your self and your life on earth when it suits You, and likewise You'll also invent 'death'."

I squirmed in my chair. "I'll *invent* death? That takes a *serious* stretch of the imagination."

"And you also created time in the first place," responded the Rector from my left.

"Time? Oh, yeah. I've heard that before. Einstein isn't it? 'We create time so that everything doesn't happen at once'."

"Excellent. You need time to make a story. And you also created space so that everything isn't squashed together."

This was more amusing than informative. I turned back to our host.

"Doctor," I persisted, "we're still not getting to the point. How can I be *sure* I will exist after death?"

"First of all, old chap, you won't *exist* after death – you need a body to exist. Anyway, why are you worried? You don't even know what's going to happen tomorrow, let alone after death."

"Well, no, maybe not, but I can make a good stab at it."

"And it's only a guess." He paused for thought. "Let's approach it another way. You say your body's your self?"

"Yeah, as far as I know."

Frostbight looked me in the eye. "Do you remember what you were saying to me before dinner: how you really don't know much about your physical self?"

"Yeah, I know, the body runs under its own steam."

"Exactly. You, like everyone else, go about your daily life with the *minimum* awareness of what's going on in your body."

"What're you talking about?"

"Digesting your food and disposing of waste; circulating blood even when you sleep; fighting off infections; maintaining a steady body temperature." He waved his hands. "And what about your various glands and hormones? D'you know how they work? Or your lymph system? Or your nervous system? Or your reproductive system? D'you know what wakes you in the morning?" He slowed. "OK, I know: it's your alarm clock. But are you aware of the increased levels of serotonin?"

I did not answer.

"You see? You said it yourself: we understand very, very little about our bodies. Want me to go on?"

"No, I've got the picture. So what are you getting at?"

"What I'm getting at is this. If you *don't even know* what your body – what you call your '*self*' – is when you're alive, how can you know what *death* is?"

That was a good question. "Maybe," I responded morosely, "I don't know what any of it is."

"Ah, progress."

"What progress?"

"Your being less sure of what you're saying. Look at it this way: so far you've thought you were alive because of your body."

" Yeah … along with anybody with intelligence."

"No doubt. Your body is the *result* of your life, not the cause of it – along with your senses, thoughts, dreams, and memories."

"All right, no need to keep banging on: they're all created by a Me-which-doesn't-exist."

"Splendid. You see? We *are* making progress." The Doctor stopped.

What was I to make of all this? I did not have the luxury of reflecting: von Lottowind spoke. "Mein Freund," he began, "we are speaking of 'your' self? Why is that important?"

"*I* don't know – it was you who started it."

"Ah so? We have said you talk of '*your*' self and '*my*' self, just as you talk of '*your*' house and '*my*' house."

"OK, OK, I get it: it's a possession."

"Das is so."

"It's clever, Professor, but so what?"

"When you die it is like losing a precious possession."

"Huh. All right, I see what you're saying, yet it doesn't cover all bases."

"Excuse me. 'Cover all bases'?"

"Oh, it's just an *expression*. What I'm saying is you've only talked about my body. What about my 'soul' or 'spirit'?"

The German stopped and turned to the Rector. "Pastor Foggie?"

The clergyman at last finished his salmon, put down his knife and fork and wiped his mouth. "Yes?"

Von Lottowind gestured. "You are experienced in this field. What do you advise?"

"I wouldn't call myself 'experienced', Professor. Nevertheless, people do indeed talk of having a soul or spirit which survives death."

"So," I came in, "what happens to *them*?"

"Ah, notice, my son, that they say they '*have*' a soul or spirit. We are back to square one"

"No, we're not."

"Yes we are – with a possession metaphor."

"Are we?"

"Yes. Just as with your 'self', you speak of *your* 'soul' or *your* 'spirit' or whatever you call it. That means it's an *object* that's *separate* from you – as though it were your *property.*"

"Hardly an object," I protested. "It's invisible."

"You're right: it's an imaginary possession that never exists."

This was too much. "Now it sounds like you're saying there's no such thing as a soul? And you, a clergyman?"

He smiled.

"All right," I grumbled, "then what *have* I got?"

"You've got your ability to imagine."

"Well, I'm glad to hear it. But presumably I lose that, too?"

"No. Death is the *product* of your imagination."

"Oh." I mulled it over. Such twisting and turning. "So you're saying I take my *imagination* into the next world?"

"Yes, but you don't '*take*' it anywhere – it's no more a possession than the 'soul'. Rather, you conjure up a different existence – *through* your imagination. Since you managed to conjure up *this* world out of nothing, you can start creating *another* whenever you want." He glanced at me. "Does that help?"

"I don't know," I replied. "Maybe I'll get the hang of it."

Part V

⌘

Entertaining Life

"Y ES," said the cleric, "you'll get the hang of it bit by bit. I'll keep it simple. You see, you interchange realities every day."

I frowned.

"Of course you do. At night. When you dream. You experience a different world."

"Yeah, Father, but those are just dreams."

"What *is* a dream?"

"You're asking me?" I gave it a moment. "As far as I know," I said, "it's a kind of alternative reality."

"Quite. And please notice you don't need your physical eyes. You can see clearly in a dream, can't you?"

"Yeah, I suppose I can."

"So it will be when you're dead: just because you don't have eyes doesn't mean you can't see – and the same applies to your other senses."

"Hey, slow down. When I'm asleep I can 'see' because *my brain's* working. It won't when I'm dead."

"Yes, we know your brain's working during sleep, just as when you're awake, but the question is: does the brain's electrical activity *create* thoughts?"

"As far as I know it does. It's certainly what any neurophysicist would say."

"Possibly. But can you tell me *how* it does it?"

I looked at the other two for help. They were saying nothing.

Frostbight resumed. "How about the alternative?"

"There is one?"

"Of course. Supposing the brain reconfigures '*pre-existent*' thoughts, so to speak, into an accessible format for use in the physical world? In other words, it's a collaborative effort. Anyhow, whichever you choose, what's crucial is, *who is making it happen?*"

"I don't know, Father. It's sort of biological, isn't it?"

"Oh, dear, we've already been through this. Yes, of course it's biological, but the point I'm making is that you stop *operating* the brain when you die."

"Ugh. So what happens?"

"You'll go back to what was going on before you were born: inventing experiences which, as Huxley might say, would no longer be restricted by your biology."

"Mmm ... hard to imagine. So *why* do I dream?"

"To inhabit a self-created Instant experience that's different from your daily life."

I rubbed my neck. "That's more gobbledygook. In what way? Dreams are pretty realistic."

"So they are. What's different about a dream is it's a chance for your Dependent imagination to tone down."

"And in plain English?"

"To reduce – or even suspend – your daily judging of the people and the world around you."

"What do you mean?"

"Haven't you noticed in a dream things keep happening with minimal analysis or commentary?"

"All right," I replied, "I'll grant you that. What are you trying to say?"

"I'm saying you could call it a taste of life after death."

"Whoops. *Really?* But a dream can be extremely scary."

"Yes," he replied, "and so can the 'afterlife'. Notice again," he went on, "that during a dream you experience a normal world, both physically and emotionally."

"I'm aware of that."

"You see? When you're awake and recount its story, the dream seems bizarre."

"OK. And when I die?"

"When you die, you'll think *this* world was bizarre. And you know what?"

"No?"

"When you're dead, you'll stop your judging."

"Huh."

"Or at least," he went on, "if there *is* to be any judging, it'll be you judging all those ghastly judgments you made during your life!"

Before I could reply, the Professor broke in. "Pastor Foggie, may I interrupt?"

"Please do, Professor. You might explain it better."

The German smiled. "I shall do my best." He looked to me. "Mien Freund, here is another way could think of your span of life." I waited while he took a little wine. "Being born," he went on, "is like going to the cinema. You enter this world, and the film begins. Soon you are engrossed and forget about the life you were having at home before you arrived. You have that picture?"

"Of my going to the flicks? Yes?"

"Das is good. Now you 'suspend' the other world while you pay attention to the screen. At the end, the screen goes blank, the lights brighten and you come back to your normal existence – without having 'travelled' anywhere."

"Oh. By 'normal experience' you're referring to the 'life' I had before I was born?"

"Das is so."

"Mmm ..." I eyed the Prussian. "You're making out my time here on Earth is a '*show*'."

"It is rather entertaining is it not?"

"Entertaining, Professor? That's a novel way of putting it!"

"Are you astonished?"

"Well, yes. Even if it were true I were creating a story, I wouldn't create *this* world."

"Nein?"

"No. The world's full of shit, if you'll pardon the expression. There's *no way* I would put together such a rotten yarn."

"I will clarify," replied the German.

"Even more than the last time?"

He frowned. "You *like* to go to the cinema?"

I tentatively agreed, cautious where this was heading.

"You e*njoy* the theatre?" he persisted.

"Yes, usually."

"And you like to read? Thrillers, tragedies, romance, crime, that sort of thing?"

"Yeah ..." I replied, eyeing him with caution.

"So you are fond of drama, are you not?"

"OK ..."

"Das is good." He raised his eyebrows. "There you have it."

I grunted. "What do you mean, Professor, 'there you have it'? Have what? You think I'm some amateur dramatic psycho creating a miserable world? And I'm doing it just for a fable? It couldn't be more screwy."

"Screwy?"

"Yes! Bananas."

"Bananas?"

"Oh, just *expressions,* Professor. Now *you* may say my life's a 'story', but what about the famines and wars and natural disasters and God knows what going on out there? You've evidently no idea what a battle life can be."

He did not flinch, but finished his mouthful and remarked, "Battles make good stories, no?"

I was incensed. "You *can't* tell me that the tragedies and horrible things going on in the world are something I've created to amuse myself. I'm not going to invent the stresses and strains and pains and fears just to tell myself a fairytale." I stopped. "Oh, *I* know. I've got it. You're not claiming that. You're trying to say it's all *in my mind.*"

He shrugged and repeated, "Of course it is in your mind."

"But I'm talking about the *real* things that go on *out there.*"

"So am I. How do you know what goes on 'out there'?"

"Because I've *experienced* it."

"You experienced it at the time, and now it has become a memory – in your mind?"

"Well, yes."

"That is what I am talking about."

I stopped to think, idly playing my finger along the rim of my empty glass. This inadvertently brought Mould with the claret jug.

"No more, thank you, Mould," I responded. "I reckon I need to keep my wits about me."

"Quite so, Sir."

I addressed the Cleric instead. "Father," I asked, "can you explain this thing about stories?"

Part VI

ℰℐ

Finding Meaning

H E PUT DOWN HIS WINE GLASS, LOWERED HIS SPECS and regarded me. "The important thing to remember is that it's *there,* in stories, where you'll find the meaning of life – at least, of *your* life."

"Huh. Will I? Sounds like another of your clever doctrines. I thought you said the meaning of life was in death."

"Yes. You need a story to make meaning possible, and an ending to make the story possible."

"Humph," I responded.

"My child, you've always thought you had to search for the meaning of life 'out there'."

"But if there *is* such a thing, it's *got* to be 'out there'."

"Trust me: it's not. The gold you're looking for is on your doorstep."

"What's that supposed to mean?"

"That you need to get into your head two things. Firstly you don't have to go anywhere, and secondly, *this isn't someone else's world. Only you* experience exactly what *you* experience."

I sighed. "Fair enough."

"And you know what?" he went on.

"No?"

"*That's* the *good* news."

"Well, I'm delighted to hear it."

He smiled. "You wouldn't want to be locked into somebody else's meaning, would you?"

"I don't know. I might."

"Well, beware. You might as well sell your soul to the devil. If you look to another to give your life meaning, you become their slave."

"Who do you mean?"

"Marxists? Communists? Jihadists? Fundamentalists? Extremists? Hitler's SS? Take your pick."

At the name of the Reichfuhrer, the Doctor ostentatiously put his fingers in his ears. The Rector paid no attention. "There's never a shortage of cults, despots, radicals and revolutionaries looking for anyone who's willing to abandon his *own* reason for living."

I paused for thought. "All right," I mused, "I can hardly disagree – and I suspect you're about to point out that they use the 'struggle' metaphor to hook them."

"Well done. They certainly do. Getting others to join their 'struggle', whatever it is, is a great way to control and dominate them."

I gave it time to settle in. "Still," I persisted, "that doesn't tell me what *my* life's about."

"My son, you told us earlier what *your* life's about."

"No, I didn't."

"You did. You told us you like to 'think'."

"Yeah, but it's not a story."

"It is. The gradual development of your thinking is your story."

"In what way?"

"Didn't you start by being lost and confused? Then, gradually, after all kinds of experiences, you've gained insight, little by little? That's a good tale isn't it?"

"Yeah, maybe, but only to me."

"That doesn't matter. It *means* something to you."

"Fine, it does. But I'm not aware of any other stories."

"What about tonight's dinner and our discussion? That's a tale ready to be told."

I thought about it while I listened to the howl of the storm – happily the shutters were holding. "Maybe," I said at last, "but what about the *future?* I want an *overall* meaning."

The Rector deliberated. "Then how about this? One of your tales could be how you learnt to see the world as your creation – and the consequences that followed from learning it."

The German took up the topic. "You also told us the tale of your 'struggle'."

"OK, I did. But I didn't tell you a 'tale' or a 'story'. I simply said life *was* a struggle."

"Ach! It is most certainly a story, and has given you a great deal of meaning – and as we've just said, that same story, with endless variations, has given a lot of meaning to a lot of people."

It was hard for me to imagine a life free of struggles.

"But," he continued, "you also have many, many other minor narratives."

"I have?"

"Ja. Every morning you begin afresh. Sometimes your stories are dull; and at other times, less so."

"What about today?"

"This evening you had an exciting one, where you were stuck in a snowstorm."

"Yes, I admit that was scary."

The Rector joined in. "You see, my son, what happened today fits into your stories of last week, last month, last year, and so on as you build the meanings of your life. Everyone does it."

"Well, maybe, but even if it all fitted together, I still don't know *the* meaning of my life."

"No? May I make a suggestion?"

"I wish you would."

"Ask a different question."

"Oh? Sounds good. What?"

He indicated with his finger. "Before anything else, stop assuming that there's no meaning to life just because you don't know what it is. Then the way is open for you to *look* for one, rather than moaning there's no such thing."

"I don't moan. Well, not much."

He smiled. "I'm sure you don't. Now here's the question: leave off wondering vaguely what the meaning of the *whole* of your life is – that'll take care of itself in due course – and approach the matter with bite-sized chunks. Ask yourself, 'in what ways is my life meaningful *today?*'"

"Mmm ... Like what?"

"Think of your journey here – *that* had meaning: you're on a quest. Or here's another idea. You could ask yourself, 'what am I doing right now that's worthwhile?'"

"Not a lot," I returned.

"No? What you're doing is a fragment of your quest. Isn't your quest worthwhile?"

"Yes, all right, it may be important."

"Of course it is. Then you could think how you might build on it day by day." He stopped eating and took some wine. "Does that help?"

I dithered. "Er ... yeah, a bit."

"Then let's go back to what we were talking about." He addressed von Lottowind. "Professor, did you want to say something more about stories?"

"Thank you, Herr Foggie. I did." The Prussian eyed me. "You listen to the wireless, do you not? You hear the news?"

"Yes," I replied, "sometimes."

"How does the newscaster begin?"

"He gives the news."

"Nein. He starts like this: 'here are tonight's main *stories*.'"

He was right. "Yeah, maybe I hadn't noticed. But he still gives us facts."

"Facts? Ja, 'facts' wrapped in drama. When he tells of an earthquake, does he call it a 'natural phenomenon'? Nein. He sensationalises it. He calls it a 'disaster' or a 'tragedy'. News is theatre – for your entertainment. All stories are designed to stir up your emotions – especially tales of hardship, trouble and sorrow." He fiddled with his knife and fork, positioning them neatly together on his plate. "And *that*, mein Freund," he went on, "is why you like stories."

I shrugged.

"Do you not understand? Emotions make the stories worthwhile. That's why you listen to them."

"Hang on, Professor, I don't like emotions *that* much."

"Please, I am not suggesting there is something '*wrong*' with emotions. Emotions take care of themselves. What matters is creating happier emotions by learning to make happier tales."

"Happier tales? Sounds good, but I wouldn't know how to go about it."

"Pastor Foggie has told you how to start: point out to yourself day by day that *everything* you experience is part of your life's tale."

The clergyman came in. "Do you remember the saying in the Gospel? 'Man does not live by bread alone, but by every *story* that proceedeth out of the mouth of God'." He looked at the butler. "Mould, I am correct, am I not?"

"Indeed you are, Sir. Matthew, Chapter 4, verse 4."

"I thought so." Talking to me, the Cleric added, "Notice that 'living by bread alone' is another story. You can make a tale out of anything. As the Professor suggested, the trick is to invent happier endings."

Part VII

❧

Self Abuse

THERE WAS SOMETHING FROM ST. MATTHEW'S QUOTE that was not quite how I remembered it, but another thing was concerning me. "That's all very neat and tidy," I said, "but what the past? What about all the stupid things I've done? *Those* didn't have 'happy endings' and never will."

Von Lottowind was quick to respond. "Ah! You feel guilty about some things you did?"

"Yes, of course. And embarrassed too."

"In that case you must consider this. Those people you wronged: they existed because you had, as Watty would say, 'set them up'."

"Whoops. Did what?"

"I am saying you brought them into existence. You asked them onto your stage."

"Hey, I've never 'invited' anybody onto any 'stage'."

"Please understand. As an illustration, imagine you are ashamed that, when a child, you stole money from your mother's purse. You did not, *at that time*, conceive that it was *you* who had put the money within reach so you could steal it."

"Well, no, Professor, of course not."

"Also you thought of others, even family, as being 'separate' from you."

"Sure. That's what they *are.*"

"Mein Freund, *everyone* is a manifestation of your own magic."

I rubbed my cheeks. It was like Father Foggie and his miracles. "I suppose when you say 'your' magic, you're referring to my higher self – sorry, I mean the 'No-self' – and not to my ordinary self?"

"Das is correct," he answered. "When you appreciate that others exist only at your – the No-self's – request, you may be sorry for what you did. You may discover a new affection for those you mistreated, and your story will have a happier ending."

"Mmm ... I'll have to mull over that one."

"You may find it strange, but only at first. Now is the time for you to learn that people behave *according to your invitation.* Even those you maligned existed only at your invitation." He stopped for a moment while he took a little wine and added, "Be kind to yourself."

"Huh? What's that got to do with it?"

"I have said you create the people around you, ja? But you have also created *your self.*"

"All right, I get that. So?"

"What," he questioned, "is the most common disease?"

"Why're you asking? *I* don't know. Probably the common cold."

He regarded me intently. "Nein. The most common disease is maligning yourself."

"Is it? Really? A disease?"

"Ja. Maligning – and shaming – yourself. That is what is at the bottom of all social and psychological ills. You, like so many, love to humiliate your own person."

"No I don't."

"Ja! You do it every time you criticise yourself."

"But I don't *humiliate* myself."

"You do. Self-criticism is self-abuse, and *any* abuse is humiliating."

"Well, all right," I agreed, "maybe *sometimes,* but usually I don't comment on what I'm doing: I just get on with it."

The cleric intervened. "Then you must find reason to compliment yourself."

"You reckon, Father? What on earth for?"

"Because it is not a sin to be kind to your own creation. And anyway, compliments make for happier stories."

I made no reply.

"Have you," resumed the Prussian, "not seen how people destroy themselves with self loathing?"

"No," I said, "not really."

"It is a pity. Maybe you will in due course. It is *insane* to humiliate what you have created."

I considered for a moment. "Yeah, Professor, but hating oneself is about rotten self-esteem."

"What is low self-esteem? It is the disease of loading criticism onto yourself. An emotional orgy."

"Lord," I murmured and took some water. Forget about the turbulence outside: there was plenty in my head.

"You OK, old chap?" It was Frostbight. I had noticed his stroking his moustache from time to time as he listened. "You're frowning."

"Am I frowning? Goodness, I don't know *what* I'm doing. Where are we going with this?"

"You want your stories to have happier endings?"

"I wouldn't say 'no'."

"Splendid. It's simple."

"Oh, yeah? You've promised me that before."

"What you need to learn is the difference between fact and fiction."

I grimaced. "I didn't know it wasn't obvious."

"We'll see about that. Reckon you're ready?"

"What choice do I have?"

"Not much!" he grinned.

"All right, Doctor. In for a penny, in for a pound."

Part VIII

☙

A World of Fiction

"**G**OOD MAN," HE RETURNED, AND SIPPED SOME WINE.
"I've got something for you to chew over."

"Doctor, I'm sure you have."

He smiled. "What is and what isn't real?"

"Is this a quiz?"

"No, it's not. Let's start with an example. Do you reckon you're worthless?"

"Funny question. I hadn't thought about it. Maybe sometimes. It depends."

"Of course. People often think they're worthless in some context or other."

"Maybe they're right."

"Only in so far as they've no idea how much they're wasting their time."

"I wouldn't know. What are you getting at?"

"This. People treat 'worthless' as real even though they can't see it."

"I'm not sure I agree."

"No? As Gusty would say, it's all about making a *story*."

Before I could comment, von Lottowind spoke up. "You have a body, yes?"

"Professor, you hardly need to ask."

"Das is good. You believe it is ugly?"

"No, I wouldn't say that."

"So you are happy the way you look?"

"Well, I'm not Adonis."

"Mein Freund, you cannot *see* 'worthless', 'beauty' or 'ugliness'."

"What makes you so sure? *I* can see them just fine."

"Nein. You cannot. They are *opinions*."

"Is that so? Well, *I* can see them – all over the place."

"Ach! No one can. As Gusty says, they are *stories* – in your Dependent imagination."

"Huh. Then they're an unusual *kind* of 'story'."

"I will clarify."

"Good. Go ahead."

He grinned. "This time I make it even more clear for you." Growing serious he went on, "It is this. Whether you think you are 'beautiful' or 'ugly', or whether you did something 'good' or something 'bad', those words are not *things*."

"No?"

"Nein. They are dramatic embellishments."

"Of what?"

"Of what is happening – of the world around you."

I gave it a moment's thought. "Not necessarily," I objected. "They might be true."

"Ach! Tonight we teach you the distinction between *experience* – which maybe said to be 'true' – and the vast majority of life which is fiction."

"What do you mean?"

"Just that. You experience what your senses are picking up, and it is meaningless. Meaning only comes from your mental embellishments: pictures, memories, words, and drama."

I made a face.

The Padre spoke. "Maybe this could help. Try it. When you're standing in front of anyone, realise that what you're seeing is the production of your sensory data, what we call your 'Instant' imagination."

"All right, if you must."

"Bear with me. Now, you could activate your Dependent imagination to embellish what you see in a couple of ways. First, you could *picture* what that person *might* look like *in the nude*. That's one way. Alternatively you could have an *opinion* about that person, such as about their choice of clothes – or about their intelligence."

"All right," I said, "but can we slow down? Opinions and criticisms are a normal part of life."

"They are indeed common," spoke the Professor. "However, when they are *judgements*, they are unfortunate or, as Oscar Wilde would say, 'careless'."

I grimaced.

"And," he added, "a thousand opinions, mien Freund, do not make a truth."

I sighed. "All right, all right." I stopped to consider. "I suppose," I admitted, "I can't *help* criticising – especially myself."

"Ach! You *humiliate* yourself and you say you cannot *help yourself*? That, also, is a yarn."

"But it's true! Lord. You're not letting me off lightly."

"Herr Evriwun, I advise you to avoid all opinions – especially opinions about yourself – like the plague. It is a world of fiction. Whether you say you are 'lazy', a 'failure', 'immature', 'worthless', 'useless', 'feckless', 'stupid', 'shameful', 'clumsy' ... *all* of it is fiction. "

I offered no response.

"And what about this?" the German went on, his voice rising. "You have *copied* them, *all of them*."

"Whoa, steady, Professor." I waved my hand about. "No I haven't."

"Nein? Being rude about yourself was *not originally your idea*."

I paused. "So whose idea was it?"

"Like everyone," he said, "when you were little you were *taught* to say critical things about yourself by your elders and betters – and probably by your peers as well."

I shifted in my chair.

"Now," he went on, "you have a chance to start anew."

The German was in full swing and I dared not ask him to repeat anything. "But," I grumbled, "how am I supposed to be different?"

"By developing your perception."

"What perception?"

"The way you 'frame' your understanding of life."

"That's more gobbledygook."

"Nein. It is easy. Every day you must rehearse."

"Rehearse what?"

"What have already said: framing – that is, thinking of – yourself and others *as your own creation*. By doing *that* you are not copying anybody."

I took a breath. "How do you expect me to 'frame' others as my 'creation'?"

"It takes practice. If you find yourself upset by someone, see – imagine – that *you* are creating what that other person is saying or doing. Advise yourself it is you who are writing the 'script'. I am sure we will come to this later."

"I bet you will." I took a deep breath. "And you reckon it's going to make a difference?"

"It will. I repeat, whatever happens in life is never accidental. Your experiences happen because … Donner und Blitzen!" he cried and slapped his chest.

The conversation stopped.

I looked at von Lottowind. He looked at us. The Rector crossed himself. Frostbight raised his eyebrows. "Everything OK, Gusty?"

"Wo ist meine Serviette?" he exclaimed. "It has been stolen!"

I got the gist of his German this time.

"Lost your napkin?" came in Frostbight. "I say, jolly bad luck."

"Bad luck? Watty, I have been robbed."

"Professor," suggested Rector, "maybe it's on the floor?"

"It is *not* on the floor, Herr Foggie. It has been stolen."

Our host brightened up. "Not on the floor? Ha! Bet I know." He held onto his smoking cap and arched back so he could see the dog bed. "Ah, thought so. Snowie's swiped it. No worries Gusty, we'll have it back in a jiff. Mould! Problem with the Professor's napkin."

The butler limped across to retrieve the object. He had to tap the dog on the nose since Snowie thought it was a game. At last she relinquished her prize and it was returned to its owner. Calm was restored.

"Sorry about that Gusty, old fellow," apologised our host. "Do you want a clean one?"

"Ach, it is no matter."

"Good show. Let me know if you change your mind. Snowie's a naughty girl when she's not getting attention. It won't happen again. Now, where were we?"

"A little more wine, Sir?" It was Mould at my side with the decanter.

I looked up. "No, thank you, Mould. With all this going on, I need a clear head."

"None at all?"

"Thank you. None whatsoever. Firm as a rock."

"Quite so, Sir." He continued doing his rounds.

Our host cast a look around the table. "I say, everyone finished?" His attention was drawn to the Professor's plate. He leant towards his neighbour, reached into his pocket and removed his monocle. "What's that I see, Gusty?" he muttered with a frown, "Salsify? Not enjoying it?"

"Ach! Watty," the German replied. "Das is a most unfamiliar schottisch vegetable. Inedible."

"It's good for you, you know ... fibre, and all that. Well, well, never mind. I reckon it's time we had pud." Talking to me, he asked, "Got room for pud, old bean?"

It had been a while since I'd heard dessert being called 'pud'. I assured him I could find space for it.

"First class!" he exclaimed. "Pudding it is. Mould?" He indicated to his butler. "Time for the next course."

I wondered what more might be coming.

Dessert

Part I

✌

Who is God?

THE ENSUING BUSTLE WITH MRS. MCWHITEOUT PUSHING the trolley in again and Mould changing our plates introduced a welcome break. However extraordinary Doctor Frostbight and his friends might be, I was warming to them and their quirky humour. I still couldn't make out whether von Lottowind was really German – or, for that matter, whether Father Foggie was really a clergyman. Nonetheless, what was I to make of the conversation? If, as they said, the universe did not create me – as I had always believed – and that it was the other way round, it gave me a lot to swallow. And I still had a problem. It would take an idiot to fail to see the gap between my skin and the rest of the world; how could I possibly have brought *other people* into existence? These chaps *had* to be away with the fairies.

Or no, perhaps not. Maybe I had stumbled upon the clandestine HQ of the wacky occult brotherhood of the Order of Creosophists. That's why Chilblane wasn't marked on the map, and they were trying to brainwash me and after dinner they would draw me into a secret ritual and we would start sacrificing …

"Apple tart, Sir?" I jolted. The butler was beside me and, in his hand, a steaming pie dish.

"Apple tart? Ah! Yes, please." Embarrassed to be caught napping, I grasped the silver slicer. "Apples from the estate?"

"Indeed, Sir."

"Thank you. They look good."

Once the Rector had also helped himself, he spoke. "So, my child, you think you've chanced upon a secret brotherhood?"

This was awkward. "You *are* reading my mind."

He didn't answer directly. "You still believe you're not creating other people? I'll tell you: everything you're hearing tonight is said because you wanted to hear it."

"I beg your pardon?"

"Nothing happens in your life that you haven't ordered with your imagination. We keep telling you: life is your creation. If you were to discover these words in a book, it would be because you had put them there yourself."

"That's inconceivable."

"So you imagine."

"Very funny, Father, but it still doesn't make sense."

"And that's because you're thinking from the point of view of the physical self."

"Look," I remonstrated, 'whether it's my self or my 'No-self' – or whatever you call it – you know perfectly well I can't *magic* people out of thin air any more than I can *make* you say what you're saying. Nor can I *make* you *do* anything. There's a gap between us." I flapped my hand. "See that? It's called 'space'."

He grinned.

"I don't see what you're laughing at. You're sitting there and I'm sitting here. You're made of flesh and blood, and so am I."

He gave me that 'look' over the top of his glasses. "You keep arguing. How many times do we have to say it? Reality exists because You made it so; otherwise there would be no such thing."

"Cream, dear?" Our cook was at my elbow.

I sat back. "Oh, yes, please, Mrs. McWhiteout, just a little." She poured on loads. "Mmm," I said, " … thank you."

"I hope that's enough," she added. "If you find the tart too sour, there's sugar on the table."

"It looks great. I bet I'll enjoy it, especially," I added whimsically, "since I'm the one who's supposed to have created it."

"Your trouble, dear," she replied cheerily, "is that you're confusing 'You' with your 'self'. It's 'You', not your *self*, who creates."

This was a conspiracy! They were *all* at it.

Von Lottowind resumed the topic as the cook continued her rounds. "It may help, mein Freund, if you start to accept there is more to you than you think. Mrs. McWhiteout is correct: you still think that you are limited to a 'self'."

"But my self has *got* to be me."

"In some ways it is, and in some ways it is not. You are familiar with your self, but you are *un*familiar with You."

"You're telling me!"

"It is so. Language is a product of your self, so it us unable to identify a 'No-self'."

"Are you surprised? OK then. Tell me this: who *am* I?"

Giving me a searching look, he replied. "You *are*."

"Is that it? Oh, my God, you're sounding like a Sufi."

He shrugged. "Maybe, maybe not. You could liken '*You*' to the conductor of an orchestral piece heard on the wireless."

"I could?"

"Ja. The role of the conductor is essential for co-ordinating the orchestra. But since he himself does not play an instrument, when you listen to the music, you would have no idea he was there."

I shrugged. "So what? That's just an analogy."

"Maybe so. Nevertheless," he continued, "you go about your daily life with no idea that You – the No-self – are orchestrating it."

"Well, Professor, it sounds very fine, but you know what?"

"Nein?"

"All your stuff, 'life's a creation', 'life after death', the 'Original Being that isn't', has no more basis than any imaginative speculation."

Von Lottowind glanced impatiently at the ceiling and said nothing.

Father Foggie raised his hand. "Could we, Professor," he asked, "take it from a different angle?"

"Of course, Herr Pastor. Be my guest."

The clergyman looked at me. "When you were at College, did you learn about Feuerbach?"

"Feuerbach?" The name rang a bell. "Yeah, wasn't he one of those boring 19th. Century philosophers?"

"Well remembered."

"Was he the one who said God's a projection of the self?"

"Exactly."

"Why're you asking?"

"We're coming to that. And were you taught those medieval debates about God being 'pure existence' and all that, and how He created the world out of nothing?"

"Kind of. It was pretty pointless. I remember they said that any attempt to describe God put a limit on Him – including the description 'limitless'."

"Top marks," returned the Rector. "I'm impressed you were listening."

"Uh! Thanks."

"There was more sense to it than you imagine."

"Really? Those debates led nowhere."

"My son, you wanted to know the answer to 'who am I?'"

That caught me off-guard. "What's that got to do with it?"

He looked at me carefully. "It has everything to do with it. That limitless Being who can't be described?"

"Yeah?"

"That, my son, is You."

I stared at him.

He was unperturbed. "I repeat. It's *You.*"

"Me? Which 'me'?"

"Good question! Obviously not your self. I am talking of the 'You' – a limitless being – who's orchestrating your world."

I laughed. "A limitless Being? That would make me like God."

"Yes," he said slowly, "it would indeed."

"Phew." I took a deep breath. "Father, that's a big statement. In the olden days they would have burnt you alive."

The Rector waved aside my concern. "Times have changed. It's not such a big statement when you get used to it. What God is said to do, you do yourself. Feuerbach was on the money."

"Think about it," came in von Lottowind. "As Pastor Foggie observed, you are hearing what we are saying because you are creating it."

Doctor Frostbight interrupted. "Well said, Gusty." He looked across at me. "I don't know why you're so surprised. We've been telling you this all evening. You're complaining that what we're talking about is simply speculation? And you're insisting that the world runs independently of you? No. It's *that* which is *speculation* – habitual, vague, universal, ancient and useless speculation, pure and simple."

"My goodness. But how are *you* getting your answers?"

"Don't you see? You invented the questions, and it's you who invents the answers – albeit via us. Yes, there *is* an 'Invisible Agent' creating the world, but how could it *possibly* be anyone else but you – at some level?"

"So you keep saying."

"And for good reason. That's because it's *You* ... Great Scott! What's *that*?"

He broke off. We ducked. A black object shot across the table, circled the room at alarming speed and swooped again. Our host whipped out his monocle and, with his tassel swinging wildly, followed the creature's gymnastics. "Good heavens. A bat! I say, what's *that* pesky thing doing? In mid winter? Mould? Where are you? We've got a bat."

"Indeed we have, Sir," replied his butler without stirring.

"What's it doing flying around at this time of year?"

"The heat of the room, Sir. It must have come out of hibernation."

"Well, come on, can't you *do* something?"

"Unfortunately not, Sir. It is too swift."

"Uh! I suppose it is." Our host replaced his eyepiece. "Anybody brought a butterfly net? OK, joke. Never mind. We'll just have to live with it – it'll no doubt tire in due course." He picked up his utensils. "Now, come on chaps, enough of that. Let's get tucked in," at which he plunged his spoon into the pastry. The rest of us followed – trying not to flinch as the bat made a pass. As far as I was concerned, the animal had been sent from Hell as a warning, and it would be no surprise if it nested in von Lottowind's mop of hair.

"Sir, shall I serve the ice wine?" asked the ever-attentive steward.

"The ice wine? Good thinking, Mould. I'd forgotten it." Frostbight saw my perplexed expression. "Want to change your mind, old boy? A dessert wine. Our own. Made from grapes picked late in the season – once they're frozen on the vine. Delicious. Try some."

My rock of resolve was less than firm. "Put like that, I suppose it would be rude to refuse."

"Good man. Life's too short."

A few moments later I was tasting the sweet liquor – Mould had filled one of my two smaller glasses. It was not going to keep me level headed, but our host was right: it was certainly delicious and complimented my dessert. The apple tart was tasty, not too sweet and with a sharp crust.

"Unfortunately not, Sir. It is too swift."

Meanwhile, there was silence while we ate, which gave me time to reflect. Finally, I spoke up. "I get what you lot are on about."

They stopped and looked at me.

"What the Greeks said, `'Know thyself'. You remember – the inscription above the entrance to the Delphic Oracle."

"A good quotation, old boy," replied the Doctor, "I remember it well." He turned to his butler replacing the decanter on its coaster. "Ever come across that one, Mould?"

"'Gnothi seauton'? The saying at Delphi? Indeed, Sir."

"Not bad, eh? Greeks ahead of their time, what?"

"Unfortunately Sir, it is misconceived. I understand the thrust of the saying was correctly, *'know your place* – in relation to the Gods."

"Huh. Fascinating. How about that?" said Frostbight to me. "Mould's up on his Classics. Today, however, a Creosophist might say, 'know your self in relation to the Non-self'." He sipped a little of his ice wine. "Mmm … excellent. I hope you're enjoying it. Now, where were we?"

"Where Father Foggie had gone off his rocker telling me I was God."

"Ah, yes," he smiled. "You think he's mad? It's marvellous how people go through life and have no idea that the world they witness is a display of their own genius."

I went back to my apple tart and ducked whenever Lucifer's emissary passed – and glad I had smeared Brylcreem on my hair that morning. As for coming up with wise sayings, maybe it wasn't a good idea. Who would have thought the butler knew Classical Greek? Nevertheless, I had other queries. "Another of my problems is this," I pronounced, "if I really *am* creating the universe as you say, then that can only mean one thing."

"What's that, old boy?"

"It means it's not *solid*."

"No?"

"No. If the world's my imagination it could evaporate at any time. How scary is *that*?"

"Or conversely," the Reverend Foggie suggested, "it's the opposite. Your imagination makes the world *more* solid."

"What do you mean? No, it doesn't."

"It certainly does. It's your imagination which *ensures* its 'solidity'."

"Huh. I don't see how."

"Think about it. If it were *not* you, but someone *else* who's creating the world, how could you trust it?"

I conceded. "All right, that's a good point. But supposing there's an earthquake?"

"Supposing there is?"

"Well then the earth *wouldn't* be 'solid'."

"Maybe not, but that too, my son, would be your invention – for whatever reason."

"Well," I snorted, "that would be a pretty crap invention. Oops! Sorry Father."

"Fear not. You may speak your mind."

No doubt the Rector had heard worse in the army. I went on. "To *my* thinking, Father, we come back to this: *if* it's I who am creating everything, why on earth would I make such a crap invention?"

He again looked at me over the top of his spectacles, and asked, "Which 'crap' invention in particular?"

"That doesn't matter. The point is the world's in a mess and it's not *my fault*."

Part II

☙

The Fantasy Courtroom

THE CHAPLAIN PUSHED HIS SPECS TO THE TOP OF HIS nose. "*If* you took it that calamities were someone's fault other than your own, that opinion would be your belief – and, as we've explained – your *story*. Can I be any clearer? There's *nothing* which isn't of your own making."

"But steady on: if someone throws a banana skin on the pavement and I slip on it, you'll say I'm to blame."

The Rector glanced towards von Lottowind. The German rose to the occasion. "Ah," he pronounced with delight, "'fault'? 'Blame'? *Court metaphors!*"

I sighed, but was getting wise about arguing. "OK, Professor," I returned with resignation, "what've I done now?"

"Mein Freund, you have done nothing. Or I should say, nothing unusual. You, like so many people, have made your world into a fantasy courtroom."

"No I haven't. What 'fantasy courtroom'?"

"You thrive on a Dependent imagination that is riddled with faults, blame, criticism, judgements, complaints, guilt, justifications and punishment: all the stuff of courtrooms."

"Wow! I beg your pardon; I don't do anything of the sort. Anyway, we *have* to have courts – to keep laws upheld."

"Those are not the ones I am talking about."

"No? Well, there aren't any others."

"There are. There is one in your head."

"No there isn't."

"Is that what you believe? You have not noticed? You, like most people, spend your life in it."

"Are you serious?"

"I am. You spend your days finding fault with both yourself and with others."

"Yeah, but only sometimes …"

"Have you not said you are always criticising yourself?"

"Well, OK, maybe I did say that …"

"And *then* you feel *guilty* about your 'sins' – which *you* invented?"

"Yeah, of course I feel guilty."

"Is that not madness?"

"What you do mean?"

"Your ideas of 'sin' are self inflicted."

"Hey, hang about. Not necessarily."

"Nein? Have you ever felt 'guilty' for eating something as innocent as too much chocolate?"

"Huh!" I retorted. "Not likely with the rationing. Anyway that sort of thing's normal. It's just talk."

"Ja," agreed the Professor, "it *is* 'just talk' – to the point of being a fashion. You, like so many, are constantly vigilant about your 'sins', and then wonder why you are unhappy." He paused, and while he took a spoonful of apple tart I watched the bat dart back and forth over his head. Was it going to nest? He went on. "Here is a common case in point. Say a person feels 'bad' or 'guilty' about her weight."

"Uh-huh?" The bat flew on.

"She has," he said, "already summoned up her invisible court."

"She has?"

"Das is so. She has already put herself before the bench and found herself guilty."

"Oh? Where? Whose bench?"

"Her own."

"But she hasn't got one."

"She has. She is her own self-appointed judge."

"Is she? All right, so who's her prosecutor?"

"She is."

"And her defendant? I suppose that's her, too."

"Nein. There is none."

"Why not?"

"Because she *never* defends herself."

I remained silent.

"She only attacks," he persisted. "She might even mete herself out a punishment and go on a diet – or something worse. It is folly, and there are innumerable men and women who go to their graves riddled with self inflicted guilt which only they know about – entire lives spent in magical 'courthouses'."

"Humph," I grunted. "Maybe they deserved it."

"Do you not understand?" The colour rose in his face. "That 'courtroom' is *fake*. It never exists *except in the mind.*"

"But not in *mine.*"

He glowered. "Ja. In yours, too."

The German was not mincing his words. He paused to take a sip of the wine and resumed. "You have heard of people being stuck in an abusive relationship?"

"Uh-huh. From time to time. It's not uncommon."

"Ja? And which is the most abusive of all?" He didn't wait. "The most abusive relationship is your own *self-humiliation.*"

"Oh?"

"Have you forgotten so soon? It is the worst human disease. What is your expression in English? 'Pissing on your own bonfire'?"

"Certainly colourful," I responded weakly.

"Please understand: your courtroom is your creation. To go back to what you asked about slipping on a banana skin: you slip on it and you slip into your court, as quickly as that – getting angry and looking for someone to condemn."

"Maybe, but what do you expect me to do?"

Frostbight spoke up. "The answer is you reframe your understanding of what life is. If ..." he jerked as the bat dodged past, "*if* you framed your life as your *creation* – instead of a law court – you would change your world."

I ducked. "What do you mean?"

"At the moment you think the world is some sort of metaphorical courtroom, and you're a judge in charge of those around you."

"Er ..." I played for time.

"Yes," the Doctor went on, "you certainly do. Nevertheless, if you think of the world as your creation, you could take the view *that you made someone* put the banana skin there."

"I could?"

"Yes, you could. Get it into your head that you invented the whole experience: the set-up; the upset and the set-down, whatever that might have been."

"The set-what?"

"The set-down, old boy. It's what you think or do about it afterwards."

"Like being angry at the person who dropped it?"

"Absolutely. But here's the thing: the set-up and the upset are over in a split second, but your set-down – your Dependent Imagination – can nurse the memory for as long as you want: months, years, or even forever – and keep you miserable forever."

"My goodness. And in this case?"

"In this case, you're angry. That's because you made an imaginary picture of the culprit – even though you didn't know who it was – and condemned him, instantly, in your fake 'court'."

"Huh!" I remarked. "Tonight's the first I've heard of a 'fake court'."

"I'm sure it is, and yet you spend your life in it."

I pulled a face.

"It doesn't help pulling a face: you judge and criticise both people you know and those you don't know: governments, countries, races, and even the weather – if it rains too much."

"Hey, come on: you're exaggerating."

He shook his head. "If only you could see the nonsense of it all ..."

The Rector joined in. "You've heard, my son, that you should forgive those who sin against you?"

"Of course."

"When you dump your magic courtroom, forgiveness and non-forgiveness become irrelevant."

"In what way?"

"You stop believing in 'sins' and 'offences' – neither against 'God' nor against other people."

"Oh. And so there would be nothing left to forgive?"

"Exactly. When you realise that *whatever* happens is *your* creation – then you'll see your make-believe justice for what it is."

"What's that?"

"Another excuse for storytelling." He paused for a second. "Even better …"

"Pardon me, Father … an excuse for '*storytelling*'?"

"You sound surprised. We've already talked about it."

"Um, yes, you did mention it."

"Well, in this case, you're making a story out of people's offences."

This needed some thought. I took a spoonful of tart. "OK," I said, with my mouth half full, "what about real life courts?"

"Good question. In *real* life, what's the job of a judge?"

"I don't know. To decide on punishments."

"To some extent. Actually, his *main* job is to listen to stories. He listens to the stories of the prosecutors, the defendants and the witnesses. If there's a jury, *it* has to decide which of the stories is more credible – the innocent or guilty one."

"Maybe so," I countered, "but *punishment* isn't a story."

"That's right. Punishment is an experience – for as long as it lasts. Later on you may make it into a tale." He stopped to take some wine before going on. "To return to what I was about to say: your fake courtroom, which no one else can see – and trust me, everyone has one – mimics a real courtroom, except that, as the Professor explained, you take on the roles of *both* prosecutor and defendant."

"But that's stupid."

"I agree, and yet you do it instantly, time and again. What's peculiar about your invisible courtroom is that, if you're criticising yourself or anyone else, you *never* declare the 'defendant' innocent."

I found myself scratching my neck. "So, what about the banana skin?"

"The same. You accuse and condemn someone unknown to you in the twinkling of an eye."

He was right.

The Rector forked a little tart on his spoon and then continued. "May I suggest you stop regarding the people in your life as prey for your judgments."

"Huh, *I* didn't think they *were* judgments."

"They are and they do nothing but harm."

"But we all have to judge."

"No, not if you convert your mind to seeing life as your creation."

I gave it some thought. "So you say, but *how?*"

"How what?"

"Well, I'm not a tap. I can't just turn it on and … poof! Life's my creation."

That made him smile. "OK, fair enough." He paused. "I've an idea."

Part III

એસ

It Starts with Imagination

"HAVE YOU? THEN SHOOT."

"All right, here goes. For a start, *imagine* the world as a masterpiece of your genius."

"Humph. A masterpiece? All right. You mean *all* of it – even the grisly bits?"

"Yes, even the grisly bits. The whole world."

"That's an awful lot."

"Then unshackle your imagination."

"Humph," I objected. "It's *not* shackled."

"It is – so far. *That's* what I hope you're going to learn tonight. Don't worry: we used to be in the same boat once. Bit by bit you'll get better at it."

"At what?"

"Going round your daily business reminding yourself – if you remember to do so – that your own genius summoned it up."

I grunted.

"A little more cream, Sir?" It was the butler.

"Cream? No, no, I'm fine thank you. I've had plenty." He remained where he was. I looked up. "Yes?"

"If I may be so bold, Sir, I recall Marcel Proust intimated that what we need is not a new landscape, but a new way of seeing it."

"Oh?" I put on an air of nonchalance. "Actually, about that cream: maybe I will have a little." I waited while he ladled on a large spoonful. "I must say, Mould, that's heavy duty stuff."

"Too much cream, Sir?"

"No, no. I mean reading *Proust*. Whose translation?"

"I prefer to read it in the French."

"Really?"

"Yes, Sir, it helps me sleep." He moved on. Landscape or no landscape, I was not gong to tell him I had never read a word of Proust in any language – not even as a sleeping draught. I mashed the apple, mixed it in the pool of cream and ducked every time the acrobatic mouse made a near miss. At the same time, I was still unsure. "Father," I said to the Rector, "despite everything you say, your whole concept's counter-intuitive."

"It is? Oh? In what way?"

"It defies normal common sense that I create the world."

"I'm sorry to hear it. What do you think *is* 'normal common sense'?"

"Don't ask *me*. It just is."

"My child, you're in danger of following the herd."

"What herd?"

"However 'intuitive', 'normal' or 'common' a 'sense' may be, a thousand opinions don't make …"

"Yes, yes, I know, Father … all right, they don't make a truth. But what you lot are saying has got to be skewed." I paused. "Here's one experience – as an illustration. I was with someone who moaned endlessly about how 'hard' it was to live with me and how she 'suffered'. So she went off with someone – and did exactly the same all over again. The thing is, her 'miseries' were not, as *you* say, *my* creation or anyone else's: it was her 'broken record' repeating itself. She dreamt up pointless problems and, as far as I know, still does today. You can't tell me she was some sort of 'masterpiece', or that *I'm* responsible for her so-called 'suffering'." I fell silent.

Father Foggie looked across to the German. "Professor," he asked, "do you feel like commenting?"

Von Lottowind was stroking his beard. "My thoughts, Pastor Foggie? Mmm …" He addressed me. "Mein Freund, your 'set-down' is your problem."

"It is? You mean what I think about it?"

"Ja. It is a set-down where you imagine the upset was her fault."

"Well, yes, it was ..."

"Ach. You could also have imagined it was *your* fault."

"It wasn't mine: it was *hers*. She loved complaining."

"You *could* decide it was neither."

"Neither what?"

"Neither her fault nor your fault."

"Professor, it had to be *one* of us."

"Ach. You still think the world is a courtroom. You cannot see it is your creation."

"I know, you keep telling me. So?"

"So you may choose any picture you please."

"I'm still not getting it."

"Nein? Now that you have had the experience, what do you do? What set-down do you choose?"

I shrugged. "No idea."

"So far, you have appointed yourself as magistrate."

I waited.

"You are free," he went on, "to play the magistrate if you wish – *or* you could take a different position."

"Oh. I suppose that would be to take the view that what went on was my 'conjuring trick'?"

The German brightened. "Wundervoll. We make progress."

"Professor," I huffed, "maybe it's 'wundervoll' for you, but to me it's pretty bonkers."

"Ach so?"

"Well yes. If I were to look at things *your* way I'd have to take responsibility for other people's behaviour – even people who don't have anything to do with me. That's not right." I jolted. The bat swooped.

"On the contrary," came in Frostbight, "that *is* right."

"But, Doctor," I returned, "it's *impossible.*"

"Do I need to spell it out?" he asked. "You wonder what would make a difference in your life. Well, here you have it. From now on, start *imagining* the world's your creation. Then you'll see for yourself that what others do *is* your responsibility."

I considered it. "Are you trying to tell me making a difference is that simple?"

"Didn't I tell you? Relax. Approach it in the spirit of an experiment. Try it on. Treat it like a new coat."

This drastically different way of viewing life was hard for me to accept. While I was running through the ideas, Father Foggie spoke again. "You've given a good example. You're at the threshold."

"What, Father? Another threshold?"

He smiled. "No, it's the same one: deciding who or what is making your world happen."

"But *nobody knows.*"

"So you keep repeating, but the same question stands – *somebody* or *something* has to have made it happen." He paused and finished his glass of ice wine. "So?"

"What do you mean, 'so'? So what?"

"So, my child, what's the answer?"

"Search me. Whatever you say, I can tell you one thing: you're going to have a hard time convincing *me* I'm conjuring up the world around me."

He ignored my resistance. "You have only one choice."

"Oh, so I've got a choice?"

"Of course. I've told you. Either *you're* making the universe, or *someone else* is."

"OK, stop there," I replied. "I hear what you say, but to go down the route of actually *believing* the universe is my creation is one hell of a stretch."

"Yes, and believing someone or something *else* is making your world is flogging a dead horse."

"Huh, flogging a dead horse? So what do I do?"

"Drop your old 'beliefs'."

"You reckon?" I responded. "That's not likely."

"Beliefs are a curse."

"Oh, come on, Father, you can't expect me to believe *that*."

"You see? *That* demonstrates the curse."

It took me a moment to get the message.

"My child," he went on, "beware of beliefs. They narrow your mind, your vision and your possibilities. They're the proverbial glass ceiling."

The German returned to the conversation. "Mein Freund, what is the *worst* belief?"

"Lord! You keep asking me these questions. *I* don't know."

"The worst is that of believing in your beliefs."

"For goodness sake, what's the matter with them?"

"Because you end up deleting anything that contradicts what you believe. *That*, in itself, renders valid alternatives invisible to you – and I am sure I do not have to spell out what troubles *that* can cause."

I deliberated. "But Professor," I said, "forget beliefs? You can't be serious: we couldn't exist without them."

"Ach! Another belief."

I pursed my lips. The bat made a rapid pass and hovered for a second over the German's hair, changed its mind and darted off.

The Professor paid it no attention – maybe he did not notice it – and waved his hand in the direction of the others. "Please observe that nobody in this room has asked you to 'believe' anything." He stopped for a moment to take a spoonful of dessert, then said, "This may help you understand: did you as a small boy believe there might be a monster in the cupboard?"

"Sometimes. Why?"

"Because really you *imagined* there was a monster in the cupboard."

"I know. So?" Then it dawned. "Oh, I see. Beliefs are about imagination."

"Ah, at last," came in the Cleric. "Yes, you must always treat beliefs – or 'truth' – with caution. First you have your imagination, and your imagination creates beliefs. That's what makes them happen."

I did not reply.

"And," he continued, "guess what?"

I looked at him.

"You need your imagination to imagine that the world is the work of your imagination!"

I briefly held my hands to my head.

"I'm sorry," he said, "if I'm muddling you. It's simple really. Here's the secret: treat with suspicion your habit of *imagining* that something other than your imagination created the world."

"But Father, it's not a 'habit'. Whatever you say, there's no *proof* I'm the creator."

He took a little water and adjusted his specs. "Why do you try to pick holes in what we're saying? Without your imagination there's no proof of anything." He glanced across the table.

"Das is so," agreed Von Lottowind. "Very good, Herr Foggie."

I held up my hands. "Could you two please stop? Maybe I'm not understanding what you mean by 'imagination'."

The German took the reins. "Ah, it is good to be clear about it. Our language is limited. In this case it is limited to a single word that refers to *all* our senses, not just to what is visual. So we 'imagine' the *sound* of a bird singing; we 'imagine' the *smell* of coffee, and we 'imagine' the *taste* of a lemon or the *feel* of fur."

"And that," added Father Foggie, "is irrespective of whether you're talking about the Instant *or* the Dependent imaginations."

I took a swig of water to give me time to think. Finally I grunted, "All right, but imagination or not, you haven't explained *consciousness*. Where does that fit in?"

"Consciousness?" responded the Cleric. "What, my child, do you think it is?"

"*I* don't know, Father. That's the problem. I'm asking you."

He cocked his head. "It's not difficult."

"No? Tell me another! Nobody's ever worked it out."

"Consciousness, my child, is another word for your – guess what?"

"My imagination?"

"Exactly."

"Oh, give us a break! *Far* too simple."

He sighed. "Listen. Without imagination, you would have no consciousness, no identity, no memory, no mind, no language and no thoughts. *Nothing.*"

"Whoa! Too extreme. What about sensory experiences? I'd have those."

"What do you imagine your sensory experiences to be?"

"Sensory experiences? They're just that: sensory experiences."

"You missed my point, my son," replied the Cleric. "I asked you what you *imagine* your sensory experiences to be."

"Oh, gosh, Father, I give up."

"At last!"

"Hey! What are you saying?"

"I didn't say anything."

"But what did you mean by *at last?*"

He smiled. "I meant that maybe you'll start to listen."

I pursed my lips and was silent.

Part IV

ℰℱ

Continuing with Imagination

"**M**Y CHILD," RESUMED THE CLERGYMAN, "YOU'VE BEEN far too busy objecting. Let me go over it again. Your Instant imagination ... no, I've changed my mind. Let's focus on your 'Dependent'."

"Fine. Whatever."

"Your Dependent: it's conventional imagination – your internal words, pictures and thoughts. It arises out of the Primary – your Instant." He stopped to reflect. "How can I best describe it? Do you play cards?"

"Yeah, sometimes. Not often."

"That's OK. Imagine you're the dealer, and you're giving out the cards face down. Those cards are your Instant imagination. They set the ball rolling so to speak – the physical world you're experiencing – but you won't see the cards until they're turned over."

"You mean until experiences happen?"

"Quite so, as the game proceeds. Now ... how are you going to play your hand? As in any card game *that's* the question which makes the difference."

"And that's my Dependent imagination?"

"Exactly: the thoughts, judgments or beliefs that arise as each

175

experience comes to pass; *it's* the stuff that gives your life meaning. We've already spoken about …"

"Sorry to interrupt, Father: I get the analogy of the cards, but you refer to 'thoughts'. What are they? As far as I'm concerned thoughts are floaty 'things'. They just kind of waft about in my head."

"You're certainly right: they do 'waft' about. But *are* they 'in your head'? It's hard to tell. In some ways they're in your head, and in some ways they're not." He looked to the German. "Professor? How would you describe a 'thought'?"

The German's face lit up. "The question is most good. 'Thought' refers to the creative stream of pictures in your Dependent imagination – tied in with language."

"Huh," I replied, "that's all very posh sounding, but it doesn't tell me what a thought *is*. They come from nowhere and go nowhere."

"By Jove, young man," exclaimed the Doctor, "you're on the money."

"I am?"

"Yes, and you know what?"

"No?"

"I can't answer it either. And nor can I say how thoughts arise. As you indicate, a thought's dimensionless, and as such, it doesn't actually exist." He caught the Rector's eye. "Padre? What about you?"

The clergyman shook his head. "It's a self-referential conundrum: any kind of an answer would be just as much a thought as the question."

"Good point." Frostbight addressed his neighbour. "Gusty, you sort it out."

Von Lottowind also shook his head. "It is a mystery. Thoughts are not of this physical world. I simply call them our magical picture gallery."

"Phew," I said. "OK, Professor, but you said, 'tied in with language'. So what's language all about?"

The German straightened. "Language? Language is a tool, a mass of sound bites associated with your picture gallery, which enables you to work your Dependent imagination – and interact it with the minds of others."

This needed time to chew over. Better to move on. I turned to the Cleric. "Father, what were you about to say before I interrupted?"

"Was I about to say something? Let me think." He looked up. "Ah, yes. It was about the 'Instant'."

"Oh," I groaned. "Haven't we finished with imagination?"

"My son, we are *never* finished with imagination: it's the beginning and end of all things." He looked over to our host. "Doctor? You wouldn't mind saying something about the Instant, would you? It'll give me a chance to get on with my pudding."

Doctor Frostbight had already finished his dessert. "Be delighted, Padre." He spoke to me. "Yes, the Instant ... I suspect you'll grumble when you hear what I say about it."

"How do you know?"

"Because almost everyone finds it a stretch too far – at least at first. As we've pointed out, your Instant imagination is the physical world and refers to your sensory experiences along with your body. For most of our students it takes some doing to get their head around the idea that the independence of our material environment is *not* just independently independent 'out there'."

"Phew. You're not joking. Now would you mind explaining it?"

"Dead easy, old chap." He waved a hand. 'Here's a demonstration. Think of standing on a mountain."

"Huh? All right ..."

"Excellent. The view of the world you would see is, yes, a visual experience – your so-called 'external' world; and make no mistake about it, it definitely *is* your 'external world'. What we're saying is that that 'externalness' is *a demonstration of your Instant imagination*." He stopped and added, "See? That's all there is to it. I told you it was easy."

I stared. "Oh. It is?" But I thought it best not to grumble any more, and asked instead, "Are you saying I need my Instant imagination to experience the world?"

"No, I'm saying reality – your three dimensional surroundings – *is* your Instant. For example, what you see in this room is, just now, your Instant."

"You reckon? So how come it's so different from the 'Dependent'?"

"The Instant is uneffected by language, and has an agenda which is quite beyond your daily imagination."

"Oh."

"Yes, it works infinitely fast – it's not called 'Instant' for nothing. It's your sensory data, the outer public stage of your normal life, while your Dependent is your private stream of mental images – cribbed from the Instant – which are, as we say, linked into speech."

"Huh! Pretty fancy." I considered the idea. "So that's it? OK, what else? I mean, what's *not* covered by imagination?"

"As the Padre's just said, *all* of life is imagination – of one kind or another."

"I know, but before that you said the world was my *'creation'*."

"It is," he answered. "The act of imagining is your creativity expressing itself."

I took a breath. Talk about 'leaping' that 'threshold'. More like bungee jumping. I could do with fewer bounces. As I considered his words, Lucifer's Agent made a pass. I pretended not to flinch. "Doctor," I said, "as far as I can see, we're flitting all over the place."

"You think so?" The bat shot by. "What we're doing is inviting you to sharpen your observations."

"My observations? Do they need sharpening?"

"There's always more to learn. Look at your thoughts, your beliefs and your opinions: notice they're *all* generated by *pictures*."

"So you say." I shrugged. "All right …"

"Likewise are reason and logic: they're also products of your imagination."

"Oh? So you're claiming they're no good?"

He shook his head. "No, I'm *not* saying that. There's nothing the matter with either. What I'm saying is every mental process demands pictures, however vague or elusive. That's why the Professor told you that it's no good believing in ultimate 'truth'. *All* of life is about pictures."

"That's quite a statement."

"Only if you're not looking."

"Doctor, I *am* looking."

He raised his eyebrows.

Part V

❧

The Pink Elephant

I SCRAPED THE BOTTOM OF MY PLATE AND POLISHED OFF THE last of my dessert. It had gone cold. This debate: what was I to make of it? Here were these men not only claiming I had created the world and everything in it out of my imagination, but also that there was no such *thing* as natural laws, my true self or any 'truth' for that matter. My common assumptions about the world were being picked off one by one. Then I looked distractedly down at my empty plate and the idea occurred to me that people have free will. Now, if they had free will *that* would mean they *must* exist separately from me; and *that* again would mean *there's no way* I could be creating them – or imagining them – unless, of course, *these* fellows tried to pretend there was no such thing as free will. I had caught them out.

"Mein Freund ..." The German broke into my thoughts. "Other people *do* have free will."

What was it with this mind reading? "Professor, I don't know how you're picking up what I'm thinking, but regarding free will, I agree with you. That proves I *can't* be creating other people."

"It does not follow. You can invent people any way you want – with or without free will."

"Well," I responded. "Either way, it means there really *is* such a thing as free will and everybody can do whatever they want quite independently of me."

"Why worry about it?" he replied.

"I got the idea from philosophy classes."

The Reverend Foggie opted in. "And who," he asked gently, "created the philosophers?"

"Nobody did. They were born – just like you."

"My child, of course they were born just like me, but that fact is philosophers are part of your imagination."

"Well whatever, I can tell you one thing: no self respecting one is going to give your stuff the time of day."

Doctor Frostbight addressed me. "You're right enough, old chum, I don't think they would either. It's a tricky business, this type of thinking – or should I say, 'imagining'? Let's see … how can we get to grips with it?"

"Well don't look at me."

He smiled. "Relax, old chap. All you have to do is think of famous persons, whether they're great thinkers, artists, politicians, charismatic religious leaders, adventurers, innovators, celebrated scientists – the list goes on as long as you want – and re-set them in your mind, not as random but as deliberate inventions."

"Doctor, that doesn't add up. I can't have created them: I haven't got *the brains* of somebody, say, like Einstein. His theories are way beyond us – at least they're certainly beyond me."

Out host ducked. The bat shot past. "You," he said, "don't *need* his brains. What you've done is invent him as just that: a great physicist whose theories you don't understand. Actually, it's the same for most of life: you 'know' virtually nothing about *most* things in life, although you created them."

"Like what?"

"We've already talked about your body – and Einstein's no different. Don't you get it? Anything you 'know' about him is what you've been told, about him – and what you've been told is *also* your invention."

Von Lottowind joined the fray. "Das is so. You *only* 'know' about famous people from stories."

I was not convinced. "But there's people who *met* him and tested his theories."

"Ja, but those people are another product of your creative genius." He paused. "It is difficult," he said, "for you to grasp this concept since you underestimate the reach of your imagination."

"Huh. Until now I thought I had a perfectly good imagination."

"Ha!" said the German. "Das is so, and you hopelessly underestimate it." He picked up his glass and nosed his wine while he pondered. "We must practise."

"Practise? Practise what?"

"I want you to think of – that is to say, imagine – a pink elephant."

"Another elephant? And pink? All right."

"So you see this elephant? It has wings and is floating over rooftops. It trumpets as it flies. You have that picture?"

"Yes, sort of," I returned cautiously, not being sure where this was leading.

"Wundervoll. But you know little about elephants, and even less about how they fly. Does that matter?"

"Well, no ..."

"Ah, now you understand."

"Understand *what?*"

"Your creation."

"Hey, hang about, Professor. You're only talking about my ordinary imagination. *I'm* talking about *real* things." I looked over the table. "Take this glass, for instance. I've no idea how the wine sits in it. Gravity? Of course. But what's 'gravity'? And this water here: it'll freeze as hard as stone at 32 degrees Fahrenheit. How come? *I* don't know. So how can you say I invented it?"

"What is your problem?"

"Obvious: it's *inconceivable I* created a world I can't understand!"

"But, mien Freund, it is *not* inconceivable because it is *your* imagination doing it. It is the same when you dream: you *imagine* a perfectly real world, but you do not 'understand' it any more than you understand your waking world. You have no need to."

I rubbed the back of my neck. "Could you take me through that again, Professor? I can tell you, it would take *a lot* of imagination for me to im- agine I create my existence with my imagination. Whoops! I'm beginning to sound like you."

He smiled. "Ach, maybe you begin to learn."

"Well, well, well," I replied, wondering how they could think this stuff was 'easy'. "So, which imagination's more important?"

"Both are equally necessary, but you always lead with your Instant."

"How do you mean?"

"The Instant is primary: it is *that* which determines your birth and death."

I fidgeted with the cutlery on my empty plate and reflected. "But, Professor, in order to *say* the Instant is primary, I would have to *think* it were primary. That means the Dependent comes first."

"My goodness!" interrupted the Doctor. "Sharp as a tack. Yes, you're right: you would have to think it. On the other hand, if there were no Instant there would be nothing to think about."

Was it the ice wine making my head spin? It didn't matter. I turned to my left. "Father," I started, "to go back a bit: I'd surely land myself in trouble if I maintained that everyone were a product of my personal magic show."

"Why so, my child?"

"Because that's where Descartes got stuck."

"You mean with his 'solipsism'?"

"I can't remember. Something like that. He thought he was the only person he could be sure existed. I'd be *insane* to believe that the world – and that includes you – existed only in so far as I existed."

"Calm yourself, my child. You're getting the hang of it, yet you're still taking your cue from the limited imagination of your local self. If you do that it won't make sense."

"Then what 'cue' *do* I take it from?"

"We keep telling you. Look at it from the perspective of You, the Non-self. Then solipsism doesn't apply."

"But I could still be accused of … what did you call it?"

"Solipsism. And if anyone accused you, they, too, would be your own invention."

I felt at the end of my tether. "So what or who *does* exist?"

"Steady, old boy," came in Frostbight. "Relax. What's important is not whether something exists, but whether you *recognise* your own imagination as the conjurer."

"I wish," I moaned, "you could make it easier."

"Well then let's look at the F.A.E."

"Delighted to hear." I straightened. "So what's *that* when it's at home?"

I caught the trace of a smile. "It's the Fundamental Attribution Error."

Part VI

⁊

The Fundamental Attribution Error

"ALL RIGHT, DOCTOR, I KNOW YOU WANT ME TO ASK WHAT it is."

"Good show. Yes, the F.A.E. is what we've been talking about: the mistake of believing that whatever it is that sustains the universe is *separate from you*."

"I presume," I responded, "you're referring to God or physical laws or whatever?"

"Spot on. It's the Fundamental Error."

"So you really *are* saying I'm a conjurer popping a rabbit out of a hat?"

He grinned. "That's one way of putting it. You see? It's not so difficult. You're a step ahead of most people."

"Huh. I don't know about that. Anyway, it still doesn't change anything."

"No?"

"No. I'm still in the same boat. However many F.A.E.s I avoid, I can't avoid the fact that at the end of my life that's it – I'm gone."

Von Lottowind spoke up. "Ach. So you are still not clear about death?"

"Yeah, Professor, that's the general idea."

"Has Pastor Foggie not already spoken of it?"

"Yeah, he has, but that doesn't mean it's sorted."

"Ah. I think maybe I know your problem."

"You do? What is it?"

"It would be best to start with an example."

"Then go ahead."

"You remember the elephant we talked of?"

"Of course."

"Good. Now, imagine that elephant. It is alive, yes?"

"Yes … alive and well."

"Now, please allow your elephant to drop dead onto the street. You have that picture?"

"Dead? All right, Professor. Dead as a doornail."

"A doornail?" he queried.

"Don't worry about it. Yes, it's dead."

"Das is good. What," he asked, "has happened to the soul of that elephant?"

"The soul? I never thought about it."

"Nein?"

"No. You told me to imagine an *elephant*."

"Correct," beamed von Lottowind. "Now you understand."

My mouth must have dropped.

Frostbight chipped in. "Not getting it, old boy? Don't worry; it'll come in time. It's just what we've been talking about: when people are faced with something they can't explain, they opt for an FAE. So when they come to understand how the world exists, they invent the various 'agencies' we've talked about. In this case, to account for the mystery of life, they cook up 'souls' or 'spirits' or 'life forces'."

"Doctor, that's hardly surprising. There's got to be *something* that keeps us alive, otherwise we're just a lumps of meat."

"My boy, what animates you is not an 'agency': neither a spirit, soul, 'field of energy', 'life force' nor 'divine energy'."

I rubbed my face. "Well then, how the heck can I be alive?"

"I'll tell you what: you can search for all your worth, but you're not going to find any of those 'agencies' that are said to create life. They no more exist than does your 'true self'."

"Das is correct," came back von Lottowind. "As we taught at Winterbad, the flying elephant does not need a 'soul' or 'life force'."

"So, Professor," I said, turning to him, "what do *you* think keeps it alive?"

"*Nothing* keeps *anything* alive."

I felt my face colour. "Then what the hell is *life?*"

"Champion," exclaimed Frostbight. "You're making definite progress."

I stopped. I realised I had asked the very question *he* had pressed on *me* before dinner.

"*I* answer," said the German.

"Please do. I'm all ears."

"It is this. Life does not exist."

"Hey! How could you …?"

Von Lottowind raised the palm of his hand. "Halt! I have not finished."

"Sorry, Prof., I mean, Herr Professor."

There was a touch of a smile. "Allow me," he said. "There is no such thing as 'life' – at least not as you understand it."

"I'm no longer sure *what* I understand."

"What you call 'life' is another contrivance of your imagination. It is not 'out there', and neither is it 'in' you."

I could not think what to say. Happily the butler was on my right with the decanter. "A little wine, Sir?"

"In the circumstances maybe I'd better," I answered, "but just a little. By the way, Mould, I bet you've been listening. What do you make of this stuff?"

"Me, Sir?" he replied, filling my glass. "We cannot see life; it is simply a word used in the context of intelligent movement."

"What? No more than that? I'm sorry, it's not on. If I sat here motionless, you'd maintain I were dead!"

"On the contrary, Sir, you would still be breathing, your blood would be circulating and your stomach digesting. Excuse me, I must attend to my rounds."

"Spot on, Mould," our host exclaimed. "Keep passing that wine."

Mould's answer was as bad as the others. "All right Doctor, despite what I said earlier about no life after death, what about the *evidence* of 'spirit': cases of people attending deathbed scenes *seeing* auras surrounding the body or *seeing* a spirit – maybe in the form of a light or cloud – departing from the newly deceased? How do you explain *that?* Either it's an illusion or there *is* some sort of spirit that goes somewhere."

"Ah," he replied, "ask the Padre. He enjoys this sort of thing."

I looked to my left. Father Foggie was polishing his glasses. "Well?" I said.

"My son," replied the Chaplain, as he perched the specs back on his nose, "they may well see something – an electro-magnetic field maybe – but they do not *see* '*life*'; nor do they *see* a '*spirit*'. As for a smoky vapour emitted at death? You think that's a person's 'spirit'?"

"I don't know. They say it is."

"You think so? Well, I can tell you, a misty vapour is not much of a 'spirit'."

"OK. OK. I suppose it isn't. So what about a 'light'? That's what some see, or even a person separating from the body and floating away."

"A 'light' is a light, not 'life'; and the same goes for a floaty body. Look at it this way. Do you recall what we said? The pink elephant was 'alive' and then 'dies' because you imagined it doing so."

"Uh-huh."

"You too are alive and will die in the same way – you don't need vapours, lights or floaty bodies."

I gave it some thought. "OK, so what about ghosts? How do you explain *them*?" I looked across the table. "Doctor, was that *really* your ex-wife?"

Frostbight smiled. "I don't know. But others have reported similar sightings."

"So why is that not evidence of her spirit being alive and still wandering about?"

He leant forward to give me a searching look. "Even if it were a spirit, old boy, the problem's the same: what *animates* the 'spirit': *another* 'spirit'? And what's supposed to animate *that* 'spirit'? Another one?"

I screwed up my face.

"Trust me," he continued. "There was no soul or spirit which came into her body at conception, and none which departed from her at death – except, of course, one that you imagine."

"So is there *anything* that's *actually alive*?"

The Reverend answered. "Yes, my son. 'Life' is the 'You' who imagines your *self* into existence."

"How can you say that?"

"Because 'You' – the No-self – never *exist* in the first place."

"But, Father," I spluttered, "this is *absurd*. How can you possibly be so certain something exists that doesn't exist … er …" I hesitated, "if you get my drift."

"I do get your drift. I didn't say I or anybody else here was certain about anything."

"*What?* So you don't *really* have any more idea about life after death than anyone else?"

"That's right, my child." He grew serious. "You see, nothing *is* 'certain' independently of you. For something to be said to be 'certain' you *have* to *imagine* it, so any 'certainty' would be your own invention."

Foggie was the strangest clergyman. Yes, I do exist; oops, no, I don't. Do I have a true self? Apparently not. And *now* there's no such thing as a soul, life *or* a spirit and, to cap it, I can't even be certain I can be certain about anything. When I found my voice again, I retorted, "So what am 'I'?"

"Apart from God?" answered the Rector. "It's an important question."

"I know. That's why I asked."

"How often must we say? You're a conjurer creating existence."

That again. I scratched my neck. Does the 'conjurer' exist? I suppose he does and yet he doesn't. I sighed and remained silent.

Our host broke the spell. "You bearing up old boy?" he asked. "Getting the hang of it? What about a break?" He cast his eye around. "How's everyone getting on? Done with dessert? I expect there's cheese if you're interested – good for the brain." He inspected the Professor's plate. "I say, Gusty, not enjoying your pud?"

"Ah, Watty," returned the Professor, "the apples are most good – as good as the apples in the Black Forest, but Mrs. McWhiteout has been too generous."

"Never mind, old chap, chickens'll get it in the morning. Everyone else finished?" I replied that it was marvellous. The Rector declared it to have been the finest apple tart ever. "Champion!" beamed the Doctor. "Mould? Any cheese on the go?"

"There is, indeed, Sir."

"First class. Bring it over would you?"

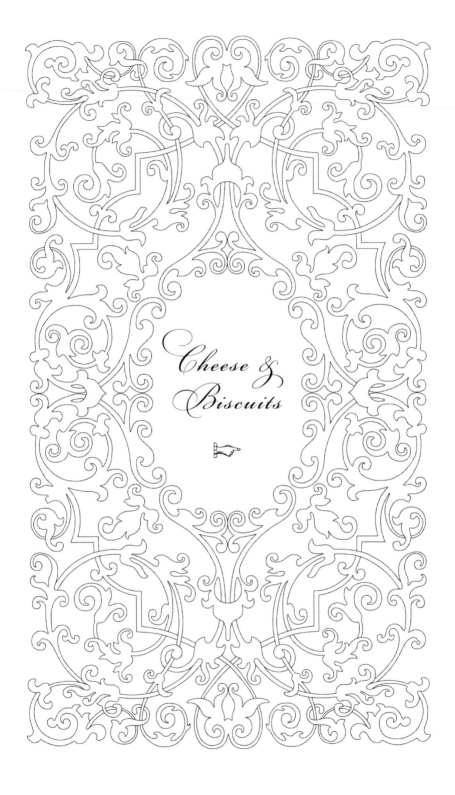

Cheese &
Biscuits

Part I

੭੨

Theatre

THANKFULLY THE BAT HAD, BY NOW, STOPPED ITS dive-bombing without nesting in the Professor's hair. With any luck it had gone into hiding behind one of the portraits. Meanwhile, Mould went from place to place, collected the dessert bowls and stacked them on the sideboard.

Taking up the cheese platter, he showed it first to Professor von Lottowind and, as he presented it, pointed out, "This one, Sir, is made from our Estate Highland cattle, and this here is our goats' cheese rolled in ash."

"Ach," responded the Professor, patting his stomach and shaking his head, "I am sure you have excellent goats, but I am unable to eat another thing."

"Very good, Sir." With that, Mould proceeded to the rest of us.

Our host cut a portion of the Highland cheese, commenting as he did, "Unpasteurised, you know, chaps," while the Reverend Foggie helped himself to goats', and I, for my part, tried both. There followed a basket of oatcakes which Mould left on the table. I hoped the Doctor was right that cheese feeds the brain: I needed it.

Frostbight smoothed the napkin on his lap, selected an oatcake, picked up his butter knife and glanced at me. "You all right, old man? You look worried."

"No, I'm OK, Doctor, it's just that …"

"I know, I know," he intervened, "it's jolly queer stuff when you first come across it. Nihil desperundum."

"What?"

"'Never despair'. So … how can we make 'life is your creation' straightforward?"

"I'm not fussy. I'm sure you've got ways."

He nodded. "Quite right. How about this?"

I prepared myself.

"Relax, old bean, it's a pushover. First, don't approach it as if it were a scientific study, or you'll never understand. It's not *logic;* it's an *art.*"

"An art?" I repeated. "But you need *reason* to figure out how the world works."

"I think we've said this already: 'reason' is useful for analysing and calculating, but *not* for explaining how come the world exists – let alone the meaning of it. If you want to explain *that*, you need unbounded thinking."

"Whoops!"

He grinned. "Look, old boy, logic and reason – and therefore, science – are all about determining boundaries."

"Er … boundaries?"

"Yes, boundaries. For example, whether or not Socrates was mortal or at what particular temperature water boils."

"And what's the matter with that?"

He waved aside my concern. "Nothing. What I want to point out is logic and science are bounded and therefore limited,"

"Do they have to be?"

"Yes, they do. They are disciplines of observations, measurements and calculations. But what you *don't* know is unbounded."

"Huh. Another of your clever aphorisms. OK. So what'll make things more straightforward?"

"*Practising,*" he said slowly, "what we've been talking about."

"Ugh. You've been 'talking about' a whole load of things."

He smiled. "You're right. Then let's have a go at it."

"At what?"

"Imagining the world is a theatre created by you."

"Oh, so now life's a theatre? Kind of like Shakespeare?"

"Yes, and more. Stretch your imagination. It's not just that the world's a stage. You're also the director of the show, *and* the main actor."

"Humph," I grunted. "Quite a show."

"It is. And you need a broad mind. So far, you *haven't* seen life as your theatre: rather, you're engrossed in it and believe in it – having no idea it's a play you've 'written' yourself."

I took a deep breath. "So what're you saying?"

"I'm saying time and again you're acting the 'patient' – and creating all the upsets and emotional storms that go with it."

"Yeah, but what 'patient'? The patient of who?"

"The other actors."

"What actors?"

"The people around you. And you know what? *They're following your very own script.*"

"Das is good, Watty," agreed the Professor. "Also you are not just the main actor playing a single part." He addressed me. "Call me pedantic, mein Freund, but the *complete* You is not only the director and main actor, as Watty indicated, but the other actors as well – including the audience."

Part II

❧

No Halfway Stations

I SPREAD SOME GOATS' CHEESE ON AN OATCAKE. "HUMPH!" I grunted again. "I still think it's seriously far fetched."

"You have a difficulty?"

"Yes, I do. If it *were* true that the world's my invention, it would mean I could do anything I wanted."

"Ja! That is right," replied the German.

"Well, in that case," I said, playing a trump card, "I am going to go out and bash everyone up and steal and rape and murder. How would you like *that?*"

He seemed to think that was funny. "Why would you do that? You have already forgotten? The world is your creation – and the people in it your masterpieces."

"So?"

He played with his beard while thought, and then said, "Imagine for a moment that you were an artist who had been painting a fine piece of artwork over many years."

"Yeah?"

"Would you slash it?"

"No, of course not."

192

"Das is so. You would be crazy."

I bit into some Highland cheese while I reflected.

"Let's say it again," came in Father Foggie. "The people – *everything* – in the field of your Instant Imagination are there because that's *exactly* where you put them yourself."

I stopped to consider. "So you're saying my world's perfect?"

"No, I didn't say that. It's obviously not perfect, but it is perfectly on purpose. I simply want you to notice that everything is *exactly* where You intended it, and it's happening *exactly* as You planned it."

I shifted my position.

"You see," the Reverend went on, "it's your stinking commentary – your Dependent Imagination with its restricted vision and bounded thinking – which screws up your view of life. If you could get the hang of *that*, it would make a difference. Remember: for the landscape to change, you need to educate yourself to a new vision. Up until now, you've fooled yourself into believing your problems are 'out there'."

Frostbight intervened. "As Gusty might say, committing a crime is pissing on your own bonfire." He stopped. "Mould? Where did that expression come from?"

"'Pissing on your own bonfire'? Shakespeare, Sir: Macbeth. The three witches. Act One, Scene ..."

"Oh, for goodness sake! Ridiculous!" He took an oatcake from the basket. "Now, where were we?"

I am sure I saw a smile from Mould, but as for my trump card about criminal behaviour, it had not been the winner I had expected. Time for personal examples. I went back to the Padre. "Right, Father," I started. "Try this. Supposing I'm young and in love and I'm jilted. I'd be distraught about it. You're welcome to your clever ideas, but I live in the *real* world."

"My son, whatever happens in external reality is your own set-up."

"I know you say that, but that wouldn't stop me being distraught." I spread some more goats' cheese. "OK, maybe that wasn't a good example. Here's a better one. Assume I were traumatised. Say, for instance, I had been sexually molested as a child."

"Were you?"

"No, Father, I wasn't, but you're perfectly aware that it happens. The trouble with your fancy pants theories is that you end up making *young children* responsible for an adult's behaviour." I took a bite.

He didn't reply immediately. When he did he simply asked, "My child, do you want to leap that threshold?"

"What d'you expect me to answer?" I responded. "I told you, I'm not a doormat."

"It's not a Royal Decree to cross the threshold or agree to any of our ideas. You will lose nothing. You'll still be just as creative maintaining your old, typical way of seeing the world – the viewpoint limited by the self – as you would be in taking this new approach."

"But it's not 'on'. *You're* saying it's the *child's* fault if he or she gets abused."

The Cleric looked across the table. "Professor?"

The German's eyebrows knitted and he glowered at me. "Fault? Did I hear *'fault'*? How many times do we have to tell you? *Your courtroom is a fantasy.*"

I rolled my eyes. "All right, Professor, all right. I hear you. So what am I supposed to think?"

The Reverend answered. "What we've been suggesting: instead of *judging* the world, *observe* that you are *always* the creator of whatever's happening."

I was having a hard time wriggling out of this courtroom stuff. The whole notion of creation really did have far-fetched implications. "But it's *hard*," I complained.

Doctor Frostbight smiled at my moaning. "Sorry, old boy. Hoping for a free lunch?"

"No, of course not. But look, what about those suffering from shell shock – something I know about. What're you telling me? Are you claiming that that shock and violence were of my own making?"

"Yes, they were, but how can I get it into your head that the Instant experiences – the physical world – are obviously not ordered by your local self. They are 'ordered' by the original You."

I suppose he was right about my expecting a free lunch, or at least a reasonably cheap one. These theories were stretching my brain. "Doctor," I exclaimed with frustration, "you said all this was supposed to be simple."

"It is," he replied, "but not simplistic. And by the way, who said they were 'theories'?"

Lord, how did he know I was thinking they were theories? "Well," I remonstrated, "what do you want me to call them?"

"Try 'perspectives'," put in von Lottowind. "Anything would get you further than 'theories'. Theories are beliefs."

"But we've *got* to have beliefs."

"If you wish. However, as we've already pointed out, they distort your observations."

"I'm not sure they do," I replied with feeling. "But – and I'm sorry to be banging on about it – whatever you *call* your ideas, you still can't go on saying that if a child, say a young girl, were abused by an adult, it was her fault."

"*Fault?*" repeated the German Professor. "You are *already* back in your courtroom."

He was correct – and *so* exasperating.

The Rector spoke. "When you're tempted to talk of your – or anybody else's – 'faults', have a go at replacing the word 'fault' with 'creation'."

"So if I'd been abused, I'd be saying, in effect, I'd planned it?"

He nodded. "Precisely."

This was too much. "Father, I *couldn't* say it."

"No? Why not? My son, in Creosophy there are no halfway stations. It's not a saccharine philosophy where" – he made a comic gesture – "ooh! I'll call life *my* 'creation' when it suits me, but somebody *else's* when it doesn't."

"But ..." My voice trailed away.

"Yes?"

"Well," I said, "I don't know about your 'Creosophy' stuff, but this thing about a child being abused: it's not right to say she's responsible. The idea of suggesting it is *itself* irresponsible. She'd be too young."

"Still hoping for a free lunch?"

"No, I'm not," I returned. "But I can tell you one thing: you wouldn't catch *me* suggesting these ideas to someone who's been subjected to that kind of shock."

"No," he said quietly, " I think you're right. That sufferer would need to be a Creosophist. If the individual's *not* one, she would understand you're saying her local, *physical* self is the creator. You would rightly get an unpleasant response."

"Humph!" I retorted. "I should say so. But what if that person *were* a 'Creosophist' thingy you're talking about?"

"A Creosophist would – even if it weren't easy – acknowledge that the experience had been his or her own idea."

"But, Father, shock is the reaction to extreme *external* circumstance."

"I know. But I keep saying: where or who did the 'external circumstance' come from? *That's* the question."

"'From,'" I suppose you'd say, "the person who experiences them?'"

"I would. But, I repeat, not as the person would commonly know him or herself. In the meantime, leave it to drama queens to claim that the origin of their experiences arise from somewhere *other* than them."

I did not respond.

"What I'm saying," the Padre went on, "is that in leaping the threshold you'll start thinking 'outside the box'."

I made a face. "Yuk! That's a cliché."

The Reverend Foggie licked cheese from his fingertips. "Yes it is," he replied, "and for good reason."

Doctor Frostbight joined in. "If that child who's been mistreated stays confined to the F.A.E. into adulthood, maintaining the belief that 'someone other than me creates my life,' she will be locked into her self-imposed victimhood. However, now she's old enough to think for herself, there's nothing to *stop* her viewing the experience as her own invention."

"Through her imagination?"

"Yes, exactly."

"But *surely*, whatever you say, she can't just *declare* that the world is her imagination."

"No? What's stopping her?"

"I ... well ..."

"She can," he went on, "either go for imagination or continue her dysfunctional beliefs. There's no halfway station."

"Is that your way of saying we're stuck in dysfunctional beliefs?"

Part III

❧

A Better Map

ERTAINLY," FROSTBIGHT RESPONDED. "YOU'RE STUCK and you became stuck as soon as you learnt to speak. You're so nearly breaking out of them, and instead you argue."

"No, I don't."

Doctor Frostbight briefly raised his eyes to the ceiling. "Very well, Ewan, think of it this way." He took a breath. "You can respond in one of three ways. You've a choice, the same as with any new idea."

"All right. Tell me."

"Champion. So listen. You can stay stuck in your box, dismiss the idea and forget this discussion."

"That's the first? Well, I haven't dismissed it: I'm still thinking about it. OK, what about the second?"

"You can stay in your box, *argue,* disagree and *then* forget it."

I smiled. "But at least I'd be using my brain."

"So you say. Now, consider a third position. Instead of trying to prove whether what we're saying is right or wrong, suspend your old beliefs long enough to assess our ideas for their *value.*"

"I do that already."

"I wish you did, old bean. Unfortunately, you spend more time arguing about whether our ideas agree with yours."

I hesitated. I had never known any approach other than proving or disproving. "All right," I agreed. "If you must."

"Splendid! Maybe a little *less* arguing …?"

The butler's refilling my tumbler distracted me for a moment. I was not arguing, was I? I thought I was being objective. I took a swig of the water: so much better than the usual chlorinated stuff.

Father Foggie took up the conversation with a question. "Can you recall your very first memories?"

"Yeah …" I answered slowly, not knowing why we were changing direction.

"In your early days, my child, did you realise you were creating your world along with your self within that world?"

"Not on your Nelly. This evening's the first I've heard of it."

"I thought so. Well, everything that's happened since those early memories has been the development of your imagination – and in your own words, your responsibility."

"OK, OK, I get it."

"I'm pleased. So now you can dispense with your traditional non-functioning perspectives." The clergyman played with a crumb on his plate while he pondered. "Didn't you say earlier that you had a map that didn't get you anywhere?"

I could see no connection. "My map? Yes, that's because it's out of date – it's my father's."

"Precisely. Don't you want a better one?"

"What, you mean one that has Chilblane marked on it?"

He smiled. "As we said earlier, this place doesn't appear on any map."

"Doesn't it? So what are you talking about?"

"It's time to ask yourself whether you're content with the same old, same old approach to philosophy for the rest of your life. One day you might notice it's never got you anywhere – neither you nor anyone else."

"Perhaps it hasn't," I replied. "But the stuff you say *can't* be right."

"What's the matter?"

"Quite a lot. For a start, it *can't* be right, for instance, that a woman who's been raped can be said to have set up the whole scenario for herself, even if it were, as you say, her 'Non-self' – as if she *wanted* to be traumatised for the rest of her life. And what about other ghastly experiences? What about someone who's been, say, tortured?"

Father Foggie didn't reply, so I carried on. "Here's an example closer to home. Supposing, as an adult, I'm driving along and a child runs out into my car. It happened to me once. There was no way I could have prevented it. And yet *you* say I'd have been responsible."

"Yes, you would have been responsible. As always, you're responsible for the set-up, the upset and the set-down."

I frowned.

Frostbight interjected. "Look at it like this. The limitation of the conventional approach is that people are said to be responsible for how they *react* to upsets."

"And there's nothing the matter with that."

"No, there isn't. But what *we're* saying is that you're responsible not only for your reactions, but *also* for the initial set-up in the first place, *before the upset.*"

I considered it. "Which in this case is the child running onto the road?"

"That's right. You set up the accident and made it happen."

"Goodness me."

"Yes," he said, "goodness me. As in that analogy of the card game, it's what you've dealt yourself."

"If you insist. And how I play my cards, is that my 'set-down'?"

"Exactly." He turned to his right. "Gusty, how would you put it?"

Von Lottowind stopped toying with his beard. "Mein Freund," he said to me, "you say it was an accident?"

"Well, of course. I didn't do it on purpose. Nor did the child."

He frowned. "There are *never* 'accidents'"

"All right: a 'misfortune'."

He leant forward and said in a low voice, "Neither are there misfortunes."

"No? Well, Professor, I'll tell you what: there are in *my* world. "

He sat back. "Ach, 'accidents' and 'misfortunes' are meaningless. They are words people use to avoid taking responsibility."

"You can say that, but I'd *know* if I actually *had made* a child run into the road."

He waited a moment while Mould refilled his glass, then said, "Maybe this will help. Let us return to that analogy of the theatre. The shows come and go. You are the theatre director in the stalls but, while watching the plays, you forget that it was *you* who made the show a reality."

"So you'd call the accident my *own* 'show'?"

"Das is so."

"Oh, come on, Professor!" I reached for another oatcake.

Father Foggie took up the baton. "What's the problem?"

"Just as I said: *if* I *were* orchestrating my outer world, I'd *be aware of it.*"

"Look, my child, you're not aware of the pupil of your eye, but that doesn't mean you don't have one; and you don't *know* you're digesting this evening's dinner, but that doesn't mean you're not doing so."

"All right, fair enough, but I'd know soon enough if I *weren't* digesting it. Who *says* I've got some unseen 'Original Being' making my world happen?" Seeing von Lottowind furrow his eyebrows, I sighed. "OK, Professor, what have I done?"

"You used the possession metaphor."

"No, I didn't!"

"Ach! You keep arguing. I repeat what we explained earlier. Nobody '*has*' an 'Original' anything. The No-self is simply You." He looked across the room. "Mould?"

"Sir?" The butler, decanter in hand, stood to attention. "More wine, Sir?"

"Not now, thank you. You studied Indian philosophy, ja?"

"Indeed, Sir."

"Das is good. What did they teach about the 'self'?"

"The 'self' it is an enigmatic subject."

"I have no doubt it is, but what did you learn?"

"Of what I read, I considered some words from the Brihadaranyaka Upanishad most instructive."

"Good man, Mould," chimed in Frostbight. "What words?"

"Something to this effect. 'If a person knows I am Braham, in this way he becomes the whole world'."

"Wundervoll, Mould," exclaimed the German. "Das is a most excellent saying."

"Thank you, Sir."

"So there," the Professor said to me. "It is an old idea. Let us return to the analogy of the theatre. You need to realise that You are all things: the owner of the theatre, the producer, director, stage manager and all the staff and back-up teams; the actors, the audience and, finally the building itself. As the Upanishads rightly state, you are the whole world."

"Humph! That certainly *is* a leap."

"Das is so. I believe even Indian sages find the idea testing."

"I can believe *that*."

The butler was about to top up my glass. Had he *really* spent time in India? "Mould?" I asked.

"Sir?"

"How long did you spend in India?"

"I was fortunate to spend a little time at the Bharatiya Girvana Prouda Vidya Vardhini Shala."

"Wow! *Where?* No, no; no need to repeat it."

"Very good, Sir."

"Well, there's one thing I can tell you: you wouldn't find *me* there. If *I* wanted to check out any of that Vedic stuff I'd go for an English translation."

"Of course, Sir. Maybe it was my translation you were reading?"

I was lost for response. "Thank you for the top-up."

"A pleasure, Sir."

Doctor Frostbight was amused. Could I make more of a fool of myself? How many butlers are likely to be Sanskrit scholars? Or was Mould pulling my leg? German? French? Classical Greek? Mandarin? Sanskrit? Surely not possible. At the same time, this mental twisting and turning was doing my head in. I rubbed my face once again. "But, look, Father," I said to the Cleric, "can't you see that this stuff you talk about implies that if I were caught in some awful earthquake, or a tidal wave – or struck by lightening – you would want me to declare, 'Oh, it's I who's made it happen'?"

"Yes," he asserted, "we've already been through that, and I repeat: it wouldn't have been caused by you *as you know yourself.*"

"Well, whether it's me as I know myself or not, if we go on like this, you'll end up telling me I invented the sun and the stars."

" … and," he added, finishing my sentence, "the clouds and the rain. My son, what part of 'life's my creation' don't you understand? How many times do we have to go over it?"

I grimaced. "I still don't get it. For all that you claim, you can't possibly *know* I'm making the world happen."

"Who said we know? We don't know."

I stopped and looked at him. "Excuse me, Father?"

"I said we don't know. We '*know*' nothing. It was the ancient Greeks who started this obsession about what we do or don't 'know'. I'm sorry: it's a red herring."

I was speechless.

He went on. "I *imagine* it. 'Knowledge' is simply a by-product of the imagination. In other words, I don't *know* the world's made by me; I simply use my imagination to imagine it is. There is no such thing as 'knowledge' – only what you *imagine* is knowledge."

I nibbled a few crumbs of oatcake while I adjusted to his idea. "But *why?*" I finally blurted out.

"Why what?"

"You say we create our own lives, but who on earth is going to *volunteer* to have him or herself abused, raped, diseased, run over, maimed, tortured or whatever? What kind of imagination is *that?* It doesn't add up."

"Nor does it add up that there are any exceptions. Creation is dynamic, and as with any active process, you make mistakes, possibly awful mistakes. Or maybe it's not a 'mistake'. Maybe it's a method for developing your own imagination. Remember Edison?"

"Thomas Edison? The man who invented the electric light?"

"Yes. How many failed experiments did he do?"

"I don't know. Hundreds I believe."

"Precisely. And what did he say?"

"He didn't say anything."

"He did. He said he had now learnt hundreds – maybe thousands – of ways *not* to make a light bulb."

"He said that? Well, it was clever, but I'm not Edison."

"It doesn't matter. What's *important* is to be ready to 'frame' any tragedies or traumas, not as disasters, but as failed experiments."

"Rather than," added Frostbight, "do what so many do: resort to amateur dramatics, saying it was 'bad luck' or to blaming someone."

"And create emotional storms?"

"Very possibly. How could you do otherwise if you think you're a 'victim' and 'patient' – but never the agent?"

I paused to consider. A particularly fierce gust outside roared in the chimney and whistled at the ancient windows. The shutters held fast. Yes, this was no ordinary storm. To my left, I saw Father Foggie crossing himself. "Reverend," I inquired, "worried about the storm?"

"No, my son: my napkin."

"Your napkin? Don't tell me *yours* has gone as well."

"It seems to have."

"What? *Surely* it's on the floor?" With this I checked beneath the tablecloth, and as I did so, heard Doctor Frostbight. "What's up, Padre? No napkin?"

"Sir?" Now it was the voice of the butler addressing me. I came up. In his hand hung the chewed linen. "The dog, Sir."

"Good work, Mould," our host pronounced across the table. "Sorry about that, Padre. I say: you chaps've got to be a lot snappier if you don't want Snowie swiping your napkins. Now … everyone had enough cheese? There's more if you want."

"No thank you, Doctor. I've done well," replied Father Foggie as he took the damp article from Mould and spread it politely on his lap. "Absolutely delicious."

"You, old boy?" he asked me.

"My goodness, no thanks, Doctor. I'm stuffed. It's a real feast." I gripped my serviette as I spoke: Snowie definitely wasn't going to get *mine*.

"Good, good. Mould? Would you see to the coffee?"

"Very well, Sir." The kitchen door creaked and the butler limped out of sight.

Snowie

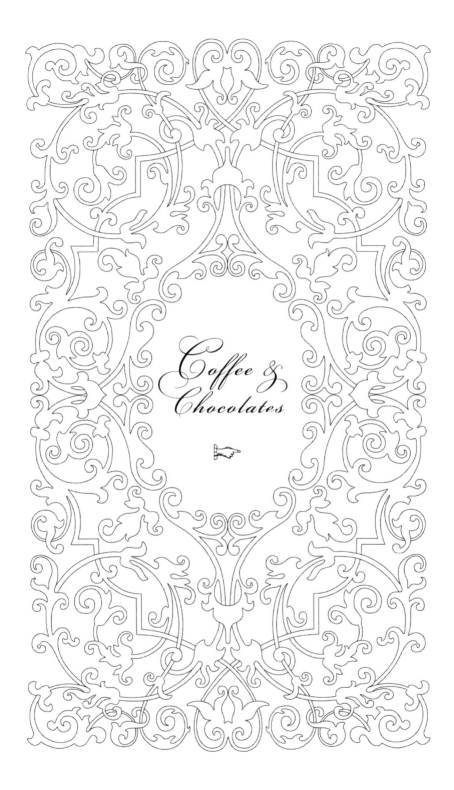

Coffee &
Chocolates

Part I

സ

The Process

THE CHANGE OF PACE GAVE ME A CHANCE TO GATHER my wits; the first one being that coffee might be a good thing, even if, thanks to wartime restrictions, it were actually chicory. I was feeling fuzzy.

Mrs. McWhiteout entered carrying a tray with a silver pot, milk and sugar, followed by Mould with demitasses. He put his tray on the sideboard, went round the table, collected the side plates and passed out the cups.

"The thing is …" I said, addressing no one in particular while we waited, "if it were *true* that life's my creation, why aren't there books about it?"

"There *would* be books," came back the Rector, "*if* that's what you'd created."

The cook was at my side. "Coffee, dear?"

"Yes, please, Mrs. McWhiteout. Lots." That was a silly request considering the size of the cup.

"Milk, Sir?" It was the butler.

"Please."

"Sir?"

"Yes, Mould?"

"It is not altogether accurate."

"Not accurate? What's not accurate?"

"That there are no books about this."

"Oh?"

"Indeed. Mr. Walsch is one such person who is quite clear about it."

"Who?"

"Mr. Walsch. He said that life is not a journey, but a creation. 'Conversations with God'."

"Oh? Really? Never heard of it. Bet it's a populist work."

"Indeed, Sir. I have left sugar on the table so that you may help yourself."

Mould was irritatingly inscrutable. Still, whatever his book was, I wasn't for giving in. "Father," I said, turning to the Cleric, "the trouble about your stuff is it's a flawed argument."

On hearing this, Doctor Frostbight burst out, "A flawed argument? I say, old boy, how old fashioned!" He turned to his neighbour. "Gusty? D'you hear? 'Flawed argument'? What do you think? Old fashioned?"

"Watty, das is most certainly old fashioned."

How could they, sporting those retro outfits in this antique monument, call *me* old fashioned?

Father Foggie came to my rescue. "The thing is, my son, at College you were taught Western philosophy, and that's a philosophy which is limited to speculation about what's said to be 'logical' or 'true'."

"I know. That's why they were so boring."

"I'm sure. You see, it's fine for old school philosophers who enjoy that sort of thing."

"So?"

"As we've said, it's restricted to reason."

"What's the matter with reason?"

"Nothing, except that, despite all the effort of brilliant philosophers, reason – or logic – is *never* going to demonstrate 'truth'. Anyway, you said you wanted a philosophy you can use."

"I certainly did. But I'm not sure your airy-fairy stuff's going to help."

"Dear me, now what's the problem?"

"You're asking me to believe the whole of life's my creation, right?"

"That's correct, although it's *not* about *believing* it. Anyway, what were you going to say?"

"I was going to say it's all very well, but this 'life is your creation' stuff is no better than any old religious myth."

"You think so?"

"Yeah. It's obvious *you* don't know what the creation *process* is. I mean, it's ridiculous. You're saying I'm making the world happen? For goodness sake, *how?* It's impossible."

"The process?" came in Frostbight. "Sorry old bean. Our fault. We didn't spell it out."

"Of course you didn't. That's because you can't."

"You reckon?" He took a sip of his coffee. "It's more obvious than you think."

"Oh yeah? It's not obvious to *me*."

"No? First of all, whether you see the argument as flawed or flawless, you're being equally creative – but bounded. You're approaching this discussion like those intellectual exercises you had at College, forever asking, 'Should I believe this?' 'Should I believe that?' 'Where's the evidence?' 'Is this true?' 'Is that true?'"

"Doctor, that's not surprising. *Your* ideas don't work because they are a closed system."

"A closed system?"

"Yeah. They've got their own bullet-proof insulation."

His eyebrows shot up. "By Jove! Not mincing your words!"

"Well, Doctor," I responded, "should anyone come along and refute it, you say, 'oh, that's just you being creative'."

"And creative they would be." Frostbight shook his head. "You won't get the hang of Creosophy by treating it like an algebraic equation."

"But I'm *not* treating it like algebra. It's just that this 'life is my creation' idea is another belief system."

He narrowed his eyes. "Ewan," he said, "you really don't need to keep holding on to your old ways," and turned to his neighbour. "Gusty, you're clever at this sort of thing. You explain."

The German added milk to his coffee and stirred. "Ach, mein Freund," he said to me as he sniffed the aroma, "you need to use your intellect less and your intelligence more."

"Oh yeah? I thought I *was* using my intelligence."

"Tonight we are not asking you to *believe* anything. This is not just dinner party philosophy. We are inviting you use your intelligence – not just your intellect – to *see* life differently."

"I'm sure you are, but you've cunningly avoided my question."

"What question?"

"*How* am I supposed to be creating this life?"

"Ah. You wish to know?" He sipped his coffee.

"Well, of course I want to know or I wouldn't ask."

He gave me a penetrating look and said, "Have you not listened? *Imagination.*"

I blinked. "I beg your pardon?"

"Imagination. That is the answer."

"What about it? We've already dealt with it."

"Ja. *It* is the 'process' you ask about."

"Is it? Huh." I wrinkled my nose. "This 'imagination' gets *everywhere.*"

He smiled. "Das is so. It does. Your question is not answered by logic because logic deals only with patterns and sequences."

"But you're still not explaining it: *if I do* create my world, *what's my method?*"

"I have said: the imagination. It is easy. You remember the pink elephant?"

"Of course."

"By what process did you imagine it?"

"I've no idea. It just happened."

He raised his forefinger. "And *that*, mein Freund, is how you do it."

I looked at the German. "Come again?"

"I repeat. *That* is how you – not the you, your self, but the 'You' you do not know – create the world. Imagination just happens. It pops out of nothing. It's a continuous instant cosmic happening."

"Whoa, Professor. Don't give me that sort of shit. I *imagined* the pink elephant because it doesn't *exist.*"

He frowned. "Das is correct. It was the action of your *Dependent* imagination. And it is by your *Instant* imagination that you create things that *do* exist."

I remained silent. The Reverend turned and regarded me from over his specs. "Does that answer you question?"

I shook my head. "Hardly."

"No?" he returned. "Listen. As soon as you engage either of your imaginations, you're engaging the process."

"Mmm … what if I didn't agree?"

"That's fine. Go on. Disagree. You'll remain sceptical as long as you limit yourself to thinking like an academic – and you'll never get an answer. What about this? There's another way to approach it."

"Tell me."

"Very well. Think of when you dream."

"All right."

"Notice that you interact with people, animals, places, bogeymen or whatever. A myriad of extraordinary things happen – and they're 'real' when they're happening."

"So?"

"Well, *you haven't a clue how those people and places come about* – they just happen."

I shrugged. "OK."

"You see," the Rector continued, "they were perfectly 'real', yet you wouldn't deny that you imagined them, would you?"

I shook my head.

"Of course not. And, by the way, what about your daily thoughts? Where do *they* come from?"

That stumped me since it was I who had said they appear from nowhere.

"So," he said, "does that make it clearer?"

"Yeah, I grant you they're valid points." I rubbed my chin. "But it still doesn't make sense that I'm creating the *exterior* world."

"How so? I say it again: you have one choice. *One* choice. Either *you* are inventing this world or some*one*, or some*thing* alien, is inventing it. And," he added, "you know what?"

I looked at him.

"My child, no alien *anything* is going to help you with the solution. Your answer depends entirely on your imagination!"

There was a pause. "But," I groaned, "as I said, if I *had* made it, I wouldn't have invented the horrid things that go on in it."

"Oh?" he replied. "What about the horrid things in your dreams?"

"What about them?"

"You invented *them*, didn't you?"

I grimaced. He was right. I made no reply. Realising I had not started my 'coffee', I loaded in a spoonful of sugar crystals, and stirred while I thought. My Grandmother said sugar boosts your energy. I could do with some.

"What d'you think old boy?" asked our host. "Coffee all right?"

Part II

✌

The Truth about Truth

I LIFTED MY CUP. "WOW!" I TOOK ANOTHER SIP. "GOODNESS. It's real!"

"Of course. What d'you expect?"

"But how did you get it? Don't tell me you grow coffee up here as well?"

"No," he smiled, "we don't, but it *is* grown at a good altitude." He took a little and savoured it. "Mmm ... so ... you're worried what we're telling you isn't true?"

"Of course. I don't want to be on a wild goose chase."

"Ach! Truth!" interjected the Professor.

"OK, Professor, what's the matter now?"

"Words, words and more words. Ja, mein Freund, there *is* something that is true, but what you believe can never be true, what is 'logical' can never be true and what you 'prove' can never be true."

"Phew!" I laughed, "I hope you're not planning to go public with this!" I paused. "Or are you trying to tell me something?"

"I am." He pulled at his beard as he pondered what to say. "The truth about truth presents no difficulty."

"No? Well, according to you it does."

"Ach so? Mein Freund, consider ..." He absentmindedly sniffed his coffee while he collected his thoughts. "If I were to tell you I felt hungry, would you believe it were true?"

"Why are you asking me? How would I know?"

"Das is so: you can believe it or not believe it. Could you prove it?"

"Well, no. I wouldn't know how."

"Again, you are correct. Now, on the other hand, if *you* were to feel hungry would *that* be true?"

"Yeah, of course."

"Now you understand."

"Understand what?"

"If you search for truth *'out there'*, you will find words and concepts and more words and concepts, but you will not find the 'truth'." He looked to my left. "Herr Pastor Foggie, do you concur?"

The Pastor removed his glasses and pulled out his silk handkerchief. "I couldn't agree more, Professor. It's just like what I was telling you," he said to me while he polished. "'Truth' is whatever you conceive it to be. No more. No less."

"Huh. What if the truth were rational?"

"The same goes for 'rational'. How do you *know* whether or not something's rational? There's no way. It's a belief. And for *believing* something to be 'rational' you have to *imagine* it's rational." He paused and replaced his glasses. "Does it bother you if what we tell you isn't true?"

"You tell me," I muttered despondently.

"Has *anyone* tonight said that *anything* is true other than, as the Professor was saying, maybe direct experience?"

"Huh, that's all very well, Father, but what about imagination?"

"What about it?"

"Which is it? True or false?"

"It's neither. The imagination is simply the imagination – just as a thought is a thought."

I groaned again and looked down at the floral decoration in my empty demitasse. This was one hell of a coffee. I could not deny I was the only one talking about truth.

"A top-up, Sir?" The butler was doing the rounds.

"Yes, please, Mould. It's amazing to be drinking the real stuff." I also needed help to keep reasonably sober: tonight's conundrums were enough even for a teetotaller. Claiming I were conjuring up the world out of nothing was a hard nut to crack – and yet my objecting to it was like the proverbial kicking against the goads.

"All right," I finally said to Doctor Frostbight. "Say I accept that life – even if I can't explain it – really *is* my creation. Say it *is* true …"

He stopped me. "*True*, old boy? Did I hear you say '*true*'?"

I rubbed my face in my hands again. "OK, OK. You're as bad as the others. But supposing I adopt this *perspective* that life's my creation. Who created whom? According to what *you're* saying, I created *you. That* means, from *your* perspective, that you created *me.*"

"And your problem is …?"

"Who's right?"

"Both are right, but your job, my boy, is to pay attention to what *you're* inventing. Tonight you've conjured up people who're telling you that you've created *them.* You will conjure up lots in the future who will deny it. And that's fine. That's the world you've made."

"So what happens now?"

"As I say, keep your focus on what *you're* doing. If you conjure up friends who say that *you* are *their* creation, how good is that? Your relationship with them will be, how shall we say, 'special'."

"I guess it would," I consented. "But, Doctor, I don't see how this creation 'viewpoint' is going to make a difference. I mean, we could talk about this all night. Tomorrow, life goes on just the same. As I said, I want a philosophy which can make life better."

"It would make a difference if you stopped fretting about whether it's 'true'."

"Why," I declared, "*isn't* it true?"

Frostbight grimaced. "Look," he said, "you're still trying to treat our ideas like mathematics. *You won't understand that way.*" He turned to his right. "Gusty, you taught this at Winterbad, didn't you?"

The Professor put down his cup. "Das is correct." The German addressed me. "It is like the game of cards we spoke of. You can only guess what cards you will be dealt: those are your 'set-ups' and 'upsets'."

"Oh yeah. Run over that again, would you?"

"Ach? Run over it?"

"I mean repeat what you said earlier."

"Ah, I understand. You do not know what cards the You-you-do-not-know will deal your self. But that matters much less than your 'set-downs': that is to say how you think and respond. So *how* you play your cards makes all the difference to your life, and is the realm of your Dependent mind. None of your Dependent mind is 'true': it is the world of words, and it is with *that* function you analyse and judge."

"Goodness. What's wrong with that?"

"Ach, more words. I did not say it was 'wrong'. Tonight we invite you to *suspend* words to allow yourself to *imagine* your experiences *are* the work of your imagination. Then maybe you will make progress."

"But only," I added, "if that were true."

I saw the Professor wince. I was not doing very well with this 'truth' stuff.

Part III

∽

The Bogyman

"**M**EIN FREUND," VON LOTTOWIND RESUMED, "WE ARE not exhausting you?"

"Certainly not." I was going to admit to nothing.

"Ah, das is good. I have an idea."

"One I can understand?"

"Of course. Maybe you remember what Pastor Foggie talked of: *test* the *value* of these ideas for yourself?"

"Yeah."

"Here, then, is my proposal. Cease analysing for a while, and *test* what we are saying. *Try on* our ideas instead of dissecting them. Try them on as much as you would a new pair of pyjamas."

"Pyjamas?"

"Ja! Ask not, 'are they true?' but rather, 'do they fit?'"

"I don't know whether they fit."

"And you will *never* know unless you try them on. We will show you how shortly. Having said that, as I warn my students, if you adopt this approach, you will have to use your intelligence."

"Hey, I've already told you, I *am* using my intelligence."

"You use it, ja, but not to your advantage."

"Then how should I use it?"

"In a new way that *is* to your advantage."

"Yes, yes, obviously, Professor, but what are you talking about?"

"I give you an example. Up until now you are nervous, seeing the world as being often 'hostile'."

"That's just how it is."

"It is not. I offer you a view that makes you less nervous."

I studied him. I realised he had green eyes. Or were they blue? "How easy is it?" I asked.

"It is easy. It is very easy. Play with a new description of life. See the world as coming *out* of you. Maybe think of it as your offspring – your child."

"My child?"

"Das is so. Your child. You have produced it."

"Really? Like I'm its parent?"

"Das is excellent. Now you become its 'agent' instead of its 'patient'."

I fiddled with my coffee cup without replying.

"What I am saying," he explained further, "is you may discover a new affection for life – and the people in it."

"Mmm …" I mused. "That wouldn't go amiss."

"In the meantime," he added, "spare a thought for those who are suicidal."

"Suicidal? Why d'you say that?"

"Because with suicide – along with psychosis and depression – the sufferer see the world, not as his or her offspring, but as a bogyman."

"Lord."

"Ja. It is a case of mistaken identity – with tragic consequences."

"No fooling!"

"It is so. People who are unhappy *always* see the world – or a part of the world – as foreign. It *never* occurs to them it is their own invention and is panning out exactly as they intended. This is particularly so for those who are terrified of life." He paused. "But do you know what is even worse?"

"No good asking me, Professor."

"Ah, so. The worst you could do – and many, many people do it – is to look upon *yourself* as the bogyman."

"What do you mean?"

"Thinking you, yourself, are the enemy."

"*I* wouldn't do that."

"Ja. You would! We discussed this."

"Not exactly. Oh, all right, perhaps we did. But *why* do we criticise ourselves so much?"

"It is more than likely because your parents treated you as the enemy when they chastised you. They trained you to see your *self* as hostile."

"They did?"

"Ja. When they criticised you."

I needed to chew that over. "Fine," I said after a minute. "I agree, parents can sometimes be horrid to their children, and yet mine weren't like that *all* the time."

"*Any* such fault-finding damages a vulnerable child. A little goes a long way. Criticism is a form of aggression."

"I suppose. But why do people do it?"

"Because that is what had happened to them when *they* were children. That is their only model. They see themselves as either shameful or dangerous." He leant forward and regarded me carefully. "Consider: if you believe your *self* is an embarrassment or danger, where can you hide?"

When I failed to answer, he sat back. "You cannot. Therefore you either attack someone vulnerable; or descend into psychosis or, depending on your character, consider suicide. It is a terrible thing to be your own bogyman."

"Phew," I responded. "Put like that, I wouldn't dare disagree."

"Ja, and do you understand this? In these cases, you are insulting your own creation, and that, as I said before, is pissing on your own bonfire."

I was silent and finished my coffee. I had had enough of bonfires. The storm still howled in the chimney.

"Everything all right?" enquired Frostbight.

"No, not really, Doctor. I'm a bit overwhelmed."

"Never mind. There's another way to look at it."

"Oh, good, it's about time."

"My child," intervened the Chaplain, "all you have to do is remember who you really are."

"Oh? I've forgotten."

He smiled. "I don't believe you have. I said you're God."

I bit my lip. "Ah, yes, Father, *that*. And I've already told you it's absurd."

"Absurd?" he said, with the hint of a grin. "I never said God didn't exist!"

"Very funny, but my trying to call myself 'God' is *insane*." With these words I heard a growl beneath the table and, almost too late, realised I had loosened my grip. With lightening reflex I grabbed my napkin, held fast and continued talking: there was no way the Doctor was going to think *I* wasn't 'snappy'. "You *are* joking, aren't you, Father, about this 'God' thing?" I kept my grip. Snowie tugged. I tugged back.

"My son, don't be alarmed. Think about it. God creates the universe, judges it and brings it to an end."

"So?"

"That's *You.*" He stopped and stared. "My child, are you feeling poorly?"

Trying to sit normally with the dog's teeth clenched on my napkin was too much. I confessed to our host. "Doctor, I've a problem."

Frostbight feigned innocence. "Oh? Don't like the idea of being God?" Then he grinned. "Ah! You mean Snowie? That's all right. Stop holding on."

I did as he suggested and loosened my grip. To my surprise, Snowie stopped tugging, wagged her feather duster, let me have my napkin and the next thing I had it back on my lap. Such a strange dog. I gave her a pat on the head.

"Sir," the butler asked our host, "would you like Mrs. McWhiteout to take her out?"

"Good thinking Mould. Snowie's a perfect nuisance," and added – with little sincerity – "such a naughty dog."

"Exactly so, Sir." The butler left, and in a few minutes Mrs. McWhiteout appeared. After accepting compliments about her splendid dinner, she scooped up the reluctant canine, cheerfully tucked it beneath her arm and retreated to the kitchen.

Part IV

❧

Where is the Universe?

"AH! THAT'S BETTER," SIGHED OUR HOST AS WE SETTLED. "Peace, perfect peace. I say, old boy," he said to me, "you've dashed fine reflexes. You know what? I think this calls for … Mould? Any chocolates on the go?"

"Indeed so, Sir. Mrs. McWhiteout prepared some only this afternoon."

"First class. Pass them round."

Reflexes or no reflexes, this was good news: chocolate was hard to come by. A moment later a plateful of dark brown goodies was offered me and I happily took a couple. Popping one in, I played it over my tongue. It was, how shall we say, 'different'? Yes, it was chocolate, but not as I knew it.

"It's raw, Sir," explained the butler. "The secret of longevity. Mrs. McWhiteout's recipe." He moved on.

The secret of longevity sounded good, and I reckoned I could get used to it more easily than I could this evening's conversation. While I sucked I asked, "Doctor, this talk about this business of my being God … promise me it's a joke."

"Padre?" he responded. "Are we joking?"

"My child," said the Rector, "if you were in India and said you were God, people would call you 'wise'."

"Really? I'm sure they wouldn't."

"And I'm sure they would. Theirs a culture that doesn't automatically assume, as we do in the West, that the body is the sum total of a person. And anyway, what about nearer home? Remember Meister Eckhart?"

"That German? He was supposed to be a mystic, wasn't he?"

"That's right. Early 13th. Century. He said the same thing."

"I remember. And I also remember he nearly got put on the bonfire."

The Padre nonchalantly waved a hand. "Things are better nowadays, but people still don't like being told they're God." He stopped a moment to consider. "I would say you're *less* than God only in one way."

"And I'm supposed to ask which one?"

He shrugged.

"Oh, come on, Father, spill the beans."

"All right. You're less than God in that you're so impressed by what you've made, you've lost sight of being the one behind it."

"So why does that make me 'less'?"

"Because," he smiled, "God at least *knows* He's at it!"

I smiled too. Nonetheless, I was still not satisfied. "You can say that if you like, but I'm *not* like God. I don't go around judging people and condemning them."

Von Lottowind spoke up. "Ach! You continue to deny it. You have spent your life judging people and de-valuing them. You believe you know better than anyone what is right and what is wrong. We have talked of this already."

"I suppose we have. So what?"

"You fantasise you are a magistrate – and believe it. You judge whether people are behaving 'properly'; whether they are speaking 'correctly'; whether their house is clean; whether they know how to dress; what they believe or do not believe; what they know or do not know. It goes on and on."

"Now, come on, you're exaggerating."

"Ja? You say this person deserves such and such, or that person does not, or you look down on someone because that person does not obey your 'rules' about how to live, and you condemn others for having different 'rules' than yours. There is no end to it."

"I'm not as bad as *that.*"

"Nein? You also judge groups; organisations; local governments; national governments; the economy. You even judge the weather."

That was too much. "Professor, I *don't* judge the weather. That'd be stupid."

"You do so," the German persisted, "even though it *is* stupid. Is it not you who says it is 'terrible weather'? That it is 'too dark'; 'too cloudy'; 'too cold'; 'too hot'; 'too windy' and so on? You even judge the poor forecaster when he makes a mistake." Von Lottowind picked up his demitasse, swilled the grains at the bottom, drank them and added, "Your judging makes the God of Scripture look like an amateur."

I felt the sting of his chastisement.

"Judging," he went on, "is an abuse of time." He paused and fixed his green eyes on me – or were they grey? "You tell me the world is hostile?"

"Yeah, well, I tend to think it is."

"Nein. Reality is mute – it is neutral. It is *you* who are hostile."

"Whoa. Steady on: *I'm* not hostile. "

"You are so. We have told you already. Every time you judge yourself to be a bogyman, you are hostile. Every time you judge another, you are hostile. Are you surprised that, for you, life is a 'battle', a 'struggle'? Are you surprised you have bad dreams?"

Without answering, I pondered for a minute and slid more chocolate over my tongue – it was really quite tasty now I had got used to it. Finally I protested. "What about the evils of the world? Somebody's got to judge *them.*"

Frostbight sighed. "Look, maybe there's something that'll help."

"You think so?"

"It might. Those 'evils' don't *actually exist.*"

"Wow!" I exploded. "Where are you off to? That's pure escapism – you *can't* pretend they're not happening."

"I'm not pretending."

"How can you possibly make a claim like that?" I kept a grip on my napkin.

"Calm, my son, calm," murmured Father Foggie next to me. "What the Doctor's saying is that evil is a furore in your Dependent mind."

"What are you on about? In my mind? *Of course* evil exists. Maybe not in *your* world, but it does in *mine. "*

"I've no doubt it does, my son, but only as an imaginary drama. We'll come to this again."

"More coffee, Sir?" Mould was back with the pot.

"God, I should say so, Mould. Pile it in." I looked at my demitasse – another stupid thing to have said.

"Very good, Sir." Could anything disturb Mould's composure?

"For example," the Rector continued again. "What're you doing right now?"

"Me? I'm downing my coffee."

"So I see. The point is you need to answer the question, 'Where is the Universe?'"

I put another spoonful of energy into my cup.

He did not wait for my answer. "As we said, the furthest reach of your Creation – the entire Universe – is simply the extent of your senses at any given moment – such as putting sugar in your cup or listening to me. In other words, it's your Instant imagination. Everything else is your Dependent." He paused to give me time. "Let's go over it again. *Everything else* is your story – including the 'evils' of the world. As the Doctor rightly says, they don't *actually* exist."

I still was not having it. "Father, I don't know about you, but I live in the real world. You know perfectly well that there are millions and millions of vile things going on, and they're all perfectly real."

"You're right. They *are* going on: but only *in your head,* so to speak." He went on. "Maybe I should explain. Of course you read in the newspapers the horrid things that happen. Nonetheless, I repeat; *for you,* they're in your mind: simply pictures and *stories* of what's *said* to be going on 'out there'."

"Well, all right, they may be stories, but they really *are* going on – you can see by the photos."

"For *others*, yes, things are going on in reality, but *for you* they're only newspaper articles, and the photos are just that: photographs. As for you, you're sitting here having dinner and talking to us, and that, *for you right now,* is the full extent of the Universe."

"Yeah, and I know jolly well there's a heck of a snowstorm outside."

The clergyman sighed. "Haven't we been over this already? *Anything* beyond this room, including the blizzard, is a scene from the theatre of your mind."

"But that implies what I drove through this evening *wasn't* a blizzard."

"The snowstorm *was* a snowstorm, but only when you were in it. As we've already said, that *was* your Instant imagination – when you were outside. Now it's gone and no longer your reality."

"So where is it?"

"In your Shadow imagination."

"Meaning what?"

223

"Converted to a memory."

"It's *not* a memory," I objected. "I can *hear* the storm."

"What you hear *right now* is a *sound* at the windows. As for what you think's going on outside, it's swirling around in your imagination."

"Yeah," I declared, "but if I went outside I would know all about it."

"Yes, my child, you would. And if you went outside, you would no longer be in here. And, I might add, you'd no longer be in the same snowstorm."

"Huh. You reckon? I'm sorry, it'd be *exactly* the same snowstorm."

"It is, but *only in your mind*. Oh dear, how can I put this better? The *real* snowstorm – the ongoing creation of your Instant imagination – is what's actually changing all the time. You know the analogy of the river? Take the Clyde. The river's a ceaseless flow – forever changing – and yet we still *call* it the 'Clyde'. The only thing about it that's static is the term by which you name it: a 'river' – not the river itself. The same goes for the blizzard – and, for that matter, the rest of your life. You see?"

Doctor Frostbight interrupted before I could answer. "Sorry to butt in Padre. May I ask Mould something? Mould?"

"Sir?"

"Didn't you study T'ang Dynasty Buddhism?"

"I did, Sir."

"Can you remember how they described this sort of thing?"

He looked up. "Let me think. I recall I was impressed by one philosopher in particular."

"Oh? Who?"

"Chih-I, Sir."

"Good man. I bet he had a thing or two to say."

"Indeed, Sir, he did. He was wont to declare, 'three thousand worlds are imminent in a moment of thought'."

"Excellent and to the point. You see," the Doctor said to me, "it's been stated before."

"Huh," I mumbled. "I don't know about that Chih-I fellow, but right now my 'Dependent imagination' is going round in circles."

There was a moment's silence. I saw the German smile and help himself to another chocolate. I waited. He looked at me. His eyebrows twitched. "Do you know …?" he began.

Part V

❧

Equality and the Insignificance of Reality

I GROANED. "I'M SURE I DON'T, PROFESSOR."

"Nein? Ach, it is this. Everybody," he stated, "is created equal."

We were sailing off in another direction and I couldn't resist the bait. "All right, Professor, who said?"

"The Creosophists."

"Oh yeah? What medication are *they* on?"

"Medication?"

"Just joking, OK, what're you on about? We've all heard this 'equality' thing. It's that communist utopia stuff, and it's nonsense. People aren't ever equal: society is *always* developing hierarchies."

"Maybe, but not when it comes to *creation*."

"That doesn't make any difference."

"You must understand. There is no thought or activity that is more or less creative than another. Even as we speak, we are being equally creative."

"Yes, maybe in our case, but generally speaking there are people who are a *great* deal more creative than others. I mean you can't say a street beggar is as creative as, say, Winston Churchill, who was running the country day by day during a world war."

"Das is not so. Sitting in silence and waiting for money is no less creative than leading the war effort."

"Oh, come on! Then put it another way: some people's lives are more valuable than others."

"Ach! More dramatic maybe, but not more valuable." The German took a sip of water and went on. "So you do not see how each way of living is as inventive as another?"

"Not in my book, Professor."

"Do not be mistaken. Whether people are beggars, world leaders, sanitary inspectors, office clerks, teachers, pupils or mothers at home, they sleep, get up, eat, go to the lavatory, daydream, look after their children, go shopping, chat to friends, do their job, play around, have sex, discuss things, smoke cigarettes, lose weight, gain weight, listen to the radio and go back to sleep again."

"Humph," I rejoined. "OK, fine, but not *everyone*'s life's like that."

"It is so. Even Adolph Hitler ..." The Professor glanced to his left as Doctor Frostbight screwed up his face. "Ja, even Adolph Hitler had a mediocre life."

"Whoa! He instigated the worst war ever."

"Yes, he may have done. Occasionally he had a grand rally or parade at which to show off, but generally he got up late, ate his vegetables, went for walks, attended meetings, looked at maps, planned his campaigns, gave orders, flew into rages, took pills for his digestion, travelled about, watched films and went to bed ..."

I interrupted. "But he turned the world upside down."

"He may have done so, yet 'world power', the 'greatness of Germany', swathes of distress and destruction: these were not *his* reality. Except for right at the end, for *him*, the destruction was only *in his head*, not in his *experience*."

"All right," I replied. "Maybe his private daily life was not much different from anyone else, but you couldn't accuse him of being insignificant."

The Rector took up the subject. "That's a good point," he said. "But insignificance too, is all in the head. The world 'out there' is not significant. Nothing 'out there' is. 'Significance' is a mental *interpretation* of what happens, not the event itself."

"Really? Do you hear what you're saying? You're condemning everyone to mediocrity!"

"Calm, my child, calm."

"Huh. Calm? What? Calm about being doomed to eternal insignificance?"

"Ah, but here's the rub: what you create *in your imagination* can be enormously significant. That's the difference."

Our host chipped in. "Cheer up, old chap. Regarding your ordinary life, yes, it's always destined for insignificance. But your thoughts ... as the Padre says, *that's* a different matter. What happens *in the world* is common to us all, but what's *in your 'head'* is unique. And for the good news?" He leant towards me and paused.

I waited. "Yes?"

"When you snuff it, it's going to be your *thoughts* you take with you. And you want more good news?" Without waiting for me, he said, "you can choose for yourself what you're going to think about."

"So?"

"So, if you want, when you die you *can* think amazing thoughts ... or ..." He slowed.

"Or what?"

"Or," he said, "you can repeat the same insignificant, mediocre judgements about life that you've always done."

I made a face.

"Look, old bean, you know where your problem lies?"

"You're not expecting me to say 'yes', are you?"

"Right enough," he smiled, "I don't suppose I am. Here's the thing: you need to stop believing your thoughts are real."

"Uh-uh, I'm not ..."

He put his finger to his lips. "Sssh. Maybe it's odd, to begin with, looking at it this way, but *thoughts themselves don't exist.*"

"Huh? Of course they exist!"

"No. They have no extension in space. If they did exist, they would die with you when you died."

The Professor interjected. "You, in common with most, are lost in a *virtual,* non-existent world of commentaries *about* life."

He paused as Mould re-filled his coffee cup. "And that is not the end of it."

I took a good breath to steady myself.

"Up until now your commentaries – and stories – have been, as you say in English, 'crap'"

"No, they haven't."

227

"So? ... you cannot see? We keep telling you."

"Hey, you're being hard on me. Anyway, Father Foggie said it was my *creations* that were 'crap'."

"He did. He was referring not just to your physical creations, but also to your commentaries."

"Huh." I found myself scratching my cheek. "Like what?"

"Like, 'I am the victim of misfortune'; 'I am overworked'; 'I am helpless'; 'somebody else is to blame'; 'life is unfair'; 'I have been wronged'; 'I have been damaged'; 'how I suffer'; 'the world is flawed'; 'I have to fight'; 'people do not understand me'; 'I need to be free'; 'my spouse does not appreciate me, respect me or care about me or ...' You wish me to go on?"

"No, Professor," I sighed. "Though if you repeat it enough I suppose I'll get it."

"You have the picture? Story upon story of a supposedly inadequate world. It is *nonsense*. I repeat, the world is not against you; it is neutral."

I slumped in my chair. "How can you say my stories are 'nonsense'?"

"Because they are not reality. They are a world of drama."

"Don't you like drama?"

"We have already spoken of that. There is nothing the matter with it."

"So why go on about it?"

"Because that is how you make yourself unhappy: by treating your dramas – that is to say, your commentaries – as things that exist."

"But they *do* exist."

He took a breath and frowned.

"All right, all right, Professor, they don't exist."

"Good," he relaxed. "Observe. You cook up your 'disasters' and stories of 'horrible people' so that you can have an emotional orgy."

"An emotional orgy?" I laughed. "That's rich!"

"Excuse me? 'It is rich'? What is rich?"

"Oh, just an expression. Don't let me hold you up."

"'Hold me up?'"

"Professor, *another* expression. Keep saying what you were saying."

"Ja? So. Your Dependent mind is where you can be both creative and significant. Why do you stuff it with other people's junk?"

I was lost for reply.

"Observing *that*," came in Frostbight, "might open your mind."

"I didn't know it was shut."

He grinned. "It wouldn't be if you listened." He helped himself to a chocolate. "Ever heard of Creosophy?"

"Creosophy? That thing you keep talking about?"

"Ever heard of it?"

"Not me, Doctor. At least not until this evening. What is it, a religion?"

"In some ways it is."

"Oh?"

"Yes. And in some ways it isn't."

"Mmm ... not very helpful. What's *that* supposed to mean?"

"It's a philosophy when you're talking about it, and a religion when you practise it."

"Humph. Sounds a pretty queer set up." I paused. "OK. What does 'Creosophy' mean?"

"It's coined from the Greek: 'the creation of wisdom' – or 'the wisdom of creation'. Either will do."

"Oh. Wisdom? So that's it?"

"Yes, in short."

"So, who started it?"

He shrugged. "St. Blane? We don't know. Lost in time."

"OK. If you teach it, where are your students? Or should I say 'ordinands'?" I looked around. "I don't *see* any."

He smiled. "They find us when they're ready."

A puzzling answer. As for 'Creosophy', it sounded like a preservative for painting my garden shed. And this Chilblane place? Some kind of Seminary? Eccentric or what?

Father Foggie suspected what I was thinking. "No, my son, Creosophy's *not* a paint product. As we've indicated, it's an extended thought experiment. It's a thought experiment explaining how come we're alive – and its implications. It's up to you how you see it – after all, it's your creation. What matters is that you start seeing your life, not only in your usual way – which is from the viewpoint of your ordinary local self – but from the You, the Self-that-isn't." He paused. "Would you like another chocolate?"

"Who?" I replied. "Me or the 'Self-that-isn't'? I can tell you, Father, I need more than a chocolate – even if it does make me live a long time."

He passed the plate to me. "What about some good news?"

"More good news? Please. Don't hold back."

"It's this: every time you let go of the common idea you're living in *someone else's* universe, you decouple yourself from your trance."

"Oh my goodness." I sucked one of the chocolates. "First I'm asleep, and now I'm poncing around in a trance?"

That made him chuckle. "They express a similar thing." His tone changed. "My son, I know it's a lot to take in, but please don't be discouraged."

"But how come you take all this weirdo stuff in your stride?"

"We're used to it. We all found it stretched our thinking when we first heard it."

"Well, I'm glad I'm not the only one."

"You're not. I fully realise the suggestion that *one* idea can encompass *all* existence flies in the face of conventional philosophy. That's what happens when you ask a different question: you get a different answer. You're doing well. I'm impressed."

Frostbight broke in. "You know what, Padre, I think it's time we cut some slack for the lad. We can come back to this in a minute. Mould?" he declared loudly, "that's not port on the mantelpiece, is it?"

The butler was at the end of the room, sweeping stray ash into the fire. He straightened. "It is indeed, Sir. Decanted this morning."

"And no dry rot spores got in it?"

"No, indeed, Sir. I kept the stopper on."

"Good work. Let's have it."

Digestif

Part I

☙

Uncreation

MOULD PLACED THE PORT IN FRONT OF OUR HOST. Frostbight put aside the stopper, filled his glass and slid the decanter across the table. "Here we are, old boy, something for your digestion. Help yourself and pass it on – to your left."

My decision to go steady on the booze had evaporated some time ago, and anyway a digestive aid seemed a good idea. I filled my other small glass, albeit not to the top and, after passing the decanter to Father Foggie, took a sip. Not being an aficionado I could not say whether it was tainted by dry rot, but it had a fine depth of flavour, and I said so. A moment later, Father Foggie declared it to be "exceptionally pleasant," and the Professor agreed that it was "of a most excellent vintage".

Our host was pleased. "Blackberry," he said simply. "Picked 'em m'self."

My goodness, I thought, talk about 'Digging for Victory': making 'port' out of brambles! War or no war, these people were seriously into self-sufficiency. I visited again in my mind's eye the dungeon below. I now had it with fruit presses; secret cauldrons; steaming vats; kettles; stills ...

Our host spoke up. "Awfully quiet, old man. You all right?"

"Oh, yes, thanks" I replied, coming back to the present. "Just a little distracted."

"We're not being too tough on you?"

"Oh, no, not at all, Doctor." I was lying. "Thank you. I'm fine. Very good port." I tasted it again to show my appreciation. "But to go back, could we slow down and take stock?"

"No problem. Fire ahead."

"Have I got this right? During this dinner you've said there's no such thing as 'truth'; no such thing as 'natural laws'; that there's no God – apart from the 'Me-I-don't-know' – and no spirit or soul, and neither is there good nor evil."

"Yup, you're getting there. All those are beliefs. And a thousand beliefs don't make a …"

"I know, I know, they don't make a truth". Silence followed. Was I 'getting there'? As far as I knew, whichever way I looked I was faced with beliefs. I rubbed my face again. "What I can't get my head around," I said, "is your implication I'm personally responsible for *all existence.*"

"Good man. You're getting the idea." He sniffed his port and sipped it. "Definite progress."

"Progress is it?" I replied. "It's one heck of a statement. I mean anyone coming in now and hearing this would think you were … well … unglued."

"Yes," he nodded, "he might, if he didn't understand. Think of Mahatma Ghandi."

"That chap in India?"

"Exactly. When he started out he said his ideas were bound to get dismissed – at least at first."

"Oh, yeah?"

"Then he said they'd get attacked, but that, in the end, they'd be accepted as self-evident." He shrugged. "And now? India's set for independence. You see, it takes time."

"Well, whatever, it's still the devil of a job getting my head around your ideas. And there's something else."

"Uh-huh? What's on your mind?"

"None of you have said anything about *uncreating* things. I mean, if we're creating all the time, aren't we also *un*creating?"

He turned to von Lottowind. "Gusty! D'you hear that? Not a bad question, eh? You like being pedantic: what d'you think?"

"Watty," responded the German with a superior air, "I am never pedantic: I am *precise*. Nevertheless, mein Freund," he said to me, "you are most observant."

"Yeah, I believe you."

He made no response to my petulance. "I perceive you are intelligent. Yes, indeed you uncreate. You do so continually: you cannot bring something into the world without releasing what is here already. You would be correct to say your life is as much an *un*creation as a creation."

"I would?"

"Ja. They are two sides of the same coin. You are here, sitting in this room which you have created, and so you have *un*created the room in which you were before and, with it, all the rest of your previous life."

"Huh? I wouldn't say I'd *uncreated* the other room. It's still there. I could show you if you like."

"Ah, but if you did so, you would need to leave here, and then you would uncreate *this* room."

"Well, no, Professor," I contested, "that's not 'on'. You *can't* say this room won't be here when I leave it."

"And why not?"

"Because it still *will* be here."

The German surveyed me intently. "We have told you," he said, "your entire Universe is what is directly around you *at this moment*."

"All right, all right, I hear you." I needed a moment to think. Uncreated or not, the old conundrum came to my mind: if a tree falls in the middle of a forest and no one hears it fall, does it make a sound? I remember I used to argue this at College, but I could not recall the conclusion – there probably never was one.

Picking up on my thoughts the German added, "You might at first find the idea of 'uncreation' problematic. If there is a tree in the quadrangle, is it there when no one is looking at it?"

"In the forest? In the quadrangle? Professor, who cares? They're there all the time."

"Nein. When no one is left looking at it, it is uncreated: it is nowhere except, maybe, in the Dependent imagination."

"Ha!" My mind went back to philosophy seminars. "I know what you are."

"Ja?"

"Empirical Idealists."

"Empirical Idealists? Ah! Do you not mean Monal Idealists?"

"Professor," interrupted the Cleric, "I think he means Empirical Subjectivists."

"Not a bit of it," argued Frostbight. "Existential Epiphenomenologists."

I raised both hands. "OK, OK," I said. "Big joke. Who cares? I'm talking about the 18th. Century chap, Bishop Berkeley and all that. You're saying things don't exist without a mind."

"That is so. Without your mind you couldn't know that there was a world."

"Yeah, that's right: that's Berkeley – apart, maybe, from his idea that existence is co-ordinated by God."

"Indeed so, mein Freund. The good Bishop made the usual mistake. He believed 'God' was someone separate from himself. Then he failed to apply his own logic."

"Oh? You mean, if *a tree* doesn't exist when I'm not looking it, why should the same thing not apply to God – who's *never* visible?"

He nodded.

"Well, whatever. Nowadays no proper philosopher pays Berkeley or his Monalists much attention."

"Nein? Why not?"

"Obvious. I can't *see* my own *brain*, and so according to Berkeley *that* means my brain doesn't exist! But if my brain doesn't exist, then *I* don't exist and so I couldn't think the thought in the first place. How stupid is that?"

The Professor gave me a wry smile. "You are indeed intelligent. It is a mystery, and I shall leave you to ponder on it. However, even if you could open your head and look at your brain, you would not find your mind – or your self."

"And you're saying that because thoughts don't exist?"

"Correct. You can search the Universe but you will never find a thought."

Part II

❧

The Story of Stories

"OK, OK," I SIGHED, "I GET YOU, PROFESSOR. BUT I'M *STILL* in the dark. What *does* exist?"

"I tell you again," he replied. "For you right now, what is happening at this very moment – *that* exists."

"I know, so you keep saying, and yet you're claiming there's no such thing as the rest of the world."

"There *is* such a thing as the rest of the world, and we have told you, it is fiction, a *concept.*"

I could see I was not getting very far.

The Reverend spoke. "Maybe you would find it easier if you remember that everything in the world is one of the two kinds of imagination we've talked of."

"You mean either the Instant or Dependent?"

"Yes. What you call 'reality' and which you experience physically and can't control with language – that's your Instant imagination. All the rest is your Dependent: your thoughts, theories, beliefs, calculations, judgements, stories and so on. What you call 'the rest of the world' is strictly your *private* world that nobody else can see."

"Or, mein Freund," returned the German, "you could say that while 'reality' as what you can see with your eyes, your *stories* are what, metaphorically, you can 'see' – in your mind – *without* eyes." He turned to this left. "Would you not agree, Watty?"

"Spot on old man," answered Frostbight.

"OK, Doctor," I asked, turning my attention to him. "What exactly do Creosophists mean by 'the mind'?"

"The mind? Simple, old boy. It's your imagination."

I frowned.

He went on. "Don't be fooled. There's no such 'thing' as the mind. The Padre told you earlier: it's another word for consciousness, and consciousness is another word for imagination."

"Hey," I objected, "you *can't* wrap it up so easily. The mind and imagination are *aspects* of consciousness."

"But don't you see? Consciousness is not a 'thing'. It's just a word we use to refer to someone being aware *of* something. The point is that you cannot be conscious in a vacuum; you are always aware *of* something; conscious *of* something or having a thought *about* something. As with the mind, it has no location. It doesn't exist."

"Now steady! It must exist or there'd be nothing to talk about."

"Look, old boy, people can talk about anything they want, but it doesn't mean what they're talking about exists."

"How can you say all this? *Of course* consciousness exists."

"Think so? Remember what Gusty said about the thunder rumbling?"

"Er …"

"The thunder *is* the rumbling, and the rumbling *is* the thunder: neither exists independently of the other. Likewise consciousness *is* whatever you're aware of, and what you're aware of *is* consciousness."

I weighed up the idea. "There *must* be more to it than that. Can we go back to 'stories'? Do they exist? I mean, what *is* a 'story'?"

"Good show. Glad you asked. No, they don't exist." He turned to his right. "Gusty? A story. How would you describe it?"

The German straightened. "A story, Watty, is the condition of a light trance, in which the Dependent imagination forms a virtual reality drawn on the creations of the Instant imagination."

"Wow!" I blurted out. "Not so simple *this* time."

The Doctor smiled. "Possibly," he said, "our Professor is being a little pedantic. Actually, yours was a cracking good question. It's by *stories* that you understand your world."

"That's what you keep driving at, but *I'm* not understanding the world that way."

"No? You are, actually. I'll go over it again. You map your whole life through stories: that's where its meaning comes from."

"I don't think sceptics like Albert Camus would agree with you: they're determined life's meaningless."

"Ah, yes. You see, for him, his claim that 'life is meaningless' is the very story that gives his life meaning!"

I gave it thought. "Oh, all right. Very smart. But we can't be making stories *all* the time."

"No, true enough. When you're making neutral *descriptions* you're not storytelling."

"Like what?"

He lifted his coffee. "'I am sitting here'. 'This is coffee'. 'This is a cup'. 'I am holding it'. Those are neutral descriptions."

"Huh. Pretty boring."

"I know. That's why we create stories to spice things up. Here, try this for size – it's an old chestnut."

"What is?"

"This: the statement, 'the king died and the queen died'."

"OK."

"Got it?"

"Yeah."

"It's a description."

"I can see that."

"Splendid. Then how about this? 'The king died, and the queen died *of grief.*'"

"Yeah?"

"Don't you see? Now you're starting a story."

"Huh. All right, so that's what you mean. But, hey, that implies there's no point in complimenting someone because it too is only a story – and not a real description."

"You missed the point: being fictional *doesn't* imply a story is useless or worthless, let alone bad. Good stories are invaluable, and so are compliments."

I rubbed my face. "I'm still not sure I'm getting it," I said, and nosed my bramble port like the others – to look intelligent. What a steeplechase! We were bounding from hurdle to hurdle. The trouble was I still had not got it into my head that there is both a 'Me' and a 'me', and I needed to remember that. It was an unusual concept that, as the greater 'Me', I invent my outside world, and as the local 'me' I create my mental world. And, I suppose, what they were saying was that I was *misusing* the Dependant imagination when I mistook my crappy stories for real experiences – and then wondered why I was unhappy.

The Doctor was having a few words with the other two, and now addressed me. "Sorry to take you from your thoughts, old boy. My late wife used to quote a wisecrack who said 'I've had many troubles in my life, and you know what? Some of them actually happened!'"

"She said that?"

"Yes, indeed." He looked round. "Mould?"

"Sir?"

"Where did she get that saying?"

The butler straightened. "I recall, Sir, she was quoting a certain Mr. Mark Twain."

"Oh?"

"Yes, Sir. An American gentleman."

"Thank you. American, eh? Twain? Have I heard of him? Not sure. Never mind. The point is, old boy," he said to me, "you can see there's nothing new about this stuff."

"Maybe not," I grumbled, "but it's new to *me*."

"Are you 'getting' how important stories are?"

"Well, sort of ... but *why*?"

"I've just told you. They're the *only* vehicles you have to conjure up meaning and make sense of your life."

"Humph!" I quipped, "my mother told me not to tell stories."

"Tch, tch! She said that?" He grinned. "Look at your own stories: whether you're a good or bad person, or a victim or survivor or hero or criminal or rescuer or whatever, there lies your meaning."

The Reverend Foggie came in. "Here's another thing. Do you know why you have problems in life?"

"Problems? Are your going to say they give life meaning?"

"That's pretty close. I was going to say you have problems because you love them."

I was taken aback. "I love *problems*? Hey, steady on, Father: not me. I spend my life *avoiding* them."

Father Foggie slowly shook his head. I thought he might despair. "My dear child," he began, "where have you been?"

"Sitting here, next to you."

"Very witty." He adjusted his specs. "Have you not noticed? Your problems are your stories."

"What? Now my stories are a problem?"

"No, no. You use your stories to generate the problems, and it's those *problems* which, as you suspect, generate meaning."

"But," I protested, "I don't *love* problems."

"As I say, haven't you noticed?"

"Noticed what?"

"You only *pretend* you want rid of them."

"Oh, I beg your pardon, I don't think *that's* true."

"Calm, my son. You'd be miserable without them. Don't you know that you *live* because of problems?"

"Huh," I responded. "I'm sure I've got better reasons."

He went on. "Don't you see? Problems are essential. You – and I – would be lost without them."

I laughed. "Father, I'm already lost with you just talking about them!"

He smiled. "But don't you see? Where would you be without obstacles: difficulties, conundrums, questions, quandaries and mysteries?"

I made a face and shrugged.

"How," he asked, "are you going to make good stories if you don't have good problems?"

"Er ... all right, Father, I suppose, if you put it like that." I paused. "So is that it?"

"May I," he said, "make a suggestion?"

"All right."

"If you call problems 'projects' you immediately convert them to better stories – as something to look forward to, rather than something to avoid. You remember we talked about your being an 'agent' rather than a 'patient'? The trick here is you're changing problems from where you're the 'victim' of your struggles to the director of your projects. You might find you enjoy yourself."

"Mmm ..." I sipped some port.

Part III

❧

The Bridge over Reality

VON LOTTOWIND SPOKE. "LET US RETURN TO WHERE WE were earlier. This time I make it easy."

"That'll be the day! Make what easy?"

"Understanding life."

"Oh, yeah? Promise?"

"Of course. Imagine it this way: as a bridge over a river."

"A bridge? All right …"

"You have that picture?"

"Uh, huh."

"Now, stand on the bridge and see yourself facing upstream."

"Right. I'm there."

"Good. Now, the river that is coming *towards* you is a stream of potential 'problems' preparing to come into existence."

I groaned. "Professor, I'm drowning."

He knitted his bushy eyebrows. "No matter. *You are on the bridge.*"

"Oh, all right, all right, keep your hair on."

"Good." He cleared his throat and resumed. "*Underneath* you is the *present moment*: your Instant imagination and *act* of creation – that is to say, reality. It is below you for less than an instant: a moving, transient experience, continuously created and uncreated."

"Phew!" I rubbed the back of my neck. "And downstream? What's that?"

"That's the Dependent imagination with its trail of private tales moving slowly away from the bridge. At Winterbad we used to say 'the water beneath the bridge is the water for tomorrow's fable'."

"Excellent, Gusty," exclaimed the Doctor. "Couldn't be clearer. I would point out," he said to me, "that the analogy of the bridge shows how your two imaginations are distinct."

"Does it?"

"Yes. With the Instant, not only is the water in constant motion, but also it never flows under the bridge twice. So it is with what happens in the physical world: it *never* repeats itself."

"Huh, I suppose it doesn't."

"You see, it's very different from your Dependent imagination."

"Isn't it the same kind of thing?"

"No. With your Dependent you can watch the flow at leisure."

"I'm not with you."

"Reality vanishes moment by moment, but your thoughts and memories are fixed. You can rehearse them at will."

"Oh, I see what you mean. That's quite useful, isn't it?"

"Yes, usually, but *not* so useful when you bore others with your same old stories."

I could not think of a clever reply.

"Actually," he went on, "to be serious, it's a real difficulty in cases of shock and trauma, but we'll address that in a moment."

I took a deep breath. Was I getting the hang of this imagination stuff? I hoped so.

Part IV

❧

The Day of Judgement

"**M**Y CHILD," REMARKED THE REVEREND, "MAY I DRAW your attention to something?"

"All right, Father."

"You remember I said you're God?"

"How could I forget? The next thing you'll be telling me I'm bringing on the Day of Judgment."

"Ah!" he replied. "Good idea. When is the Day of Judgment?"

"What? The Day of Judgement? You're asking me?" I turned round briefly. "Well, I can tell you, it's not today."

"You'd be surprised."

"I would? You're kidding?" I again turned round. "I don't hear trumpets. And, oops, no skeletons hopping out of graves."

"No, no, no. *Your* Day of Judgement is not, as in the Bible, one event. It's continuous."

"Mmm ... haven't we been here before?" The Rector made no reply. "Oh, all right, all right, I do judge occasionally."

"Exactly," he said. "It doesn't have to be that way."

"But I don't judge *everything*."

"You still think so? Not much escapes you. Even now you're at it in this room: you're trying to make out we're talking a load of rubbish."

"I …" My voice trailed away. He could be right.

"It's *such* a habit you're not aware of it."

I took a deep breath. "OK," I said, "maybe I do judge. *Why's* it such a bad thing?"

"Because your judgments are a hierarchy thing. They're 'put-downs' of people and events you've created. It's a way of devaluing them and pretending you're more important." He hesitated. "Still, it's not always a bad thing. You're right to assess whether we're talking rubbish … but are you judging us?"

I shrugged. "I suppose I might be."

"Yes. It's a rotten use of your Dependent mind: you think your private judgements *about* experiences are intelligent."

"So?"

"That's what makes your life an emotional rollercoaster."

Frostbight broke in. "Padre, I think we should make one thing clear before we go on. We're talking," he said, addressing me, "about your typical daily criticisms. As the Padre pointed out, we're not talking about judgements in the sense of *assessing*."

"I'm sorry?"

"We're not referring to judgements that are reasonable calculations – or miscalculations."

"Like what?"

"We need to calculate whether doing something is safe or sensible – safe, for example, to cross the road. And of course we like to avoid *mis*calculations so we don't get flattened by an oncoming bus."

"Yeah, Doctor, OK. I get that. But going back to this business of judging people, adults have to be critical: everyone has faults."

"Sorry, old boy, the same goes for 'faults'."

"No it doesn't. Why?"

"Why? Because it's *machines* that develop 'faults'."

"I know. So?"

"*Humans* make *mistakes*."

"Oh, yeah? Tell me that's not linguistic hair splitting."

"It's not. Machines start off all right and then develop faults as they grow older. Mistakes, however, are part and parcel of people starting any creative process, but grow *less* with experience."

"Maybe, but what about convicted criminals? Crimes are faults."

"Real crimes are assessed by real judges. Yes, they may be judged to be crimes, but that doesn't make them 'faults'. Crimes are mistakes – or misjudgements. They are part of the creative story telling processes of a human being. In due course, the criminal could well change his mind, his behaviour and his story."

"Huh." I chewed over the idea. "I'm not sure. OK. Let's put aside actual criminal stuff. You can't deny it'd be a dull world if nobody was allowed to judge anyone."

"You think? First of all, it's nothing to do with 'allowing', and secondly, why judge any man to be less than you? Would that make him interesting?" When I said nothing, he continued. "Your judging people is just a pompous ego-trip that does nothing." He paused. "While we're on this subject, there's something else."

"*More?*"

Frostbight raised a hand. "Are we tiring you?"

"Oh, no, no. I'm fine." I wished it were true.

"First class. It's about self-judgements."

"I'm not with you."

"All judgments are the product of your Dependent imagination."

"I know."

"So they repeat themselves, and any of your judgements can go on for the rest of your days – especially self-judgments."

"Lord. But hold on. We've got to judge ourselves or we'll never learn."

"I wouldn't judge yourself if I were you. You'll be guilty forever."

"Ugh! That's a long time."

"It is a long time. Funnily enough, you never apply the same kind of judgement to your own judgments."

"How do you mean?"

"*You fail to judge your judgments.* If only you did you'd see for yourself how stupid you're being. Sorry to be so frank, old chap, but look: you're no better than anyone else and your invisible courtroom never existed. That's the first thing. Now, let's go back. As I was pointing out, there's a difference between declaring someone has a 'fault' and someone is 'making a mistake'."

"You did. So?"

"Whatever someone's done, claiming they have a 'fault' is a judgement – and denigrates them, and by so doing you're denigrating your own creation. That they made a 'mistake', however, makes what they did a *mis*judgement and does not devalue them." He looked across the table. "Padre? You're better at explaining this sort of thing."

These had been unusually strong words from the Doctor, and I looked to my left. The Reverend dabbed his lips with his napkin. "My son," he began, "think about it. If you were unfortunate to make a poor investment and lost your money, you wouldn't call that a ' guilty offence', would you?"

"No ..."

"That's right. It was a case of misjudgement or, rather, a miscalculation."

"All right, Father, I get that, but it doesn't apply elsewhere. What if I'd been a victim of abuse?"

"Yes?"

"Surely you're not telling me the abuser wasn't guilty – but was simply making a *'misjudgement'*?"

"I am. He was guilty, yes, *and* he made a mistake."

I stopped and thought. "Oh, I see what you're saying. You're saying there's *two* things going on."

The Rector waited for the penny to drop.

"A person can be guilty according to a country's law, but that *philosophically*, no one's guilty?"

"Well done," he replied. "And when the perpetrator comes to review what he's done – either in this life or in the life to follow – he'll find out what effect he's had on those he targeted – and will learn whatever he needs to learn at that time."

I interrupted. "But what about the victims of crime? What are they supposed to think?"

"My son, that you've been a 'victim' is *not* a *fact*."

"No? Seems like one to me. Call me old fashioned."

"Well, it's not. 'Victims' don't exist in the landscape."

"Huh. They exist *somewhere.*"

"My son, victimhood is a belief."

"Yeah? Well, if *I'd* been abused, *I'd* exist in the landscape!"

"Don't you see? *People* exist, but *'victims'* don't – it's poetry. Can't you tell the difference?" He did not wait for an answer. "Going back to what we said earlier, believing you're a suffering 'victim' is an act that plays the role of 'patient'."

"And?"

"*Any* belief that you're suffering demonstrates you're playing 'patient'."

"But it's not just a belief: people really *do* suffer – from pain, physically and emotionally."

"They think and do whatever they think and do; and feel whatever they feel, whether or not it's pain, but are they 'suffering'? Who can say? It's an *opinion.*"

"Crikey. Just an opinion?"

"Yes. Or, if you like, poetry."

"Bloody queer poetry," I snorted.

The Rector shrugged. "I agree."

Part V

❧

Do Beliefs Exist?

NOBODY SPOKE. THE WIND STILL PUSHED AGAINST THE windows and, from time to time, draughts flustered the candles. I wondered if conversations at Chilblane were always like this. I took a breath. "I don't know," I said to no one in particular, "about this business of facts versus beliefs – or opinions."

Frostbight raised an eyebrow. "And the difficulty is …?"

"It's not a 'difficulty', Doctor. I mean it's a *fact*, not a story, that in coming here tonight I nearly got stuck in a blizzard."

"Ach," countered von Lottowind, "we have already said, it was a *fact* that you were in the blizzard when you were *in* the blizzard."

"But I could have died."

"If you had died, that too would have been a fact. However, you would never have been the '*victim*' of the storm. *That* would be fiction."

"Fine, but it's 'fiction' which would *reflect* the facts."

"Ja, you are correct. Your Dependent mind embellishes the facts to dramatise them. And that is how you imbue facts with meaning. Your virtual world has much more of an impact on you than what's going on 'out there'."

"Like what?"

"I am talking, of course, about your endless stream of beliefs, judgements and, above all, stories. And it is they which fuel your secret courtrooms, victimhood and emotional storms."

"But why does life have to be such a struggle?" I said half to myself, and realised I was rubbing my face again.

"You do not understand?" he replied. "You suffer because you *believe* what you *think*."

"Gosh! Doesn't everyone believe what they think?"

"Das is correct. They do. That is why you see so much misery." He gave me one of his piercing looks. Yes, his eyes were definitely blue. "There are," he said gravely, "three great lessons in life."

"Oh? Three?" I replied.

"Ja. Would you like to hear them?"

I made a face. "Try me."

"They are these. The first is, do not believe what you think."

"OK. Got that. And the second?"

"The second is, do not believe what you think."

"Huh. So what's the third?"

His eyes sparkled. "Do not believe what you think!"

"Very funny, Professor." I sat up and stretched my shoulders. "Now I'm wondering what I *am* supposed to think. Anyway, may I ask you something?"

"Of course."

"What *is* a belief?"

"Das is a good question. Firstly, I can tell you what a belief is not."

"That's helpful."

He disregarded my sarcasm. "It is not something in the landscape."

"Yeah, yeah, you're always saying that."

"I explain. If you think that the world is a sphere circling the sun, that is a reasonable belief – an assessment of what you can see. Tonight, however, we are discussing *superstitions* extracted from reality."

"Oops! Superstitions?"

He smiled. "It is so. Let me illustrate. You think the world is created and kept in order by some kind of intelligence?"

"It's got to be acted on by *something* like that."

"Ah so? And you *believe* 'life is a struggle'?"

"Sure. What's that got to do with it?"

"It is an example of your way of explaining your life: by believing there is some sort of intelligence 'out there' that often opposes you."

"Humph!" I took a moment to consider. "OK. What I'm battling may not be solid, but it doesn't mean there's *nothing* 'out there'."

"Can you *see* it?"

"Well, no, obviously not."

"There you have it. It is not a fact. It is an *embellishment* of reality: a belief."

"Good show," exclaimed Frostbight. "What you haven't noticed," the Doctor said to me, "is you've spent your life believing there's such a thing as 'evil' when actually it's pure superstition."

I deliberated.

"Not positive about it, old chap?"

"No. There *is* evil in the world, and people have always talked about it."

"Of course they've talked about it, but that doesn't mean there's any such thing. I say again, *beliefs don't exist*. As the Professor pointed out, if you can see something with your eyes, it exists. If not, it doesn't. Do you follow me? It's an artificial reality that you *pretend* 'exists'."

"Well, whether or not it exists, *something's* going on."

"Yes, it is, but it's not 'out there' in the world."

I groaned.

"Dear me, maybe we'd better try another example." He considered. "Do you ever hear yourself being criticised?"

"Criticised? Yes, often."

"Can you hear it in the landscape?"

"I don't need to. I can hear it in people's voices."

"No," he said, "you don't hear it *in* people's voices. You *interpret* people's voices. Your trouble is you think those 'criticisms' exist."

"But they *do.*"

"No they don't. You believe they do because you can't yet tell there's a difference between the colourful and biased inventions of your Dependent mind and the neutrality of your landscape."

"Huh," I grunted. "All right, then, what *is* reality – or rather, as you call it, the 'landscape'?"

"We keep telling you: your fleeting experiences from moment to moment."

"But I thought you said what I experienced was the product of my Instant imagination."

"I did. And *that's* how come it's 'real'."

"All the rest," added von Lottowind, "all the millions of things you think about are fiction: they're mirrors in your Reflective imagination."

"Huh," I responded, "my brain must have a lot of mirrors." I fell silent. I could do with time to digest the ideas, and a diversion would be good. The portraits had been catching my eye from the beginning, and it was tempting to see their resemblance to Doctor Frostbight – especially the one on the panelling behind my host. It was of a funny fellow in a black Seventeenth Century hat. "Doctor, may I change the subject?"

"Of course. Go ahead, old chap."

"Well, it's that portrait behind you. I keep noticing it. An ancestor? Looks awfully like you."

Without turning round, he replied, "Yes, indeed. Horatio Frostbight."

"He seems a fine fellow. Was he famous?"

"In his own way. He was a Creosophist Grand Master."

"Really? That sounds important. So, then, who's that?" I referred to another in a horned helmet behind Father Foggie.

"That one? Ah! That's Sagacious Frostbight. An earlier Grand Master – long time ago."

"Gosh, so it's hereditary?"

"It can be. Not always. These days I'm waiting to find out whether my daughter will take over."

"Wow. A Grand Mistress?"

He smiled. "Whatever. It can have its dangers. Sagacious was executed for 'heresy'."

"You don't say?"

"Yes. Nasty business. You can see him being hanged in the neighbouring picture."

He was quite right. There he was, swinging from a gibbet. "Gruesome," I mumbled. "Nasty times."

"They certainly were." He turned to some more works behind von Lottowind. "You see over there?" It was a lively scene of warriors in kilts. "That's the Battle of Chilblane Bridge."

"Oh? Looks fierce. When was that?"

"I don't remember exactly. During the Anti-Creosophist Crusade."

"A *Crusade*? Against Creosophists? I've never heard of such a thing."

"No?" replied Frostbight. "'I suppose you wouldn't have. Thankfully things are different these days."

"I'm glad to hear. I wouldn't like your daughter to have to swing for it."

He made a slight nod. "Moi non plus."

Part VI

❦

Does a Brick Exist?

WHILE WE WERE SPEAKING, FATHER FOGGIE HAD taken out his pocket-handkerchief and resumed polishing his specs. "My child," he said as he seated them on his nose, "I'd like to return to where we were."

I groaned again. "There's more?"

"There is."

"All right, if you must ..."

He put away his handkerchief. "Do you want to hear the good news?"

"There's *more* good news?"

He grinned. "Of course. It's this. Once a brick has fallen on your head, it's uncreated."

I laughed – more from surprise. "A brick? A real brick? I didn't think we were talking about bricks."

"No, maybe we weren't, but I want to be clear about what exists and what doesn't. So, as I say, the dangerous brick's uncreated."

"But, Father, the brick would still be there, lying on the ground."

"Yes, but it wouldn't be the same brick."

"Of course it'd be the same. You can't say it'd be a *different* brick."

"Ah! It *used* to be a dangerous brick. Now it's a *safe* brick."

"Is that so? Then what's happened to the dangerous one?"

"You've uncreated it."

"Huh! I can tell you, Father, whatever the brick is, if it had fallen on *my* head, I'd have a cracker of a headache, and there wouldn't be anything 'uncreated' about *that*."

"My son, the body starts healing instantly; so even the worst of your sore head would be fractionally better than it was a minute ago. As for the brick: it's done its mischief."

"Pleased to hear it."

He didn't react. "You see, your Instant experiences uncreate themselves automatically. On the other hand, as you've heard, your *response* can repeat itself forever. You need to get the idea that the *memory* of being hit by a brick will probably remain in your Dependent imagination forever – along with your words."

I frowned. "Which 'words'?"

"The words which drive your Dependent mind: your commentaries and your judgments."

"What you call my set-downs?"

"That's right. Meanwhile you pay little attention to the *real* world."

"But if someone had thrown that brick *on purpose, that* would be real."

The Rector took a breath and paused. "Look," he said, "the *brick's* not dangerous any more. What're ultimately dangerous are your *set-downs*. It's *they* which land you in trouble. What you created in your Instant imagination was an unpleasant experience, but it's over and it's already moved elsewhere – apart, maybe, for your sore head. What you are now *left with* is what you *think and believe about it*."

"Oh? You mean pissed off because I think someone was being irresponsible?"

He grinned. "Quite likely. And yet it was You, the No-self, which decided the brick landing on your head was a good idea."

"I don't see how, especially if someone chucked the brick at me."

"There you are again, looking for someone to blame. Or maybe you believe that the brick fell because of 'bad luck'? It's all the same – misusing your Dependent imagination by adopting fantasy."

"Yet how do you know someone *didn't* throw it?"

"So what? The experience is finished."

"What am I supposed to think instead?"

"Use your Dependent mind differently. Instead of blaming someone, remind yourself 'You' created your own unpleasant experience – whether or not someone threw it. Then you avoid becoming another self-appointed magistrate looking to find someone guilty. I assume you don't like bricks hitting your head?"

"Most amusing, Father. But it wouldn't have been *my* fault I got walloped."

"My child, *that's* what I keep showing you. You're *still* in your habitual courtroom. 'Faults' are for machines. Humans make *mistakes.*"

I screwed up my face.

He waved his hand. "Let's leave it. What I want to emphasise is that any botch-ups you made are automatically uncreated. Even today's mistakes are uncreated."

"Yes, but they exist in my *memory.*"

He sighed. Slowly he said, "My child, nothing *exists* in your memory."

I looked at him. "What? Now hold on, Father, how can you contradict yourself like that? Doctor Frostbight said the whole point of memories is that they can hang about forever."

"Yes ... of course they can, more or less – in our Dependent imagination. But memory doesn't *exist* any more than your Dependent imagination does."

I held my head and shook it. "Father, you're frying my brain. What have we been talking about all night?"

"What exists and what doesn't exist."

I paused. "Oh. I think maybe I'm getting the picture: the Instant imagination exists and the Dependent doesn't?"

He gave me time to think.

"Ah!" I said. "Thoughts can't be weighed or measured?"

"Precisely. They don't have boundaries."

"But, Father," I blurted, "if all the stuff we've talked about tonight doesn't exist, what *is* the Dependent imagination?"

He shrugged and said nothing.

It was difficult to contain myself. "And, I might add, *how come we're talking about it?*"

The Rector remained silent.

"Well?" I pressed.

"Because," he finally said, "neither our thoughts nor imagination need to exist for us to talk about them."

"Oh? They don't, huh?" I hesitated. "Do you realise where this leads?"

"Yes, I expect I do."

"You're claiming that everyone is spending his or her life engaged in an activity which doesn't exist?"

"Uh-huh. That's just about the sum of it."

I shook by head again.

"To be more accurate," he added, "*what* they talk *about* may have existed when it existed, but their thoughts? They never exist."

How confusing could this get? "But," I complained, "the thought that a thought doesn't exist doesn't itself exist!"

"Good man!" exclaimed Frostbight across the table. "You've cracked it."

"Have I?" I asked in exasperation. "Then what *does* exist?"

Von Lottowind answered. "Must we keep repeating, mein Freund? Reality is what is *actually* happening – including the sounds bites of your voice – *only* in this second, even this split second." He paused. "Actually in less than a split second – it is, as we say, continuously instant."

I stopped and considered. "No, Professor," I objected, "it couldn't be *'instant'*"

"Nein?"

"No. Because if it's *'instant'* it's not subject to time, and if it's not subject to time, it can't exist."

"Das is well said." He leant forward and remarked quietly, "but does time exist?"

"Well, yeah, of course it does."

"Have you ever seen it?"

"No ... but I can measure it."

"Ach. You cannot measure *time*. You can only measure the movement of objects through space."

I expelled a long breath. What next? I was beginning to doubt even reality existed. "Is this," I asked, "supposed to be that 'unbounded thinking' you talked about? Because *that* means this conversation isn't really happening!"

He smiled. "It is happening, but it does not exist."

"Whoa!"

"The sound of our voices is happening, but not so the meaning of what we are saying."

Doctor Frostbight broke in. "Gusty," he said to my neighbour, "I think you'd better go steady."

I was not having it. "Hey," I said, "you can't fob me off like that: you lot are nihilists."

"Sorry you think so, old boy."

"It's no use being sorry. If *meaning* doesn't exist, then nothing *matters*." I could feel my temper rising.

"Dear me, does that matter?"

"You bet. *Of course it does.*"

"Splendid. There you have your answer. Thoughts are not just metaphysical: they're immortal. They matter a great deal." He came to a halt. "You know what? I think it's time to move on."

Part VII

❧

Recognising Agency

"P HEW." I WAS SECRETLY PLEASED. "WHERE TO NOW, Doctor? This is a marathon."

"Too much for you, old boy?"

I raised my eyebrows. "Too much? No, no, it's a doddle."

He grinned. "That's the stuff. We know it's a lot to take in; nonetheless, we need to press ahead."

"I gathered that."

"Tip top." He looked to my left. "Padre? Did you want to say something?"

"Thank you, Doctor, I did. Yes, I think we should say a little more about uncreation." He turned to me. "You know, it's a strange thing how we still react today to events we *un*created long ago."

"Do we?" I replied. "What sort of events?"

"I was thinking about traumatic experiences."

"Lord. OK."

"You see, even though, technically, you *un*created the experiences maybe years ago, you recreate your reactions as if they were current. I'm sure, as someone left shocked by the war, you don't need reminding."

"You're telling me, Father. Are you claiming there's something I can do about the shock?"

"Of course there is."

"Well, no, actually, I don't agree with you. How am I supposed to control nightmares? Or panic attacks? Or stop myself breaking out in a cold sweat when someone pops a paper bag?"

The Rector shook his head. "All right. Let's say your problem's not so much that you *can't* control it, but that you don't *know* how to."

I considered it. "Fair enough, but however much I might think of my past as 'uncreated', it wouldn't stop the affects in the present."

"You're right." The Rector tapped his chin absentmindedly. "Your magical theatre freezes you with terror."

I sipped my bramble port. This was difficult. "Father," I replied, "I would hardly call the things I'm terrified of my 'magical theatre'. The attacks scare the shit out of me."

"Good show," chimed in Frostbight.

"Good show, Doctor? What good show?"

"You've hit the nail on the head, old chap. Here, have a top up." He pushed the decanter across the table.

"Have I?"

"Absolutely." While I refilled my glass, he went on. "You've raised the issue of shock – and trauma."

"It wasn't me, it was Father Foggie."

"Was it? Dear me. Anyway, I agree with what you said about the affect. When a shock is re-triggered, the fear can be sudden and savage. Apart from closed minds and rank prejudice, nothing's more difficult to deal with." He stopped and turned to his right. "Gusty you're 'up' on this. What d'you think? Padre, pass the bramble port to Gusty, would you?"

"Thank you, Herr Pastor." Von Lottowind took the decanter from the Rector, poured some of the 'digestif' and addressed me. "In your case, do you suppress the way you respond when you hear a loud noise?"

"Yeah, I try to."

"The original Instant creation has not been properly converted."

"I'm sure it hasn't, but that doesn't tell me anything."

"Nein? It has not been turned into a normal story."

"How's that going to help? Shock is shock. You can't make it into a 'story'."

"Ah! You think of a 'story' as something that is only – how do you say? 'Trite'? Just because it was a harrowing experience does not mean it cannot become your story. Do you not agree, Herr Pastor?"

"I couldn't agree more, Professor." The Pastor addressed me. "As you rightly pointed out, shock *itself* isn't a story. The story is your set-down. The upset – the actual shock – was an experience."

"So?"

"You no doubt need assistance from those who specialise in treating shock. With Creosophy you can, however, sweeten the process."

"By doing what?"

"The same as before: by visualising whatever happened as the invention of your own genius. And bear in mind that if you do find someone to help, that person will *also* be your invention."

"What do you think, old boy?" asked Frostbight. "Shock's a tough subject, and I hope we'll come back to it. What we're pushing is the idea that, *whatever's* happened, you always were and always are its agent." He stopped to consider. "I think we'd better turn down the heat and look at easier stuff."

I was quietly relieved. "Like what?" I asked.

The German answered. "You may take any daily experience."

"Such as?"

"You go to the cinema? Or to the theatre? Ja?"

"Yeah, when I have the chance."

"Good. You must understand that it is You who creates the entertainment."

"Oh yeah?"

The Reverend Foggie joined in. "Or what about this? Would I be right in thinking that you enjoy classical music?"

"Yes, Father, very much."

"Well, the next time you go to a concert, hold in your mind that You composed it – and played it."

I still found this kind of talk loopy. "Father, now you're pretending I'm *Mozart*? I can't write a note of music – nor play an instrument."

"Calm, my son, calm. Think outside the box."

"I *am* thinking outside the box."

"It takes practice. In time you'll get more used to the view that the entire world's your creation, whether it's a case of shock or of listening to music. No, of course you're not Mozart: you are you. But the You who created your self also creates every composer, including Mozart; and not just him, but also all the music ever written – and the musicians who perform it. You conceive them and recreate them every time you listen. Remember that when you next go to a concert. You might find the performance engaging."

"Huh," I commented. "I'm sure I will!"

The Rector waved a hand. "Look at the stars," he said, " … if it's not too cloudy."

"It usually *is* too cloudy – in this country."

"I know, but whatever you're looking at, clouds or stars, say to yourself, 'they're in the sky because I put them there'. And at sunrise – if you're up early – say, 'it's rising because I'm making it come up'. You may discover a new relationship to nature."

I was nonplussed. "Father, if you don't mind my saying, I thought earlier that it would be a *joke* if you ended up telling me I made the sun rise."

"That's where you need practice," he replied casually, "until the idea becomes normal."

Part VIII

 ❧

The New Vision

"**A**LL RIGHT, FATHER," I RESUMED, "BUT AS ENTERTAINING as it is, I don't see why my thinking like that would make a difference."

"No? Well, firstly it'll help you to keep your emotions level."

"It will? OK, I admit that'd be good."

"Yes. If you're worried or nervous, remind yourself time and again that everything is *exactly* how it's meant to be because *you're* the one creating it. Ultimately, you're always in control of every experience – even if it doesn't seem like it."

"But not if I'm, say, depressed."

"The same goes if you're depressed. You created it. Remind yourself again that, behind the scenes, *you're* the one in charge. Thanks to You, and *only* thanks to You, *everything* is *exactly* as it should be."

"Phew. Hard to imagine. It really helps?"

"I can recommend it." He lowered his specs and regarded me. "My son, don't get the idea that we, here, are immune from getting discouraged. We need to apply this as much as you."

"Oh?" I made a face. "I thought you lot were super humans!"

He grinned. "I don't know what made you think that. By the way, I might also add you can use these thoughts to enhance enjoyable experiences."

"I can? Like what?"

"Well, when you're having sex."

"Sex? Do you mean that?"

"I do. It, as you might say, 'livens up' the experience. When in the act, you remind yourself, 'this is my own brilliant invention'."

"What?" I could not hide my surprise. "You, *having sex*, Father?"

"What's the matter?"

"Aren't you celibate?"

"Who said? What makes you think I haven't had a life?"

I made a face and shrugged.

"I used to be married," he explained. "I lost my wife and child in an air raid four years ago."

"Oh, dear." I lowered my eyes and my voice. "I'm so sorry to hear that."

He went on. "Our having a long life together wasn't to be, but at a time like that, when I needed help, Creosophy was invaluable. My framing the world as my own creation got me through the bad times – and helped with the better ones when they came." He looked across at the German. "Your family, Professor? Have you heard anything?"

"Unfortunately not, Herr Pastor."

The Rector returned to me. "You see, he doesn't know where any of his family are, or even if they're alive. I'm pointing it out in case you think we've all had an easy ride. But right now, what about a typical, everyday troubles? Any thoughts?"

I was silent for a while. "Well," I replied, "one thing I hate is being criticised."

"Ah! You mentioned criticism not long ago. Did you deserve it?"

"No. I mean when I *didn't* deserve it."

"And it was definitely a *real* criticism – not just, as you said, a 'tone of voice'?"

"Absolutely no doubt, Father."

"Then it was a bum bit of creating. If you were a Creosophist you'd remember."

"Remember what?"

"That the person being rude to you would be following *your* script which *you* had 'given' him."

I couldn't help smiling at his 'bum creation', and idly toyed with my port glass. "I want to accuse you," I replied, "for making me take the blame for anything that goes wrong in my life – only I know the Professor will swoop down on me with his 'court metaphors'."

"Well done, my child, you're getting wise. Now, one more thing …"

I grimaced. "There seem to be a lot of 'one more things'."

"Are we tiring you?"

"No, no. Go on. I'm fine – well, sort of."

He nodded. "I'm pleased. Now, I was about to ask you: what's worse than a shitty experience?"

"I'm sorry, Father?"

"I said, what's worse than a shitty experience?"

When I shrugged, he lowered his specs again. "The answer, my son, is a shitty *response*."

"Huh, clever." I paused. "Are you referring to the way I usually react to criticism?"

He waved a finger. "Exactly. And you know what?"

"No?"

"You *really believe* in your response!"

"Huh? Yes, of course I do."

"Well, *that's* what 'suffering' is all about. OK, enough – it's nothing new. Right now I want to point out that it's pretty easy to see *pleasant* occurrences as something you've created. But *un*pleasant experiences – like for me when I heard about my family? That's different. It was a hard task seeing their deaths as something I'd fabricated."

"Gosh, I bet. That was terrible they were killed." I felt bad hearing about his loss. Nevertheless, there was something else I wanted to clear up. After a moment I turned back to the German. "Professor, for all the talk about life being a struggle, what about people who think life's a bowl of cherries – and *don't* find it either hostile *or* dangerous?"

"Das is well said. They may well not be interested in this discussion."

"That's what I thought."

"Ja. There is hidden value in 'struggles' and 'suffering'."

"Such as?"

"It makes the sufferer ask questions."

"And they're the only ones who benefit?"

"Nein. *Everyone* could benefit – if they want. As Pastor Foggie said, seeing the universe as your own creation enhances pleasant experiences."

I took a sip of my drink and mulled over these matters. "So, Professor, if I see life your way, things won't go wrong any more? No more shocks?"

"Ah, mein Freund, we have answered that already. Your magic show will still generate unpleasant experiences – many of them. Please understand: they keep you bescheiden."

"Besch *what?*"

The Rector translated. "He means unpleasant experiences keep you from getting too cocky."

"Oh." Silence followed. The wind was still at the windows, but I didn't think it was so fierce. As for my head, it was tossing about with ideas – mixed with bramble port.

Our host ended my reverie when he sent the decanter on another round. "Here, have a top-up, old boy."

It was lucky I didn't need to drive my car. I poured just a little more into my glass and pushed the decanter to my left. "You know, Doctor," I said, "I was imagining my going home and saying to my friends, 'Hey, your life, even the ghastly bits, are your creation. Oh, and by the way, you created Mozart.' They would have me sectioned."

"And if, old boy," Frostbight replied, "you did end up in a psychiatric ward, it's because *you* would have created it. Anyhow, you don't *have* to tell *anyone*. It may well not be appropriate. Consider it private, unless someone asks."

"So, Doctor, why're you telling *me?*"

"Because you *did* ask – when you arrived."

"Oh, yes, so I did."

"Whatever happens," he went on, "you can use this evening's discussion how you want. It's like life: you can treat it as entertainment and then forget about it – which you're more than likely to do. On the other hand, you can treat it as a lesson and an inspiration to put into practice." He stopped. "This is a long session. Let's give it a rest for a mo'. There's something on my mind."

"Ah," cut in the Professor, "I believe I know what it is."

"I bet you do, Gusty: we haven't had the Loyal Toast. Need a refill? Padre, pass the Professor the port, would you?"

Loyal
Toast

Part I

☙

Victims?

"**D**ON'T LOOK SO WORRIED, OLD MAN," OUR HOST SAID TO me. He signalled discreetly to Mould, and, while the decanter was making its way round the table, the butler limped to a mahogany cabinet between two of the windows. To my surprise, he opened its doors and raised the top to reveal a gramophone. I waited while he bent over, wound the handle, checked the needle and then, once he saw we were ready, lowered the arm onto the disk.

As soon as the speaker picked up the record's crackle, Doctor Frostbight adjusted his smoking cap and rose from the table. "Gentlemen," he commanded, "please be upstanding."

Father Foggie and the Professor obediently scraped back their chairs and stood at attention. I followed suit. The record burst into life with trumpets and a thunder of drum rolls followed by an all male choir bellowing God Save Our Gracious King, loud enough I imagined, for Mrs. McWhiteout to hear in the kitchen.

The National Anthem's first stentorian verse drew to its close. Our host turned and held up his hand. "Right-ho, Mould. That'll do."

The butler pushed the 'off' lever.

In the hush Doctor Frostbight picked up his glass and raised it. I did likewise.

"The King!" he announced.

"The King!" we chorused, and downed our port.

I was glad we were toasting the 'King' – although I wondered which King they had in mind.

"Right," beamed our host while we resumed our seats. "Time to relax. Now, where were we?"

With my worldview being turned upside down, it wasn't so easy to feel 'relaxed'. I spoke up. "Doctor, can we go back to what we were talking about a little while ago?"

"Certainly. Go on, old chap."

"I'm not saying there haven't been good times for me, but as you've guessed, I've had all kinds of shocks in childhood and again later in adulthood, to say nothing of what happened during the war. Life's no pleasure trip."

"I understand," he said. "That's why we're suggesting a 180 degree change of view."

"I say, how awfully modern."

"I know, I know. I dislike it as much as you. Still, I want to be candid. At the time you were shocked, you saw yourself as the victim of people, circumstance, divine justice, bad luck or anything else you chose."

"Well, yes, I was the victim of *something*."

"No. You were shocked because you gave it to *yourself*."

"But I *didn't*."

He leant towards me. "Look, old boy, nobody is ever at the mercy of anything other than themselves."

"It's easy for you to say that," I replied morosely, "but I *was* a victim."

He sat back and sighed. "How many times do we have to go over this? Whatever you *created* happened. *That* was the 'Instant' experience."

"Yeah, and nobody can change that."

"No, nobody can change that. However, as we go on telling you, 'I'm a victim' *is a story – victims don't 'happen'*. They have to be invented – by you." He stopped and idly nosed his port. "You know what?"

I looked at him. "What? Don't like the port?"

"Most amusing." He put down his glass. "No, I'm thinking of my late wife and what she used to say about what stands between a man and his peace of mind."

"What does?"

"His voice."

"Oh?"

"Yes. Odd, don't you think?"

"Odd? I should say so: we weren't talking about voices."

"No? Well, we are now. Vocal chords: if there were no such things there would be no words and therefore no thoughts; and with no thoughts there would be no stories, and without stories there'd be no 'victims' and, incidentally, life would have no meaning. How about that?"

"I don't know. What's wrong with my vocal chords?"

"Nothing," he smiled. "They're fine. The point is words inform and modify every aspect of experience. We all of us have a variety of experiences over the years, yet it's our voices that deal with the set-downs: and it's they which really matter, as you know only too well. We live more in a world of words than anything else, and this dinner party is no exception. Simple as that."

"So why do we suffer?"

"Just as I've said: through the incompetent use of words."

"Sounds good to me," I mocked. "Sort out what I say, and bingo! No more problems from now on?"

He shook his head. "If only! But it's a good start. Remember that problems are not necessarily a problem. You *need problems* just as you need friction to light a match. On the other hand, vocalising rotten stories, now that *is* a problem."

"What do you mean?"

"That's your way of stirring up foul feelings."

"Humph. Is it? What in particular?"

"Fear and shame come to mind. Remember about being either the 'agent' or the 'patient'?"

"Of course – you keep bringing it up."

"Excellent. Now you, in *your* stories about life, put yourself in the role of 'patient'."

"When?"

"When you say that life's a struggle or when people criticise you. Or when you claim they don't love you or don't appreciate you or don't respect you. Then you drum up stories to persuade people you're a victim."

"But," I mumbled, "I might well have been ..."

"No, no, *no*! You were *not* a victim. What happened happened. Nothing

271

more. The idea that you're a '*victim*' is simply the set-down description you've chosen. In other words, it's the 'spin' *you* freely decided to put on the original upset. Do you see?"

"Mmm … possibly."

And *then* what do you do?"

"Me, Doctor? I'd call myself a 'survivor' instead."

He sighed. "We've gone nowhere."

"Yes, we have. It's much better than saying I'm a 'victim'."

He shook his head again. "You've gone nowhere because you're *still* not *the agent* of the event."

"Oh."

"And you know what you end up doing – apart from telling yourself self-destructive stories?"

"Me? No?"

He waved a finger at me. "You create distractions."

"Do I? Like what?"

"You take to drugs; or turn to drink, or get hung up on addictions or eating disorders; or you keep constantly busy or you overwork; or you take unnecessary risks or maybe you just get angry and slam the door. You name it."

"Hey, I don't do those things – at least not all of them."

"No, I'm sure you don't, but do you get the picture?"

"Sort of. So what would make a difference?"

"*Tell better stories.*"

"Oh. As easy as that?" I stopped to run it over in my head. "Yeah," I said, "it's great as an idea, but I wouldn't know where to begin."

"It's not difficult, old chap – although I'd admit it needs cultivating. The starting place is the same, and guess what it is?"

"You mean stop using the language of being a patient?"

"Tip top. Tell stories where you're the agent. And you would do that by …?"

"Recognising that my life's my creation?"

"Top marks. You know how to begin perfectly well. See how easy it is?" He paused, took up his glass, sat back and, with a twinkle, asked, "so, old boy, how are you getting on?"

"I'd like to say 'fine', but I suspect there's more."

"Absolutely." He turned to his neighbour. "Gusty, I think you wanted to say something."

"Das is so," replied the German. "There is certainly 'more' … including, I believe, more chocolate?" He looked enquiringly at the dish.

"More chocolate, Gusty? Of course. So sorry. I'm glad you're enjoying it." He pushed the plate towards him. "Here, pass it round."

Von Lottowind selected one and pushed the rest across the table to me. "As you have seen, Mein Freund," he stated, "the distinction between what is and what is not can be elusive." He lifted his napkin to wipe a piece of chocolate from the corner of his mouth. "We did not finish," he continued, "talking of shock. I have a question for you …"

"Ugh," I grumbled, "another?"

Part II

ꕥ

The Hammer Syndrome

"Y OU ARE SURPRISED? NO MATTER. IT IS THIS. WHAT keeps reactivating past shocks?"

I grimaced. "Lord. Search me, Professor. I thought we had dealt with that. The Doctor would claim it comes from telling stupid stories."

"Ja, maybe, but what else? What *emotions?*"

"Emotions? I don't know." I reflected. "Fear? Or if I had been abused, a combination of fear and shame?"

"Das is most likely. What keeps fear and shame alive?"

"Well, Sigmund Freud said it was suppressed childhood memories, but I bet you'll tell me that's twoddle."

"'Twoddle'? What ist?"

"Nothing, Professor, just slang."

"Ah, slang. Das is good. You are correct that they are memories, but what is it you remember?"

"The shock, of course."

"Ach. You remember a belief *in response* the shock. I wish to stress, it is the belief which locks you into the shock."

"Huh. Beliefs *again?*"

"Ja. And I wish to talk of those stories – or your beliefs – that mark you as the 'patient'."

"Humph, back to stories. You mean where I make out I'm vulnerable?"

"Das is so. Distress arises when you are convinced you both helpless and in exceptional danger. It is a toxic cocktail."

"A toxic cocktail? Goodness. What if I were helpless and safe?"

"If you were helpless and safe, that would be neutral. And if you were in danger, even mortal danger, but knew you could handle it, that would be fine – you might even find it stimulating. But when you believe you are both helpless *and* in mortal danger, then you are set up for the Hammer Syndrome."

"Oh my God. The *what* Syndrome?"

The butler interrupted us. "A little coffee, Sir?"

"I should say so, Mould. I could do with a bigger cup."

"You wish for a larger cup, Sir?"

"No, no, just joking. Yes, please, I'd love some."

While the butler poured me some coffee, von Lottowind resumed. "I understand you are not familiar with the Hammer Syndrome?"

"Don't know the Hammer Syndrome, old boy?" interjected Frostbight.

"No, Doctor, actually, I don't."

"Well, it's the old Chinese idea: if the only tool you have is a hammer, everything looks like a nail."

"Oh," I replied brightly as I helped myself to sugar, "like a conspiracy theory?"

"Sorry? What's that?"

"You know: if someone demonstrates a conspiracy theory is nonsense, then he's assumed be part of it."

"Jolly good show. It's just the kind of thing, although I wasn't thinking of that. What the Professor had in mind about the Hammer Syndrome is that if you suffer shock and that shock is not converted to a story, *anything* resembling the initial trauma tricks you into being a 'patient'."

"Humph," I responded again. "You mean like going into a cold sweat when there's a loud bang?"

"Ah, you are correct," came in the German. "It is the same for many such situations – such as if you faint at the sight of blood or when someone describes their hospital operation. The story will re-enact an old shock, whatever it was: you are locked in the Hammer Syndrome."

"Why? Because of memories resurfacing?"

"Nein. *Not* because of memories. Because of your *belief*."

I rubbed my neck. "What belief? I'm still not getting it."

"Nein? Let us take a different example. Supposing you were a woman who had been molested when a child."

"Goodness, that's pretty extreme, but OK let's go with it."

"It is 'extreme', but I remind you that Creosophy is not just intellectual entertainment. Now, as I was about to say, any time you came to sexual intimacy, the Hammer Syndrome could kick in. You would find yourself in 'patient' mode, *believing* your lover was dangerous."

"But that's totally irrational."

"No, no, it is perfectly rational."

"Well, if you ask me it's irrational."

"Nein. There is no such thing as an irrational belief."

I raised my eyebrows. "I'm sorry, Professor? Say that again?"

"People call their phobias 'irrational'. They are nothing of the sort. It is important to honour your fears: all beliefs are perfectly reasonable at some level, or you would not believe them. The difficulty is you *believe* your beliefs."

"Humph. All right, put like that, I can't argue. But *why* are beliefs such a big deal?"

"Because your beliefs hold you captive. I might also add, your fears also hold your beliefs captive. That is the Hammer Syndrome. Now, I want to say this: the *memory* is in the past – and you can do nothing about the past – but your *beliefs* are in the *present*, and you *can* do something about *them*." He paused while he sipped his coffee. "May I ask you a question?"

"Do I have a choice?"

He frowned. "At the moment, what happens when you suffer your panic attack – in your case, when, perhaps, you felt faint at a clap of thunder?"

"Gosh, I don't know. I try to pull myself together."

"Das is correct. You chastise yourself for being weak, fearful, irrational or whatever."

"Sometimes. I might also try to calm myself."

"Ja, and you know how little effect that has."

"Yes, but what else *can* I do?"

"For you to change your reaction, you need a strategy."

"Yeah, tell me another!"

"Another?" he asked. "Another what?"

I sighed. "Pay no attention, Professor. What were you saying?"

"I wished to say," he went on, "you need to identify the beliefs you are holding."

"Yeah, I hear you, but I wouldn't know what they were – they're unconscious."

He leant forward and studied me. "Mein Freund, they are not 'unconscious'. If they were unconscious you would not respond to them. You know *exactly* what they are."

"No, I don't."

"Ach, you do. You simply have not articulated them."

"Then what are they?"

"You believe someone or something is attacking you and is about to hurt you – maybe kill you."

"Do I?"

He straightened. "Of course. And that is why it is perfectly reasonable to be afraid. You believe you are both in danger and absolutely helpless – a patient. *That* is the toxic cocktail."

"Gosh. All right, I agree that sort of thing would get me fainting." So I asked, "What am I supposed to do?"

Take to thinking differently."

"So you lot keep saying."

"Turn onto a different road."

"I *did* turn onto a different road. So what?"

"Change your 'set-downs'."

"No doubt. That tells me nothing."

"I say it in other words. Whatever your beliefs, you must 'reframe' your *overview* of what happened. If you can remember the original shock, stop framing it as either 'bad luck' or someone's 'bad behaviour'."

"And ...?"

"Remind yourself that while it is completely reasonable to be afraid, the event itself was your invention in the first place."

"Oh. Then what?"

"Then make your story more useful: maybe it was an experiment – your own experiment – that misfired. What is your expression in English? You 'screwed up'? Maybe, as Watty said, you bungled your creation – and scared yourself to hell."

"You're telling me!"

"It is so. You shocked *yourself*. Or maybe you wanted to experiment to see how you would *react* to the event. Maybe you needed a shock to make you re-evaluate you life. But whatever the reason or whatever the shock, you are *never* the victim of a hostile universe. *That*," he added gravely, "would be a poor story indeed."

"Goodness me, Professor." I looked around the table. "Maybe I need one of those chocolates."

The Rector passed me the plate.

"Thank you, Father. I think, Professor," I admitted as I took one, "I've got a long way to go." I paused for a moment. "But what about this? If an infant needs a hospital operation and the operation's for his own good, that is what he needs; and yet it may traumatise him for life. You *can't* say someone of that age has made some sort of 'hash' of his creation."

"A hash?"

"You know: a cock up." I saw his expression. "All right, all right, a mess. A shambles. You know what I mean."

"Ah so. Das is good. However there are no exceptions, even if you were very young. Life is your creation from conception to the grave."

"Huh. It's a tough nut to crack."

"A 'tough nut'?"

"Oh, just another saying, Professor …"

Part III

⌘

Death

"MM …" MURMURED THE GERMAN. "I HAVE ANOTHER question."

"You have? What?"

"It is this. What is the worst affliction that ails mankind?"

"*Another* affliction?" I groaned. "Haven't we had enough? I thought you said it was self-hatred."

"I did?" the Prussian replied with a grin. "Ah, that is certainly bad, but I have changed my mind." He went on. "The worst plague for mankind, mein Freund, is a *belief* – the false belief that we are helpless."

I considered it for a moment. "You're certainly pushing this thing about beliefs. I'm sorry, but I don't think you're right. What about when a loved one dies? We *are* helpless, beliefs or no beliefs."

"Das is so. Indeed your *physical self is* 'helpless'. However, as Pastor Foggie told you, when you become familiar with Creosophy you will react differently in times of sorrow."

"I will? But that doesn't stop me being helpless when someone dies."

"Ah, you must observe that whoever or whatever you first created and then 'lost', nothing happened by accident. I repeat: you invent life and death – both yours and that of others." His eyebrows twitched. "Mein Freund," he said with apparent seriousness, "your life is an example of German engineering."

He saw my surprise.

"Your life," he said, his smile growing, "is *precise* and *efficient*."

"Huh, Professor. *Highly* entertaining."

The Reverend Foggie interrupted. "You must excuse him," he said to me. "The Professor has odd ways of describing things. Anyway, further to what he explained, another way of looking at it is that people don't just 'die'."

"I beg your pardon, Father. They certainly do."

"No, what I mean is everyone puts *him or herself* to death – sooner or later."

"Not if they're murdered."

"Yes, even if they're murdered. We create our own lives, and we create our own deaths."

"Phew. Alternative or what?"

The clergyman made no reply.

I drew in a breath and blew a silent whistle. "Well, whatever …"

"You'll get the hang of it all in good time," he said. "Meanwhile, I too have a question."

"Oh yes, Father? No shortage of those."

"There certainly aren't. So, where," he asked, "is yesterday?"

"What? Yesterday? What's that got to do with it?"

"You'll see. Where is it?"

"*I* don't know. The question's crackers. Yesterday's gone. It isn't anywhere."

"You're right. It's died."

"Oh? I didn't know days 'died'."

"They do, in that you've uncreated them."

"Oh, I get what you're saying: back to the 'uncreation' stuff."

"That's right: uncreation is the flip side of creation. Creation can't exist without it. Think of your body: yesterday's body has changed and gone. It's no more. My son, you're 'dead' to yesterday – the past – and every day of your life, and you've not yet noticed it."

"You're right," I commented with a touch of sarcasm, "I hadn't."

"So, my son, what about the future?"

"The future? You tell me."

The Padre scrutinised me. "You're only alive now – today – that's it. By tomorrow *today* will be dead."

"Huh," I muttered, "I suppose that's *one* way of looking it."

"Yes, it is. It helps to see how death is a constant in your life – not just something at the end of it. When your body finally comes to an end, it'll simply be a death in a lifetime of deaths."

"Lord." I realised I was rubbing my neck again.

"Look on the bright side," he said. "If ever you find yourself frightened of dying, remind yourself you're an expert at it."

"Well, I'm glad to hear it." I took a little port and thought. "But what about the war? What about the friends of mine who were killed?"

"Mein Freund," came in von Lottowind, "it is time for you to learn that the untimely death of someone was *not* 'bad luck', nor 'random'. It was *your intention* that they died."

"*My* intention? Oh, come on, Professor, you're making out I'm some kind of evil creature going about getting friends killed."

"Nein, you are no evil creature. I say again: during your life, the 'You-who-you-do-not-know', creates friends – and family – for your self, and also uncreates them sooner or later."

"You must not forget," added the Padre, "that just because you're creating the world, doesn't mean it's going to be 'perfect' – whatever that may mean." On seeing my expression, he paused. "Yes, I realise it's an unusual 'take' on life."

I felt my temperature rise. "I should say so. Try telling this sort of stuff to a child who's parents have committed suicide! Or what about a young woman who's husband has been killed on honeymoon? Or a community that's been devastated by an earthquake?"

Von Lottowind remarked again. "Telling this to those people? Did we suggest it?"

"No, Professor, you didn't," I rebutted. "But what do you expect me to do?"

"It would be disrespectful to speak to them in this manner."

"Well, then ..." My voice faded.

"Mein Freund, the Creosophist mindset is only for all those who want a bigger perspective on life. It is for those who have had enough confusion; enough sorrowing; enough fearing and enough worrying."

His feelings took me aback.

"You do not expect me to say these things? Ja, your *self* is helpless when a loved one dies, but the original '*You*' is never so." He quietened. "Herr Pastor? Do you recall the prayer of Heiliges Francis?"

"The prayer of who?" replied the Cleric.

Our host interrupted. "Mould'll know. Mould?"

"Sir?"

"Are you up on the prayer of Heiliges Francis?"

"Francis of Assisi, Sir?"

"Ah, yes, that'll be the chap."

"In that case, it was indeed a fine prayer."

"I've no doubt, but do you remember it?"

"I do, Sir."

"Well come on, how does it go?"

"It goes thus: 'Lord, may you show me in what way I am helpless, and in what way I am not; and be granted wisdom to know the difference."

It was an interesting prayer. Mould's version wasn't how I recalled it, but maybe I was splitting hairs.

The Professor had more to say to me. "Perhaps this will help. Imagine your consciousness is a cine camera making a film of your life. Even if the story on the screen is of bereavement, grief, shame or fear, the *camera* is perfectly safe and happy."

"By that you mean *I'm* perfectly safe and happy?"

"Ja. Maybe your local self *is* helpless, but the camera – the You who is doing the filming – suffers neither loss nor is in danger."

"Huh. Sounds like I'm living in two worlds at once."

The Doctor stepped in. "That's a good observation. Look, there's nothing new about this: people even sing about it. Do you remember the words, 'Years cannot age you; fear cannot scare you; pain cannot hurt you; death cannot kill you'? Sorry to say I can't recall who wrote it."

"A poet by the name of Gary Nicholson, Sir," came the butler's voice from the corner of the room.

Our host looked round. "My word, Mould. Excellent memory." He turned to me. "You see?"

I said nothing.

Part IV

ↄ

Poisonous Beliefs

ALL WENT QUIET FOR A WHILE. FROSTBIGHT WAS STROKING his moustache. Then his eyebrows rose briefly. "Let's," he said, "return to beliefs."

I groaned. "Surely we're done with beliefs?"

"Afraid not, old boy. You'll see why. What're your most deadly ones?"

"For goodness sake, you're like the Professor: it's no good asking me."

"Of course – silly question. What I had in mind was that the worst ones are those you turn against *yourself.*"

"Oh. Haven't we been there already?"

"Maybe, but you need to get wise to the poison of beliefs. Like almost everyone, you're riddled with abusive beliefs about yourself; and likewise, but even worse, they're so habitual they're invisible."

"For example, what?"

"An example? Imagine someone," he said, "who thinks he or she's 'ugly' for some reason – you know the sort of thing: 'wrong sort of body', 'too fat', 'too thin', 'too spotty', 'nose too big' …"

"All right."

"It's that sort of self-belittlement I'm talking about. Now, the point is you can *believe* you're ugly, but you can't *be* ugly."

"Why not? Of course I can be ugly."

"You're not listening. We've already said, it's a *belief* – not a fact. The same goes for depression. If you feel 'low' or whatever, that's what you feel. But if you say, 'I'm depressed', that's a belief. *Neither ugliness nor depression can be seen by the naked eye.*" He waved his hand. "So there you have it, old chap. Don't say I didn't tell you!"

"But, Doctor," I persisted, "supposing it were *true* I was ugly?"

I had no sooner said these words than Professor von Lottowind smashed his fist on the table. I jumped in my seat. He glared from under his eyebrows and growled, "*How many times do we have to tell you there is no 'truth'? 'Truth' is only another belief.*" Then he settled back and sipped his port as though nothing had happened.

My heart fluttered. Doctor Frostbight cupped his hand against his mouth as though the German could not hear him. "He livens up the old shock response, eh, what? Now, where were we? Ah, yes, you can always remove the idea of ugly. It's never more than a belief, and beliefs don't exist."

"Ugh! It's all right for *you* to say that."

"Relax. It's obvious once you get used to it."

I took a breath. "So what's this got to do with my battling against myself?"

"Don't you see, old chap? Your attacking yourself is a total spoof: you're attacking something that doesn't exist."

I frowned. "Is that right?"

"Trust me. *None* of what you accuse yourself of is actually real."

"If it's not, then what is it?"

"It's a stage; drama; theatre; a show business. Call it what you will."

"Oh."

The clergyman took up the reins. "What about another example?"

"Phew. Thank you, Father. I could do with it."

"Well, I'm not going for a trite illustration. Take this. Supposing you were a woman who'd been raped?"

"Crikey. OK."

"What do you think you would *believe* about yourself?"

"Gosh, how do you expect me to know?"

"Fair enough. As we've said, you would no doubt call yourself a 'victim' or a 'survivor'."

"Yeah, I would."

"Now, both words demonstrate the deadly cocktail of shock: the combination of being, at the time, helpless and in danger – and in this case humiliated as well."

"And that's that?"

"Not at all. The psychological system goes into a kind of vicious cycle. Anything remotely resembling the original danger ignites the sense of helplessness, and the sense of helplessness confirms the idea of danger. You may remain locked in the Hammer Syndrome for the rest of your life."

"Ugh! Awful. So I'd be stuck?"

"Yes. But there're ways to extricate yourself – if you wanted."

I took a little of the bramble port in preparation for a lecture. "All right, Father. Fire off."

"I'm sorry if it sounds like a sermon. How're you going to learn otherwise? There's one way to extricate yourself – and it's the *same as always.*"

"And I suppose I can guess what …"

"I'm sure you can. You *must* visualise that, however horrible, what happened was the work of *your own genius.*"

I took a moment to consider. "Well," I commented, "it's damned stupid 'genius'."

"Let's say it was a misjudgement."

"God, I should say so."

"Think about it, my son. Shock, shame, terror, trauma, panic … you're the conjurer."

I took a breath. This was certainly a curious attitude to life.

"Doing all right, old chap?" enquired our host.

"I'm not sure."

"That's why we keep going over it. Never mind, do your best. There's more."

"No surprises there."

He grinned. "You ready?"

"Not really, but plunge in anyway."

"Good show. You see, if you got yourself abused, don't ask me why you would have made it happen – that's for you to decide – but the sooner you stop attacking *yourself* and see that the set-up was your own idea and your own responsibility, the sooner you can convert your *set-down* into a story from the past – where it should be."

The Rector joined in. "Let's look at it this way: is there anything else you would believe about yourself?"

I fiddled with my glass for a moment. "You mean if I'd been raped?"

"Yes."

"Well, I would probably think I were 'soiled goods', or guilty and probably shameful."

"Precisely. That would be you attacking yourself again. And for good measure you might add that you were also 'ugly' or 'worthless' or whatever, in order to push shame down your own throat."

"Huh, a colourful way of putting it. But *why*?"

"Why what?"

"Why would I shame *myself*?"

"Because the rapist was externalising his own drama – that is, his *own* shame. It was a power play, and it's worked: he's infected you."

"Huh. So can I get *out* of it?"

"To get yourself out of the cycle, it's vital you *see* that the courtroom beliefs we talked about are *theatre* – and that includes 'soiled goods'."

"Yeah? I would hardly call it 'theatre'."

"But it is. 'Dirty', 'soiled goods', 'worthless', 'damaged' are the same as 'ugly': they don't exist. It's amateur dramatics, *invisible to everyone* except the sufferer." He paused for a moment to reflect. "You see, being convinced of *any* belief is a misuse of your imagination." He adjusted his specs and turned to our host. "Doctor, what's the name of that woman who teaches that it's beliefs that're behind suffering?"

Part V

☙

The Self-made Prison

"HAVEN'T A CLUE, PADRE." FROSTBIGHT LOOKED TO the butler at attention beside the mantelpiece. "Mould? Who teaches it's beliefs that create suffering?"

The butler put his fist to his mouth and cleared his throat. "In this instance, Sir, I suspect the Reverend has Ms. Byron Katie in mind."

"Oh? 'Byron' as in 'Lord Byron'?"

"Indeed, Sir."

"Then don't you mean Katie Byron?"

"No, Sir. I mean Byron Katie."

"Huh? Jolly queer name, Mould."

"She's American, Sir."

"Ha! That explains it. So, Padre, there you have the answer. Katie Byron. I mean Byron Katie."

I butted in, not being sure if Katie Byron or Byron Katie was real. "Never mind who said what," I objected, "beliefs are part and parcel of daily life."

Doctor Frostbight looked at me intently from across the table. "Be suspicious of them, old boy – very suspicious."

"I don't see why."

"No? After all we've said? Try these, none of which exist: 'I'm a failure'; 'he or she doesn't love me'; 'you can't trust people'; 'I'm alone'; 'I'm worthless'; 'I don't have enough money'; 'my boss, my parents, my husband or my children don't appreciate me'; 'the government's no good'; 'money's evil'; 'Hitler's evil'; 'infidels are evil'; 'it's bad luck to walk under a ladder'; 'I'm suffering'; 'it's unfair'; 'life's meaningless ...' The list goes on forever."

"All right. Fine. I see what you mean. But how do you know some aren't true?"

"Aren't you getting it? They're spoofs."

"*All* of them?"

"Yes, all of them. Let's take another example." He ran his finger over his moustache. "What about this? Say the woman who was molested as a child belittles herself with self-loathing ..."

"Gosh, back to that. All right."

"The self-loathing is an almost universal set down, and it's strictly her decision: nobody else on Earth can see it. It's a belief that's madness or, as Gusty said earlier, it's a disease."

"Yeah, but it's an obvious response."

"Of course it is, but that's not the point. In order for you to be shameful, you *have to believe it*."

"But *why* would that person humiliate herself?"

"It's self-aggression in reaction to shock."

"I'm sorry?"

"She was helpless during the attack. And because she couldn't fend off the attacker, the unfulfilled retaliation turns inward and she abuses *herself* instead."

"And so she ends up with a battle metaphor?"

"Yes, and the same could happen if she had been excessively criticised in childhood. Her life becomes a 'struggle' to counterbalance her failure to defend herself. And *that* can result in all kinds of aggressive behaviours: self-harm, anger, eating disorders, sexual dysfunction, you name it."

"But *why?*"

"Because her rotten beliefs have lost her her sense of safety in society."

"Ugh!" I exclaimed. "That's miserable."

"It is. We're back again to mistaken identity."

"What, you mean the *real* culprit is what she *believes* – about herself?"

"Well done. Yes, the belief that she's shameful. And yet we have the same old story: *'shame' is never an actual thing.*"

"Fair enough, I'm getting the idea."

"Good man. The same goes for 'I'm ugly'; 'I'm a slut'; 'I'm worthless'; 'I'm bad'; 'I'm a failure'; 'I'm depressed'. They're *all of them* a load of ghastly fiction. And I might add this: while humiliating of *others* with that sort of fiction is cruel, doing it to *yourself* is a disaster."

I took a deep breath. "Goodness. Heady stuff."

"It is. I'm sorry about that. Want to keep going?"

"Yeah, Doctor – having got this far."

"Good choice. So now maybe you can see what I meant when I said that the way you *describe* yourself can make or break you." He paused and sniffed his port. "But you know what's extraordinary?"

"A leading question?"

He grinned. "It could be. As with all beliefs, self-criticism isn't even clever."

"But it could be honest."

"Never. We've said it before: it's a destructive behaviour *you've copied from others.* Whatever you do: *distrust your beliefs.*"

There was a moment's silence. "But Doctor," I objected again, "beliefs aren't all *that* bad. I mean, what about things like 'beauty'? According to you, *that's* also a belief and therefore a spoof. And *that* means nobody's beautiful."

"Ah," he replied, "it's not that you can't *call* someone beautiful. That's fine so as long as you know it's theatre, and that beauty's not something that *exists* out there."

"So it can never be true that someone's beautiful?"

"That's right."

"Then you're saying it's a lie?"

"Nope. It can't be a lie either. If there's no truth, there's no lie. Look … all these things people say about being beautiful is nothing to do with 'truth'."

"No? So what is it about?"

"It's about colouring your life … only this time, with a brighter palette and a healthier script." He paused to take a little port. "Maybe this would help: are you clear about the difference?"

Part VI

❧

Prose, Poetry and Beliefs

I LOOKED AT THE DOCTOR. "I BEG YOUR PARDON? THE DIFFERENCE between what?"

"Between prose and poetry."

I smiled. "I suspect you're about to tell me."

"Good man. So I am. Let's have a look."

"All right. Into the deep end ..."

"Excellent. Now, take the statement, 'he's a man'."

"Go on ..."

"Note that it's prose. It's neutral and describes something in your Instant imagination."

"OK ..."

"However, saying he's 'ugly' – or any such comment – is poetry."

"Uh-huh, if you say so."

"Tip-top. 'Ugly' is an embellishment: it embellishes what you see with greater or lesser value. And it's that, by the way, which generates emotions."

"And?"

"Well, that's the difference. You see, old chap? ... Couldn't be simpler."

I waited. "Is that it? Sounds like pretty stupid 'poetry'."

"Exactly. It's total crap. But it doesn't stop people. No matter how intelligent people are, they love spouting loads of appalling poetry."

"And that means spouting loads of appalling beliefs?"

"Just so. God knows why, but people are loathe to wean themselves off that sort of mental poison."

The Reverend Foggie interrupted. "May I point out something?"

"Of course, Padre. Go ahead."

"It's about this holding onto damaging beliefs. Do you remember," he asked me, "the picture of the pink elephant?"

"Uh-huh ..." I replied slowly.

"What happened to it?"

"What do you mean? Apart from 'dying'? Nothing. I forgot about it."

"How much effort did that take?"

"Effort? Funny question. It didn't take any effort."

"And when you were visualising the elephant in the first place, how much effort did *that* take?"

"None, of course ..."

"And this evening ... how much effort did it take to circulate blood around your body?"

"That's another whacky question: I'm not aware of it."

"And digesting your dinner?"

"OK, OK, I'm getting your point: a lot of life happens automatically."

"Sort of. Better to say it's a matter of noticing the effortless power of your imagination. How much effort did it take to create today? Or to uncreate yesterday? Or conjure up tonight's snowstorm?"

"I hear you: they just happened. But there are *some* things that take effort."

"You're right, my son, there are some, and they're part of your physical life. Keeping awake when you're tired, for instance, or lifting weights – *they* take effort. But all the rest: while around most of your Instant, material world happens of its own accord."

"Oh?" I paused. "I hadn't thought of it like that, but I suppose you're right. Why're you telling me?"

"Because firstly, *if* you noticed and remembered how many of the good things of life are effortless, you might calm down."

"Calm down? OK, I could do with that."

"I'm not surprised. Secondly, it's time for you to ask yourself *why* you cling to *so many* beliefs when it's effortless to change them. OK, you love the drama, and you love copying others, but since your beliefs do so much damage and it doesn't cost you a penny to drop them, why not abandon them? After all, as we keep saying, they never existed in the first place."

"I don't know … I suppose I haven't been aware of them."

"I'm sure you haven't." The Rector reflected for a moment. "Take Adolph Hitler," he said. I noticed our host making a funny expression. "Pay no attention to the Doctor, my child. Adolph was a good man."

"A good man?" I remonstrated. "No he wasn't. He was evil."

"That, my son, is a judgement."

"Well, he deserves it."

"And *that's* an opinion."

"No, it's not."

"And *that's* a story."

I was silent.

"You see," he said warmly, "you're riddled with judgments, beliefs, stories and rotten poetry and you hadn't even noticed. Your mind is a cesspit of other people's fabrications. None of it actually exists or benefits you. It won't cost you a penny or an ounce of effort to dump them. And finally …" He took out his handkerchief and removed his spectacles.

"Yes?"

He began polishing. "You created him."

"Who? You mean Hitler?"

"Exactly."

"Hey, steady. You're taking this 'life is my creation' thing a step too far. I wouldn't create *Hitler*."

"You would, actually, and you did."

"It's impossible. Maybe I'm creating my life, but Hitler? It's like saying I've created history!"

"Yes," he replied quietly, "it does."

I screwed up my face.

"And," he went on, "it was effortless. The same applies to what you believe about Adolph. Good or evil?"

I had no answer.

He replaced his handkerchief and perched the specs. "You're free to call him what you like. What about a 'lost soul'?"

"*I* don't think he *was* a lost soul."

"There you are again: stuck in your beliefs."

"Good show, Padre," declared Frostbight.

I took a deep breath. "All right," I said, "but hold on. What about this: you keep talking about beliefs. What *is* a belief?"

"You've asked that already," replied Frostbight. "Remember?"

"Oh, yeah, maybe I did. I think you said it was superstition."

"That's right enough if you're convinced there are invisible agencies like 'laws' governing the universe." He turned to von Lottowind. "Gusty, this is just up your street. What's a belief?"

The German sat up straight. "Up my street?"

"Gusty, you know perfectly well what I mean."

"I do?" Von Lottowind smiled, shrugged and turned to me. "Mein Freund, a belief is a fragment of a story characterised by light trance."

"Huh," I replied, "you're as bad as the Doctor. A 'trance'? What, you think I'm seeing visions?"

"Ah! You *could* see visions – if you wanted. I was thinking of *light* trances."

"Oh? How 'light'?"

"Those that are part of daily life when you suspend analysis."

"Like what?"

"Like when your attention is taken up with stories, gossiping, films, music, songs, poetry, meditating, daydreaming and so on – the various activities of your Dependent imagination. We regularly go in and out of trances."

"Humph! I can tell you Professor, nobody's ever said *I'm* going in and out of trances."

"It is perfectly normal. What I want you to notice is the misuse of trance."

I frowned. "What, you mean like hypnotism?"

"Nein. Hypnotism is a deeper trance. Here is a question: do you not realise your Instant imagination – the natural world around you – is meaningless?"

"What's that got to do with it? Are you saying *reality's* meaningless?"

"Das is correct."

"Huh, you sound like an Existentialist."

"Nein. The Existentialists fall for the common mistake of looking for meaning in the world."

"So where does meaning come in? Oh, I know: you're going to say from my Dependent imagination."

"Das is correct. It comes from your *embellishments*." He paused while he stroked his beard. "I make it clear to you."

"Yeah, yeah."

"It is not difficult. The statement, 'she wore a dress' is, as Watty said, prose: a neutral commentary about something in the world. There is no meaning beyond the description."

"If you say so."

"But the statement, 'she wore a *beautiful* dress' is an embellishment of the description."

"Sounds like a perfectly good observation to me."

"Nein. *Beauty* does not exist in time and space. That dress is of a certain size, but 'beauty' is not. You cannot *see* something which does not exist."

"Oh, back to that. The test is whether I can measure it?"

"Das is so. Beauty is not reality, but a development of it – created by your Dependent imagination. It is poetry, not an observation. You use reality as a springboard to invent meaning."

"Humph. Maybe. But what's this 'trance' business you talk about if it's not hypnotism?"

"Any belief, any meaning, is a trance – albeit, as I say, a light one. Take the quotation, 'Life lasts four score years and ten'. Can you see that it is an observation of reality?"

"Uh-huh, not very accurate, but, yeah, I suppose it is."

"Das is good. It is prose. On the other hand, if you state, 'life is a *struggle*' you are generating meaning – in a trance."

"Well, if it's a trance, it's not much of one."

"That maybe so. There are many possible levels."

"But I *still* think life's a struggle."

He smiled and shook his head. "How may we wean you from your trance? I repeat, the 'struggle' exists only as a metaphor – it is not in the landscape."

"So you keep reminding me. OK, *maybe* it's not real."

"Good. Here is another one. The statement, 'she weighs 6 stone' is a straight commentary."

"Fair enough, it's a measurement, so it's real. Got that."

"Das is also good. However, to say 'she is *anorexic*' is poetry. It has grown into a belief – and a story." He paused for a moment. "And that, mein Freund," he said, "is why we say that you are frozen in time."

"But I'm *not* frozen!"

He grinned. "You are in a trance-like stupor."

"A trance-like stupor? Crikey! Tonight's the first I've heard of *that*. Maybe a teeny bit of exaggeration?"

The German did not respond directly. "Earlier this dinner," he said, "Watty told you that you had not yet learnt to distinguish between what you *see* in the external world and how you *describe* what is happening. The more you see the difference, the more you are awake."

I suppose I was getting some sort of idea what they were on about. I would probably need to mull over it when I got home – *if* I got home. I turned to my neighbour. "Father, can we retrace our steps?"

"No problem, my son. Where to?"

"It's that business of believing in God. How does *that* fit into this reality stuff?"

"What about it?"

"Well, if we're talking about beliefs. What about God?"

"Is God visible?"

"Well," I joked, "I certainly can't see Him – not with my eyes. I wish I could!"

"And there you have your answer."

"Humph," I responded. "It's too quick. You can't see electricity, and you can't say *that* doesn't exist."

"Electricity is something you can test and predict."

"So?"

"Ever tried doing that with God?"

I stopped. "Granted, I agree that that would be difficult." After a moment I said, "But supposing I accept your idea that life's my creation? That, too, is a belief rather than an observation."

"It can be a belief and/or an observation. If you are willing to believe the world's your creation, that's a start. But so what? It makes no difference. On the other hand, using your imagination to *observe* it as such reinvents your whole approach to your life."

"But what happens if I don't believe it?"

"While that's also a perfectly creative thing to do, I suggest you return to the same old question: if *I'm* not inventing the world, then who is?"

I sighed.

The conversation stopped. Our host spoke up. "You're doing a great job, old boy. I think you'd better have a top-up."

"Gosh! Do you think so? I've had rather a lot already."

"Then pass it to the Padre."

I handed the port to my left.

Part VII

ɐɔ

Why I was Ever Born

I TOOK A SWIG OF WATER INSTEAD. I MIGHT HELP ME SOBER up. Was it because I was drunk, or could it really be that my adopting Creosophical ideas might, after all, help me in managing my life? Yet there were things I wanted to ask, and if I did not grab the moment we might not get to them. I turned to my left. "Father Foggie, may we talk about something else?"

"Of course. What've you in mind?"

"Well, a while ago you told me that I'm in 'eternal life' all the time."

"Yes?"

"It's been bothering me, because it must mean I *can't* have created this world."

"No?"

"No."

"And why not?"

"Well, it's the same kind of problem. *Why on earth* would I conjure up this world if I were going to screw it up, be miserable, terrify myself and live a life riddled with disease and shock?" I paused. "If, as you say, we're *immortal*, by all accounts it'd be *much* better *not* to have taken on a body."

"What are you thinking?"

"Obvious. Anyone with sense would want to keep himself safe and happy rather than go about inventing a stupid physical world and get himself terrorised – *and* spend a life on Earth not knowing what happens after it's all over."

The Rector looked across the table. "Doctor, would you like to take this one?"

"No, not me, Padre. You're much better at it."

The Rector adjusted his specs. "I'm not sure I *am* better at it. Anyway," he said, regarding me, "it's a reasonable point. Where do I start? Firstly, it's not a 'stupid world'."

"It is if you ask me."

"Listen. Reality – that is, your Instant imagination – is innocent."

"So you've said, but it doesn't seem innocent to me."

"My son, the world's *always* innocent."

"Yeah, well, even if it were innocent, the people who *inhabit* it aren't."

"No. It *includes* the people. They're just as innocent: after all, they too are your creations."

"Huh. Creations or not, I still can't see why I was born."

"Can't you? You got *yourself* born."

"Yeah? At a stretch, maybe, if I adopted your ideas. But *why?*"

"Because you wanted to experience *not* being eternal."

I made a face. "Not being eternal? What's the point of *that?*"

"You wanted to test the dynamics of operating within the constraints of being an animal and with a restricted imagination."

"Did I?" I paused. "Well, I must be nuts."

He grinned. "You're less nuts than you think. As you know well, you enjoy making up stories. More importantly, it's made you ask valuable questions."

"Maybe it has, but that changes nothing. If you ask me, questions or no questions, making the world with all its crap was a rotten idea."

"But not if you attend to what's *really* going on."

"Oh? *Now* you're going to tell me what's *really* going on?"

"I am." He lowered his glasses. "My son, this world is a fantastic opportunity for you to test your imagination under physical restrictions and limitations."

"Is that so? A test for my imagination?"

"Yes – to develop it as much as you want. It's a grand thought experiment. Remember? Your thoughts are all that you take with you when you leave."

"But why's it not *obvious* this world's my creation?"

"Because *that's part of the experiment.*"

"Humph." I sat back and gave it some thought. "Well, whatever, I still don't see why I had to come down to this planet."

"Then look at it another way. It's the difference between live concerts and sheet music."

"How come?"

"You can hear music in your head when you read the music, but it's nothing compared to experiencing it physically. It may not turn out as you expect."

I could not disagree. "All right, carry on."

"You remember you asked earlier what's the meaning of your being alive?"

"Well, yes. It's *the* great question."

"So here you have the answer."

"What? To experience my ideas in space and time?"

"Yes, within its constraints. Excellent. You've got it."

Von Lottowind joined in. "What Pastor Foggie says is good. You cannot *experience anything* unless you create a world of some kind."

"Maybe."

"So … you like to go on holiday?"

I nodded.

"Which is better: the *idea* of a good holiday, or the *experience* of a good holiday?"

"Well, some holidays go disastrously wrong."

"Occasionally, but that is not what I am talking about."

"Fine, yet I still wouldn't describe life on earth as a 'holiday'."

"For you, possibly not. Maybe we look at something else." The Professor paused. "You like to paint pictures, do you not?"

"Yeah," I replied, "when I get time."

"Have you asked yourself *why* you paint pictures?"

"Yes. It's because I enjoy it."

"Das is good. You have the idea of a picture, and then you produce it?"

"Yeah …"

"Sometimes you like what you have painted, and sometimes not?"

"Of course."

"So it is with your life."

"So what?"

He leant forward and fixed his eyes on me. "If you worked on a portrait of a beautiful woman and made her look ugly by mistake, does that mean it was not worth painting the picture?"

I shrugged. "Well … no."

"Ja. You might well do more work on it. And would you deny you painted the picture?"

I smiled. "Not unless I had to."

"Das is good. So why would you claim that what is *ugly* in this world is *not* your artwork?"

I remained silent.

"And claiming that life has dealt you bad luck," he added, "is as absurd as saying your ugly portrait dislikes you."

"But," I objected, "supposing real people take a dislike to me for no particular reason – to say nothing of the various terrors of life – it's hardly holiday entertainment, and certainly not enjoyable."

"Das is so. However, tonight is your chance to abandon your story of being a 'victim'."

"How do I *know* I'm not a victim?"

He closed his eyes for a second, to compose himself. "*Pastor Foggie has just told you: external reality is innocent.*"

"Oh."

"Ja. *It does not victimise people. Saying you are a victim is merely a stunt.*"

"All right, all right, no need to shout …" I mulled over it. "A 'stunt'? You're sure about that?"

His face coloured. "*Of course. How many times do we have to keep telling you? You are not at the mercy of life: you are its origin.*"

Our host made a point of clearing his throat to get our attention. "I think this is getting a bit steamy. You're doing well, old chap," he said to me, "and you know what? It's been a long evening. We could do with a break." He stretched. "Anyone need the facilities?" When the other two didn't respond, he glanced at me. I realised I hadn't 'been' for ages. Before I could reply, the Doctor addressed his butler. "Mould? Would you show our guest the plumbing?"

"Of course, Sir." The butler picked up the oil lamp on the sideboard and waited. I felt dizzy. The bramble port must have got the better of me. I scraped back my chair, checked for the bat, swayed a little and made for the door in what I thought was a straight line.

"This way, Sir," said Mould as he led me from the dining room to the end of the corridor. "There it is, directly in front of you." He pointed to a Gothic door across the hall, handed me the lamp and turned back.

Following his directions, I found myself in a small vaulted chamber. Faded team photographs and certificates decorated the walls, but it was not the time to study them. To my left there was a shelf on which I could rest the light, and in the far wall a slit window, beneath which sat a polished mahogany bench. When I lifted the middle section, words came to light on the lavatory bowl, 'Thomas Crapper. London.' There could be no better name in a privy. I took off my jacket and jersey, hung them on a hook on the back of the door, released my braces, pulled down my grey flannels and, on sitting, drew breath. I was unprepared for the temperature.

Chilly or not, WCs are ideal locations for musing. I thought first of how it was a travesty that Mr. Crapper's name was a synonym for shit: he whose invention of the flushing cistern revolutionised sanitation. He deserved better. Unlike my brain, his sewage systems never got overwhelmed.

My mind turned to the dinner conversation. Who *were* these characters? They were still a mystery. Comedians? I half expected Billy Bunter to jump out of a cupboard. And where did Mould come from? And the 'Ancient Order of Creosophists'? Were they 'having me on'? And the Creosophy 'Crusades'? And Winterbad? As for their 'creation' stuff ... *was* that *really* why I existed? *Was* that the 'difference that made the difference'? As much as I tried I could not refute it, and the more I tried the more creative I became – and the more I proved the point. Maybe what they were saying really *was* the missing link in the puzzle of existence – although now I was beginning to wonder if existence really existed. Oh, dear, so confusing. And yet, my following what they said really did make sense: I did not *ask* to be born – or die – because I never needed to. It was my idea in the first place: I had every intention of being born. In the end, maybe this Universe *is* intelligent after all – as these fellows keep telling me – and it is not someone *else's* intelligence, it is *mine!*

Yet for all the talk, life would be going on just the same when I got home ... hoping I *did* get home. Was this 'Creosophy' merely an amusing conversation? Or was it really and truly, as they claimed, going to re-invent my life?

I shivered. This was not a place to linger. I reached for the loo paper. My God, it was Bronco! That horrible slippery stuff they gave us in the army. Freezing cold, too. But then again, maybe tissue paper would not work in this damp. What did the Jocks say? One up, one down and one to

"Mould, would you show our guest the plumbing?"

polish? I enjoyed the return of the warmth when I pulled up my trousers – and was glad for my tweed jacket and jersey. Now all I needed was the flush handle. Or was it a chain? It was neither, but there, inserted in the mahogany, was a porcelain lever with the word 'pull'. I did as instructed. Initially there was a silence. Then as I waited the pipes began gurgling and, of a sudden, the lavatory basin thundered like the clap of doom as the Cataracts broke upon 'Thomas Crapper'. Nothing beats good Victorian plumbing. I slammed the lid abruptly before the splashes soaked me; washed and dried my hands, retrieved the lamp and unlocked the door.

Gingerly I stepped outside in the silence, held my light aloft and glanced about. Any sign of the late Mrs. Frostbight? All was clear. I quickened my step back to the others.

Cigars

Part I

❧

Practice Matters

TOBACCO AROMA WAFTED THE LENGTH OF THE COR-ridor. I opened the dining room door. "Ah! There you are," came our host's voice. He was difficult to see in the haze. "Come on in. Fancy a cigar? We're getting stuck in."

"I gathered that," I said as I waved smoke away from my face. Happy to be back in the warmth, I replaced the lamp and returned to my chair. "But thank you," I said. "I won't. I've not had one for ages – in fact since before the war."

"My son, the war's over," the Reverend Father reminded me.

"I know, Father, but life just isn't the same any more."

"Well, I'd have one if I were you: nicotine's an adaptogen."

"A what?"

"An adaptogen, my child, like Creosophy: it lifts you when you're down, and calms you when you're over-excited. Just the thing for a stormy night. I recommend it. Helps the brain, too. 'Every man should eat and drink and smoke, and enjoy the good of his labour'. Ecclesiastes, remember?"

"Oh? No I don't remember."

"Chapter 3, Sir, verse 15," announced the butler from the smoke.

"Ah, thank you, Mould," said the Rector. He returned to me. "Mould's up on his Bible. So there. Feel free to enjoy yourself."

There was something odd about that quote from Ecclesiastes, and yet it wasn't every day that a man of the cloth urged me to smoke. "All right," I relented, "just a small one."

"Good show, old man," exclaimed Frostbight warmly. "Mould? Hello?"

The butler emerged from the fog.

"Splendid, there you are. Could you fetch a cigar for our guest?"

Mould was already holding a silver box, and he opened it to show a neat row of Havanas. There was no option regarding size – they were all large – so I took the nearest.

"Allow me, Sir," he requested, holding out his hand. I let him have the one I had chosen, whereupon he removed the label, cut the rounded tip, lit a taper from one of the candles, held it to the cigar, and once the end glowed handed it back to me.

Gosh, I thought, I could do with a Mould at home. On thanking him, I drew in the flavour of the Cuban leaf, and as soon as I did so I relaxed. The Rector was right: nicotine's a fine 'adaptogen'. "Thank you, Doctor," I said to our host. "It's very good. But look, changing the subject, I was thinking about this in the loo: in *real* life, what happens when I get home?"

"You mean," he replied, "how can Creosophy make a difference?"

"Well, yes. This has been a wonderful dinner – thank you – and a marvellous conversation, but guess what? When the weather clears, I'll get back to reality. What's changed?"

The Doctor blew a cloud of smoke. "Glad you asked." He pondered a moment. "Firstly, don't be fooled: there's a fashion these days to discredit the enjoyable bits of life as though they weren't reality. Pleasure is no less real than pain. Apart from that, things in your home *will* be just the same …"

"So all this talk's for nothing?"

"Let me finish. If you treat it simply as an information dump, then yes, it *is* for nothing."

"And if I *don't* treat it simply as an information dump?"

"If you *apply* what we've been telling you, well, that's another matter."

"Oh? Apply what? Simply agree that I'm creating the world, and Bob's your Uncle, I'm enlightened?"

The Chaplain next to me shook his head and said, "Enlightened?"

"What's the matter with that Father? Sounds good if you ask me."

"Did you as a child look up at the sky and ask what was beyond it?"

"Yeah …"

"Good. I am sure you were told there was sky beyond the sky, and more sky beyond that." He blew out a cloud of smoke. "So it is with enlightenment. There's no such thing."

I groaned. "You mean I never get there?"

"That's right. But you *can* get *more* enlightened." I waited while he took a draw of his Havana. "Don't look despondent, my child," he continued. "May I suggest getting *wiser* instead?"

"Wiser? OK, not a bad idea. In what way?"

"Well, almost everyone sees the world solely from the point of view of their local self, but if you want to go beyond that, the more you learn to see the world from the point of view of the 'You' outside time and space, the more you will develop your imagination."

"Humph. Sounds great, Father, but I bet it doesn't take five minutes to learn *that.*"

"Ah, you could be right. *Hearing* these ideas," he said, "takes only an evening," and added in a lower voice, "on the other hand, *integrating* them *may well* take a lifetime."

There was a short interlude. The door opened and Mould entered with a fresh batch of logs. He threw some into the basket and others into the grate, and arranged them with the poker. The fire crackled into life.

I resumed. "Father, did you say a 'lifetime'? That's *awfully* long."

"It depends. Your understanding is only as good as your practice."

"I'm not with you."

"No? You could *talk* about the difference this stuff will make until the cows come home, but only practice will make the difference." He raised his eyebrows. "Don't you see?"

"See what?"

"None of us here could talk like this if we didn't rehearse."

"Oh? It hadn't occurred to me."

"Didn't we say? *Every day* we visit this material. It needs constant vigilance. If we didn't practise, we'd revert to our old lives, spellbound by words."

"'Spellbound by words'? Lord!"

"Yes. You need to convert words into personal experience, otherwise everything we've said never gets beyond an intellectual exercise."

"What's the matter with that?"

"You can do what you want, but you'll have wasted your time being here." I did not expect the Cleric to be so forthright. "On the other hand," he said, softening his tone, "we're glad to hear you want to take it further."

"Father, all I know is I don't want to be shooting blanks all my life."

That made him grin. "And nor you will, if you *apply* what we've talked about."

"I see. Looks as though you'd better tell me what to do."

"That's why we're here. I wouldn't say it's necessarily easy, but then nor is it difficult. Remember the difference between theory and practice?"

"Oh? What's that?"

"In theory it works in practice."

I made a face. "What's *that* supposed to mean?"

"It means in theory these ideas are a no brainer, but *applying them* is tricky. Yet that is the only way you're going to get results."

"Results? What, get pregnant?"

I caught him hiding a smile. "Patience," he said. "I promise you this stuff's confusing more in the telling than in the doing. You see, if you want to learn to ride a bicycle, you can *talk* all you want about the physics of forward thrust, centres of gravity, potential energy and so on, but in the end the only way to really learn is to start peddling."

Von Lottowind interjected. "And it is pointless to build a ship if you do not launch it."

"Well put, Professor," responded the Rector. "So picturesque." He turned to me. "What we're saying," he went on, "is that this entire evening has been pointless unless you *practise* developing your view of life."

"I get the message. So what happens?"

Frostbight answered me. "You apply what we've been telling you."

I looked at my host. "*I know.* But by doing *what?*"

"Ah. Good question." He smoothed back his moustache. "Let's think. How can we get you started? What about the next time you're looking down a street?"

"OK."

"Check out the road and the buildings."

"Yeah. And ..."

"Now, if you were told that everything you saw was the spontaneous product of your Instant Imagination generating what you see out of nothing, would you be surprised?"

I groaned.

"It's straightforward, old chap, although I admit it's a bit strange – at first. Keep at it. It requires no effort."

"No? *I* reckon it'll require a lot of effort."

"Don't you believe it," he said. "It always comes back to imagining. Don't fuss about whether it's 'true': simply *imagine* the world's your instantaneous creation. Try it. Or this: on a summer's day in the country-side, look at what's around you – birds, bees, the scent of flowers, a breeze in the trees, the sky, the clouds and the distant landscape. If you're with a companion, so much the better. Now, *imagine* that *all* of it – including your companion – is being conjured up by you at that very moment."

The Cleric joined in. "The same goes, my son, wherever you are. You could be in Church. You could be at a lecture or on the lavatory. But let's return to that street. See the people and the shops and houses: see them as being exactly where they are because you've put them there. You're creating them precisely, right then, moment by moment – out of nothing except your Instant imagination." He paused. "See? It's a picnic."

"A picnic, Father?" I rubbed my eyes. "Some picnic!"

"It's a start. As the Doctor said, keep at it. Wherever, whoever or what-ever: it's a display of your genius."

"Huh? I didn't reckon on having *that* much genius." I stopped and considered. "I can't argue," I said, "that I'm creating my thoughts – my 'Dependent' mind, as you call it – but seeing the *whole world* as my own work ... phew! That *is* a leap."

"And that's the threshold we've been talking about."

"It certainly is."

"Look," remarked Frostbight, "there's nothing to it: you can practise *at any time* – that's the beauty of it."

Von Lottowind took up the reins. "Watty is correct: anytime."

"Yeah, sure, Professor," I said, turning to him. "What about when I'm brushing my teeth?"

"It is so, even when you are brushing your teeth. You may rehearse whenever you remember."

"When I remember what?"

"To pay attention to the idea that you are creating everything you experience." The German made a gesture. "You could do so the next time you are driving your motorcar."

"Really? *Actually* while I'm driving?"

"Ja, when you are at the wheel. Pay attention to the vehicles in front of you and those passing you on the other side of the road."

"OK."

"Remind yourself that you have put each one there."

"I have?"

"Ja. Look at the makes and models as they pass. You invented every one of them."

I ostentatiously looked to the ceiling.

He paid no attention. "Look at the white lines painted on the tarmac: they are *your* invention – to make your driving easier. Look at the tarmac itself: the same applies. Look at the signs and advertisements: you wrote them. Observe everything."

"Oh," I said, "and that's going to make me a Creosophist?"

"If nothing else," he grinned, "it will make you a better motorist – you will pay attention."

"It would certainly make for a different *kind* of motorist!"

"Ach so. And the same goes for responding to other road users. If someone overtakes you and cuts in too close, it is you who have made the driver do so."

"But it's just bad behaviour."

"So! You are back in your courtroom?"

"No, no, not me. It's just that some people really *are* bad drivers."

"Nobody asked you to judge. You have no need to make that sort of comment."

"And why not?"

"How many times do we have to repeat it? Their so-called 'bad' behaviour was *your idea.*"

"Huh," I mumbled. "A pretty dangerous idea."

"Das is correct. It was dangerous and it was your idea. What I am talking about is a new vision of life. Do you wish another example?"

I smiled. "Go for it."

"I 'go for it'?"

"Pay no attention, Professor. What's your example?"

"It is this. If you happen to be late and come to red traffic lights, you have no need to fret. Instead, remind yourself that you put the traffic lights there and you made them go red. And if you become stuck in a traffic jam, instead of becoming impatient, imagine that you created the jam."

He must have read my expression and stopped for a moment. "Maybe, mein Freund, you are astonished?"

"What do you think?"

"Ah! We have hardly begun."

"You're not kidding?"

"Nein, I am not 'kidding'. You like to be invited to parties?"

"Yes," I replied cautiously, "if it looks to be a good one."

"I am glad. The next time you go to a party say to yourself, 'I am accepting my own invitation to this party. I invented this gathering – it was my idea – and I have asked myself to attend it'."

"Professor, it's bonkers."

"Bonkers?"

"Sorry. Forget it. It's just that the Creosophist way of looking at things is seriously different."

"But you want a different way of living?"

"Yes, of course I do."

"Das is good. It becomes more normal with practice. Here is another example. Maybe you wished you had *not* accepted a certain invitation?"

"What, you mean to a party?"

"Ja. Maybe you agreed to it and then regretted it, but were obliged to attend. If that should happen, when you arrive, remind yourself it was *your own idea* to have invited yourself. You may find you enjoy the party after all."

"Huh. That'd be nice."

"Good. Or again, supposing you are nervous because you are asked to give a speech? The same holds true: you will have accepted your *own* invitation to give the speech – and have created your own audience."

"Public speaking scares me like hell."

"Das is so? The audience is there at your bidding."

I took a deep breath. "I'd have my work cut out to think like that."

"As we say, it takes no *effort* to think like that."

"So what does it take?"

He glowered. "Must we keep repeating? *It takes your imagination.*"

The Professor had perhaps good reason for getting impatient: I was not too quick at getting the hang of this stuff. Anyway, several questions needed answering. I looked across the table. "Doctor," I asked, "what about bad moods? Are you telling me I can say good-bye to them? I mean, let's say I go home, accept that life's my creation and do your exercises. Is that the end of my getting depressed?"

"In some ways nothing will change, old boy, and in other ways, *everything* will change."

"What's *that* supposed to mean?"

"That your life will continue the same, but your *understanding* of how the world works will change."

"OK, I'm kind of getting the hang of that."

"Good, that's the stuff. Now a consistent and reliable understanding of the world will necessarily modify your responses and, as the Padre told you a while ago, your responses are what generate mood swings. So practise seeing that everything around you, and *everything* you experience – including your depressions – are exactly as you intended, exactly as you wanted and it's all for your benefit." He paused. "You know what?"

"What?"

"You'll wish you'd come across Creosophy years ago!"

I could not hold back a smile. "All right, very funny, Doctor. And then what?"

"Then keep doing it. That's the difference which makes the difference." He stopped. "How does that sound?"

I chewed over the idea. "Worth a try, I suppose. I'll see what happens."

"Good man."

The Reverend came in. "Nonetheless, even if you do take up the practice, there's a problem."

"Oh?"

"You like problems, don't you?"

"So you tell me. What's it this time?"

"It's that irrespective of whether you treat this evening as entertainment or as a lesson, you will surely forget it." He blew one, two and then three smoke rings.

Was he 'having me on'? "Forget it, Father?" I said. "After an evening like this? Not likely!"

He blew another ring. "You'll forget. Believe me, everyone does. You'll forget it a thousand times … ten thousand times – and more." He looked at me. "My child," he persisted, "you'll need daily rituals."

"Rituals? Kind of like in religion?"

"Yes. Why do you think Mahommedans pray five times a day?"

"You're asking me? Haven't a clue. It's what they've been told to do."

"That may be. What's important is that it's a constant reminder about what, for them, matters – otherwise they'd forget." He looked at me from over his specs. "You see," he said, "you'll leave here, maybe think about what we've said for a few days and then it'll fade."

"No it won't. How could it?"

"Because," he explained, "seeing the world in the old way – as someone else's creation – is your 'default mode'. It's like poor posture. Unless you deliberately rehearse every day, you'll submit to your habitual position." He stopped and blew another ring.

"Mein Freund," came in von Lottowind. "Waking yourself out of your stupor requires *arbeit*."

"'Arbeit'? What's *that*?"

"It's 'w*ork*'."

"'Work'? Oh my God! That's a four-letter word. I thought you said this stuff was effortless?"

"Excuse me? A four letter word?"

"Sorry. A joke. What were you saying?"

"I correct myself." He tapped his cigar on the edge of the ashtray. "I mean it requires *regular attention* to keep yourself from reverting to your old posture. You must understand: you will be so fascinated by the activities in your life outside here that you will forget everything we have told you."

"I think you're exaggerating."

"I wish I were exaggerating."

"OK, then if you're not, *how do* I remember?"

"As with daily prayers, you must set aside times to go 'off-stage' from your public life."

"What does that mean?"

"Take QPs."

"Take *what*?"

"QPs."

"What're those?"

"Quiet Periods: time out."

"Oh."

"Do you take time for Quiet Periods?"

"Who? Me, Professor? Not likely. I'm too busy."

"Ja. Das is so. You spend all your time 'on stage', so to speak. None-theless, even when you are on stage, doing exercises while looking down the street or driving a car as we have described, take up none of your time – you can do them whenever you wish."

"I'd prefer that. What's the problem?"

"The problem is you will soon forget to do them."

"You're as bad as Father Foggie. I promise you I won't."

"And *I* promise you that you will."

"No I *won't!*" I almost stamped my foot.

"Mein Freund, unless you deliberately set aside a time to rehearse there is *no doubt* that you will forget. You need a way to remember to remember."

Father Foggie explained. "That's why you need regular Quiet Periods. We, in the Creosophist Order, set aside time for QPs each day."

"You do? Really?"

"Yes, we need to. Even if life is quiet, during any typical day 'on stage', we know how difficult it is to remind ourselves we're writing the script."

"Huh. So how often do you set aside Quiet Periods?"

"As a minimum we like to rehearse twice a day: before breakfast and at the end of afternoon tea."

"I don't take afternoon tea. But you reckon if I do that I'll be sorted?"

He raised his hands. "I wish! Anyway, as soon as you try to keep aside a few minutes you'll come straight against resistance."

I screwed up my face. "I can't think what."

"You'll find out. That's the way it goes – I don't know why: your Dependent imagination will suddenly load you with urgent things to do."

"You think so?"

"I *know* so. When rehearsing on your own, it'll be fine for a few days and then any number of 'obstacles' will get in the way."

I still could not see it happening, so I went back to where we were. "OK, let's pretend I *do* keep going. What's the QP routine?"

He glanced towards von Lottowind. "Professor?" he said. "Would you describe a typical QP?"

The Prussian blew some smoke. "I would be happy to do." He addressed me. "There are many things you can do. Where do you wish me to start?"

"No good looking at me, Professor."

"Ah, I understand. An effective way to begin might be to look at what is around you."

"Like when? Out jogging?"

"That," he frowned, "depends on whether you like jogging. You could equally well be on a bus or train, but I have in mind you will be indoors, in which case you will be sitting down. You may look at the windows, the view through the windows, the walls and ceiling around you and the furnishings in the room – it does not matter what. Point out to yourself that here before you is your creation and the full extent, for the moment, of the universe."

"Huh," I said. "The universe? Well, all right, if you must. I suppose I'll get used to the idea. What else?"

"Settle down to your QP. As you look at or think about each thing in turn, repeat, 'this is my own creation'; or 'this is exactly how I intended it to be'; or 'everything is exactly the way it should be'."

"And then?"

"You can make up any words you want, but whatever you choose, keep repeating it – for as long as need be."

"Call me old fashioned, Professor, but that sounds awfully like a mantra. I am supposed to say it out loud?"

"You may say it aloud, or say it to yourself, or you may chant it with others. You must be clear that it is not the words which matter, but cultivating your imagination to see it for yourself. *That* is what matters."

I wondered what it might be like to have a go at it. "All right," I said, "that seems to be straightforward. Then what?"

"Then, mein Freund," answered von Lottowind with a gesture, "you celebrate!"

There was a brief silence as I stared at him. "Celebrate, Professor? Celebrate what?"

"Celebrate your creation."

"What d'you mean? Pop a champagne cork?"

The Rector spoke up. "As long as it's good champagne! Don't look so puzzled: I'm joking. No, it's easy to celebrate."

"Yes, but what do I do? Shout 'hip, hip, hurray'?"

He waved a hand. "That's a great start. Any ejaculation will do."

"I *beg* your pardon, Father. *Ejaculation?*"

"Whoa, steady up," exclaimed the Doctor. "I know what you're thinking. The Padre doesn't realise grammar's moved on. It's now called an 'exclamation'."

"I'm pleased to hear it."

"You can," continued the unperturbed Cleric, "ejaculate with any sound that denotes rejoicing. You could say, 'whoopee' or 'yippee' or 'Geronimo' or an emphatic 'yes!' – whatever whets your whistle."

"So what're you telling me? I should say three cheers for this cigar?"

"Why not?" answered Frostbight. "How many people do you know who celebrate *anything?*"

I puffed on it and allowed the smoke to rise. "Well, Doctor," I admitted, "not many. Maybe at the birth of a child or when it's someone's birthday, or when their football team wins …"

"Spot on. Now think about it. Your football team may not win, but there are a thousand reasons to rejoice: a good dinner; good friends; refuge from a storm; a safe journey; the sun coming out – at least in Scotland; the dentist assuring you your teeth are ship-shape; having a roof over your head; a hot bath; a good night's sleep; going on holiday; finishing a project …"

"What if I can't think of anything?"

He shrugged. "Then celebrate a success you've enjoyed in the past."

"What if I haven't had one?"

"I think you'll find you've had plenty – if you look. But if not, what about other people and their successes? You can celebrate those too."

"Tell me," interrupted the Reverend, "how much do you rejoice normally?"

"Me, Father? Almost never. It's not the 'done thing'."

"Too bad. What's important is to honour your creation. Say it while you're having sex."

"What? Say, 'this is delightful' in the middle of a romp?"

He grinned. "No, not out loud: *in your head!* Mind you, during sex you might prefer something a little more emphatic than 'delightful'."

Frostbight remarked, "Bear in mind, celebrating is also a kind of instant meditation to bring you to your senses – yes, even during sex. As a Sufi might say, 'wherever you are … *be there'*."

I was not sure a Sufi would really say that, and nor could I imagine finding this sort of advice in any book on lovemaking. Still, I liked the idea of 'instant' meditation.

"I would add," commented the Cleric, "that you might also like to say 'thank you'."

"Oh? Who would I thank? Myself?"

He sighed. "No, no. It's your 'self' who's *doing* the thanking."

"Then who do I thank?"

"Oh, dear, I'd hoped you'd 'got' it by now. You, as your self, thank the You who's orchestrating life behind the scenes." He went on. "If you have trouble with it, don't worry: simply address your gratitude to 'whom it might concern'."

"Ah, so you're Unitarians?"

Von Lottowind growled from across the table. "Why do you keep wanting to know who we are? *Simply say, 'thank you'.*"

"OK, Professor, OK." I thought better not to make further remarks. Doctor Frostbight started the decanter on another tour of the table. I was finding the port tasty and helped myself to a little more. Oops! It came out rather quickly. Never mind, I did not spill very much. With my cigar gripped in my teeth, I shot the decanter to Padre Foggie. It scooted off faster than I expected. Fortunately he caught it before it hit his tumbler.

The butler's voice came from behind me. "A little water, Sir?"

"Gosh, Mould, where did you spring from? Not a bad idea. Actually, maybe quite a lot." I waited while he filled my tumbler to the brim, and took a swig. It was just the thing. I needed time to collect myself and drew on my cigar. Nothing happened.

In a moment the butler was back again, this time with a lighted taper. "Allow me, Sir." With his applying the flame and a bit of puffing on my part, the tip flared and all was well.

"Thank you, Mould." A few moments of puffing gave me a chance to ponder. "Professor," finally I said, "what about the rest of the QP?"

"Ah, it is good that you ask. You must experiment."

"Experiment? I thought a QP was some sort of meditation."

"That is what meditation is: an experiment."

"Oh, is it? So what do I do?"

"You spoke of those parts of your life which are going 'badly' ... ja?"

I shrugged.

"It is not a problem. Look on your difficulties with the eye of your mind. Now, keep your attention on any one of those difficulties and repeat, as before, 'this is my creation'." He stopped while he blew smoke. "You could also do it for agreeable topics. For example, think of members of your family and the people who are close to you. Look at where you live and the kind of work you do and at those who you work with."

"And repeat, 'this is my creation'?"

"Most precisely. Take each one in turn and learn to understand that their existence is an example of your genius."

"Huh ..." I took another draw of my cigar. "Doing that," I said, "would make people a kind of extension of myself."

"Das is a good observation. You will see yourself less as an outsider."

"Oh?"

"I am sure you will find it a pleasant experience."

317

I did not mind the idea of trying out an 'experiment'. "All right, Professor," I accepted, "so maybe I'll test it out, and maybe I'm in for a pleasant surprise. Is that all?"

Von Lottowind raised his eyebrows nonchalantly. "That is your choice."

"What choice?"

"There are many exercises."

"There are? I suppose I shouldn't be surprised. Go ahead, then, get them off your chest."

"They are not on my chest."

"Professor, that's an *expression*."

"Ach? An expression? I see. Now, we have talked of your present life. You may also review your past. Choose any particular event from recent days or from days long gone. Imagine how you might have responded differently if you had understood the events had been your own creation."

"What are you talking about? Things which happened last week?"

"It could be, or from your earliest childhood."

I flicked the end of my Havana over the ashtray. "But going over my *whole life*? That's an *awful* lot to do in five minutes."

"Don't worry, old boy," Frostbight joined in. "We *know* it's more than you can do in five minutes. As the Padre said, it's a lifetime's project. And on top of that, you're going to find your mind wanders all over the place."

"I don't see why it would."

"Look, old bean, we've been at it for years. We know only too well that during QPs thoughts have a party. It's the very devil to keep to the subject."

"So you weren't pulling my leg when you said you do this stuff yourself?"

"Of course we do it ourselves. It's a daily ritual. Doesn't stop the thoughts and distractions, though, going every which way. Padre," he said to the Chaplain, "how do you get on with your QPs?"

"I confess, Doctor, when I focus intently, I fall asleep. When I awake, I do the same thing again, and so it goes on. Very difficult to direct the mind."

Frostbight turned to von Lottowind. "What about you, Gusty?"

The German closed his eyes. "Watty, my concentration never wavers."

For a moment I thought he was being serious.

"Steady, Gusty," said the Doctor. "You'll scare the poor chap. You see," he remarked to me, "we all find it tricky. Your mind's bound to wander: it's normal."

"But how do I stop it?"

"You don't. Whenever you realise it's gone off somewhere, point out to yourself that whatever's distracted you is equally your creation – whether it's a person, thing or event. That way every lapse of concentration *becomes the exercise*." He paused. "Don't look so glum, you might enjoy it – and then you'll spend more time at it."

"But if this is a kind of meditation, aren't I supposed to observe my desires and attachments – you know, like Buddhists?"

"Not exactly. You're aiming to see that your desires and attachments are *also* your creations. Everything in your consciousness is your invention."

I think I was getting the idea.

"Also," added the Rector, "you'll find these daily exercises help you take your foot off the accelerator."

"What accelerator?"

"They calm your stress levels."

"Oh, that's what you mean. Less turbulence?"

"Exactly. You'll find the ups and downs of life much less distressing when you *see* they're your own idea."

"It's like this, old bean," came in Frostbight. "When you revisit your past during your QP, face it that *you* created your own set-ups and upsets, but what's important is you don't play the magistrate and criticise yourself. You can now re-create new set-downs. Instead of chastising yourself, treat what happened as lessons, misjudgements or simply as bits of conjuring that misfired."

"You realise you're talking to someone who's spent his life kicking himself?"

"I suspected that. Not a good idea. Time to stop. That's how you make bad situations worse. Never make war on your self, or you're stuck in your battlefield for eternity."

I took a deep breath.

"Beware," he continued, "of treating yourself like a machine and expect to run without a hitch. *Allow* for inexperience. What's that saying? 'Only beginners blame the clay for their wonky pot'. Remember, Padre?" he asked the Rector.

"I haven't heard it before, Doctor. Confucius?"

"Confucius you reckon?"

"Nein," corrected the Professor, "More likely Lao-Tsi."

"Huh? Lao-Tsi? Mould? Where are you? Who do you think it was?"

"It was you, Sir."

"Good heavens. *Me*? Was it really? Well I never, it's rather good." He paused and said, "So there we are," and turned again to Rector. "Padre, what else do you suggest?"

I waited while the Chaplain blew a smoke ring. "Yes," he said at last, "we're all in the same boat. When we've blundered, it's essential to admit it." Turning his attention to me he added, "And it's equally important to admit that at some level *we made those blunders on purpose*."

"Good work, Padre," complimented the Doctor. "You see, old boy," he said to me, "reviewing the past is never time wasted. And by the way, here's another thing you can do."

"Oh, yes?"

"Yes. Use your QP to review your stories."

"Oh. Stories?"

"Yes. Have you forgotten they're the lynchpin?"

"No. I remember well."

"Champion. Look at it like this. Really you've got a creation within a creation: your Dependent within your Instant. Now, it was bad enough when, as we've been saying, you invented crap experiences, but you made it a good deal worse when you conjured up crap *stories* – criticisms – to decorate those experiences."

I must have looked perplexed.

"You embellish them," he said. "Remember?"

I nodded.

"First class. Now, during your QP, go over those beliefs and judgements about the things that happened, and separate out what is reality, and what are your own decorations added *onto* reality."

"Yeah, I suppose," I replied. "And then what?"

"You could rename those experiences. Maybe rename what you call your 'misfortunes' as 'failed experiments'. It's a more attractive decoration." He looked at me with mock seriousness. "Then you could save you a great deal of money in psychoanalysis."

"Oh, good. If I practise Creosophy I'll be right as rain?"

"Whoa, steady. I didn't say that. It depends. It's not good to pretend you don't need help when you do." He looked at his Havana. "Damn, it's gone out. Mould. D'you have a match?"

The butler helped our host relight the cigar. As he held the taper, he said, "Excuse me, Sir."

"Yes? What is it?"

"Sir, regarding narratives …"

"Uh-huh?"

"I recall a certain saying."

"A certain saying, eh?"

"Indeed, Sir."

"Well, come on. Out with it."

"Very well, Sir, it goes like this: 'you can stand, sit or lie down. The rest of your life is a story'."

"My word, Mould, that's spot on. Who said it? Some Zen chap?"

"No, Sir. Ms. Byron Katie."

"Her again? Ah, thank you – that's smoking nicely now. Well, she's got her head screwed on." He addressed me. "How about that? It looks as if you'd do well to study Ms. Katie." He turned back to the butler. "Mould, do you remember: 'I'm here, and the rest of my life's a belief – thousands of them'? My late wife, wasn't it?"

"No, Sir, that was you again."

"Me again? By Jingo."

"I also recall, Sir, the Buddhists express the idea simply thus: 'come to your senses'."

"Jolly good, I bet they do."

Mould returned to his duties and for a period all was quiet. Even the rumbling in the chimney was subdued. Did I really know what they were talking about? Maybe it did not matter. If I did the exercises I would probably find out. "So," I remarked, "are we done with the QP?"

"Not quite," responded the Reverend Foggie.

"Phew. OK, Father, what next?"

"I want to emphasise that your guilt and your judgments are *essential* subjects to review."

He could be right. "OK, but you know, here's what's troubling me. This stuff about revisiting my past? There's some of it I don't want to visit: it freaks me out."

The German interrupted. "Excuse me. 'Freaks me out'?"

"Yes. You know, Professor: puts me in a stew."

"A stew?"

I sighed. "*It upsets me.*"

"Ah, so. I understand. Das is why seeing your day-to-day experiences as your creation is valuable practice. Thus you develop mental 'muscles' to tackle upsets from the past."

"It'd be a tough job."

"Only at the beginning. You will become better at it."

"Yeah, but as you said: it's great in theory. What about shame, embarrassment, fear, sorrow and so on?"

"Examine your *beliefs*. Find out which ones feed them. You have been telling yourself in a thousand different ways, 'I am guilty'; 'I have failed'; 'I do not deserve to be forgiven or be happy'; 'I have been a naughty boy' or a 'naughty girl'. Those and all the rest of them are no more than ugly decorations and, as you say in English, 'crap' poetry."

"Also, old boy," butted in Frostbight, "you can review *happy* times in the past but which ended in sadness. Pay attention to how you now feel if you understand it was 'You' who *made* those good times to be uncreated. In the meantime," he said, looking at my glass, "you've uncreated your port. Here." He pushed the decanter towards me.

I had uncreated my port? A funny way of looking at it, but yes, he was right. However I had had enough, and passed the decanter to the Rector – this time with more care. It was apparent my daily 'Quiet Period' was going to be busy. "Doctor," I asked, "there's nothing *else* to pack into five minutes, is there?"

"Hold on, old chap. The 'five minute' idea is simply a practical amount to get you up and running. If you find it helpful, you'll spend more time at it – or do it more often. And remember, you can always invent your own exercises."

"I can? What like?"

"You won't be short of material. In fact you could review everything we've been talking about this evening. Here's another one. Bring to mind a 'difficult' person with whom you have regular contact. You know: someone who's a 'problem'."

"All right."

"Practise framing that person in a new way. Whatever they're doing, they're following your script. Recall what the other person does or says, and *imagine* it's *you* who's 'asking' them to play that part. Notice the difference in your attitude. I would also add that if someone's kind to you, celebrate it – that's also your script."

"Humph. And you say it's easy?"

"Like taking candy from a baby."

"Oh yeah? Hilarious." I drew on my cigar and said, "What about my family? I'd find it difficult to imagine that my girlfriend or my parents or my brothers and sisters are *really* products of my ... how would you say, my 'inventiveness'?"

"You'll get the hang of it."

"Huh. You mean, *actually* thinking of my family in that way? Sorry, I *still* think it's weird."

The Cleric looked at me over his specs. "You still think it's weird? Didn't you say your interior light wasn't working?"

"My interior light? In my car? What's that got to do with it?"

"Do you want to stay in the dark and go on travelling without a map?"

"All right, Father, I get the point. I'll have a go at it. So, all done?"

The Rector smiled. "Nearly. Here's another idea."

I groaned. "Fire away."

"It's easy. How about reflecting on how much your life and your experiences are effortless? They are absolutely free of charge and to change your ideas costs nothing."

"Or," suggested the Doctor, "you could recall that life is a string of mini-deaths. Focus on yesterday and observe that it's 'dead', along with yesterday's self. And tomorrow will soon be dead too. That way you'll get used to seeing death as a normal event of life."

"Huh. I still reckon it's whacky."

"It's a lifetime's work. Keep reminding yourself your QP is an exercise in thought. And thoughts don't exist. Any time you're thinking, you're engaged in an exercise that's not altogether of this world."

"Phew."

"Yes, 'phew'." Anyway, the more time you give to your QPs the less whacky this stuff will be. The exercises are invaluable in teaching you to attend to the world differently – and, of course, building new habits."

I deliberated. "Do you *really* think Doctor, after all this, I'd forget?"

"Certainly, old boy. I can't stress enough that you'll need to remind yourself to remind yourself every day. As you'll find out, it's *very* hard, when you're on stage, to engage in your daily activities *and,* at the same time, remember it's entirely your creation."

I leant to my left to allow the butler to remove my empty wine glass – he was clearing the table of unnecessary clutter. Dinner must be drawing to a close. There wasn't a great deal left of my cigar and the end was getting soggy. I stifled a yawn. Surely these fellows weren't giving me any further work? "So," I said to no one in particular and trying not to appear sleepy, "you all reckon I'll go home, do my daily QPs, and the next thing I'll be a Creosophist?"

"Slow down, old man," grinned Frostbight. "Looking for miracles? For a start you won't suddenly become a Creosophist; it's a mindset that grows over time. Apart from that, you've no idea at the moment what the You-who-you-don't-know has planned for yourself."

"Oh dear. No earth shattering marvels?"

He smiled. "Sorry, old chap. Your life will go on just the same. If, say, you've got an insufferable boss at work, he'll continue like that, but at least you can do something about it. It may be that he's a crappy bit of creating. Whatever – it's your conjuring trick, and that is what you pay attention to."

"So what's different?"

"In a funny way, everything is. If your stupid beliefs are the problem, you can drop them. And if it's a rotten creation, you can leave the job – so long as you don't hold other rotten beliefs that stop you. The same applies with any of your 'struggles'."

"And," put in the Rector, "you will still have highs and lows, good days and bad days, but that's OK, because they won't be the same 'problems' any more. As a wise Creosophist once said, 'I've had problems all my life, and as I get older they get better and better'. No, no, Mould," he added hastily, "I don't need to know who said it."

"Very good, Sir."

"However," joined in the German, "it is not for us to be your Kinder-madchen ... Watty, how you say in English?"

"'Nanny', old man."

"Ah, yes, thank you. It is not for us to be your 'nanny'. You are intelligent, ja? You have imagination? It is for you to explore."

"Or," commented Frostbight, "you don't have to do a thing. Just keep disbelieving what we say: putting your head in the sand is a perfectly creative thing to do even if it's not very helpful. However, why not suspend for a while, your analytical mind and its beliefs? Take a leap of imagination. You can return to your conventional way of thinking once we're through ... if you want to. Now, imagine: you're giving yourself this dinner party tonight. We're here because you put us here, and I'm saying this because you wanted to hear it. Call it a magical show, if you will: we are here because you conjured us up. Later, in days to come, you may forget, or you may not. Nevertheless, at the moment, you're creating what we're telling you. In a sense, it's your own words which you're hearing."

"You once wondered how come you have a body. Now you know: you invented it, and have been re-inventing it every day of your life. You yourself are constantly re-fashioning the miracle of your biological system – your senses, your eyes and ears and your feelings – along with your personality and your character."

He paused for a moment and I was unable to hide my yawn. I let the butt of my spent cigar sit in the ashtray. My eyelids felt heavy.

Father Foggie quietly took over. "My son, think of yourself as more, much more than you believed. For a moment, go back to the very earliest memories of your childhood – that was the beginning of your creating this particular physical life and you've been expanding your world ever since.

"Go back to your days at school and what you learnt, and what you were taught to believe about the world. Think of the lessons in history; or geography; or religion or science and about the so-called 'laws' of the universe. You invented all of it. You taught yourself those things because you wanted to participate in this world you were devising. It's not you, as you know yourself, who brought the world into being, but rather it's the whole You, as someone infinitely artistic, who manifests the world out of nothing. You're making your world 'real', and that's the way you wanted it. But having created it, you've become so engrossed that you've lost sight of the 'You' who's running the show.

"Think now, if you will, of your daily life as an adult. Every day that the sun rises it rises at your bidding; and sets because you ordained it. It's a constant all through your life because that's how you've put your world together. The sun, the stars, the moon, and their regular movements – they're what they are because it was your idea. Do you complain about the damp and the clouds, the snow and the rain? You've forgotten they're your inventions.

"Whether or not you make mistakes, *all* experiences happen *exactly* as you intend: it's you who engineer them, on purpose, every moment – even though you, as your ordinary physical self, don't know you're doing it. Your physical self only observes the effects."

Von Lottowind now spoke in his customary accent. "Think also, mein Freund, of the things you do not like: of the troubles in your life, both in your own life and in the world around you. You may be frightened. You may not be comfortable in your own body. Or you may not be comfortable with others. Or you may not be comfortable with the news of what is going on in the world. However, strange as it may sound, it is all of it your own idea. You, as your local, physical self, may not know why or how you are making it happen, but that does not mean you are not in control."

His voice was growing distant, and it was difficult to concentrate. Probably the port. Or the dinner – I was stuffed. Maybe the cigars? Where was this Castle? Was the Professor really German? Was there really such a thing as the 'Order of Creosophists'? Who *was* Mould? Was Doctor Frostbight really an old gold miner?

The last thing I remember was our host. "Bring to mind," he was saying, "the good things in your life, old chap. Think, maybe, of your family. Recall the people you love; and your home; maybe also your work or your colleagues; or the holidays you've enjoyed; the things you've learnt and discovered, the good times you've had; and all those things that interest you – and the laughter … these have happened because you manifested them yourself. They are displays of your genius. *All of your life is a display of your genius.* It always has been … give yourself a pat on the back … rejoice … congratulate yourself … *celebrate!*"

"He blew one, two and then three smoke rings."

Epilogue

I GREW CONSCIOUS AND OPENED MY EYES TO THE SOUND OF rain. It was drumming on a skylight in a combed ceiling not far from the end of my bed. I propped myself up and looked around. I was in a small room with an iron fireplace where glowing ashes still gave a little heat, and to my left was a curved wall and a small window letting in the morning light. I slumped back. Where was I? Oh, yes: Chilblane. They seemed to have put me in a bedroom in one of the turrets. I sat up again. There was my suitcase, open on a stand – Mould must have gone out into the snow, retrieved it from my car and brought it up.

I was happy to see a carafe of water with a tumbler on my bedside cabinet, and I poured myself a glassful. Water never tasted so good. While I drank, I cast my mind back. Doctor Frostbight had been going on about something, and I may have fallen asleep. How embarrassing. And how come I ended up here, in bed, wearing my pyjamas? I rubbed my forehead to try and dispel the fogginess. Since daylight is slow to come in mid-winter, it was obviously not early and I looked at my watch, but I forgot – it was not working. I pulled myself from under the blankets and went to the window. A steep roof had the rain bouncing off the slates without any sign of the snow, and beyond, a curtain of fog.

I become alert, aware now that a thaw had followed the storm. It meant I could leave – I knew how worried they would be at home. My clothes were not hard to find, neatly folded as they were over a chair by the bed, with my shoes keeping warm on a trivet in front of the fire – such old fashioned hospitality. Before long I was dressed. I packed my pyjamas into my suitcase, clipped it shut, made for the door and stopped, aware of my manners. Taking out my wallet, I wedged a ten bob note under the carafe.

It was a clumsy business carrying a leather suitcase three floors down a narrow spiral staircase, and I hoped the noise did not disturb anyone asleep behind the doors. Finally, I found the entrance hall, only to discover Mould on a stepladder replenishing the chandelier.

He stopped what he was doing and came down. "Good morning, Sir."

"Good morning, Mould. You're looking busy."

"Jobs to be done, Sir. Would you care for some breakfast?"

"Thank you, but no. I really must be on my way: this rain will have cleared the road. Did I make an awful fool of myself last night?"

"Not in the slightest, Sir."

"Well, I hope you're right. Is Doctor Frostbight around?"

"I regret he is not. He is outside checking for storm damage."

"Ah, well, in that case, would you thank him very much for rescuing me ... and for the dinner?"

"There's a Visitor's Book on the hall table. Maybe you would care to make a comment?"

"Certainly. Good idea." I could see the book he was talking about and a fountain pen beside it. After filling in the date, my name and address, I wrote profuse thanks for the hospitality. "There," I said when I finished, "that should do it. What do you think? You reckon I'll ever make a Creosophist?"

"Of course, Sir. You are one already. That is the easy part."

"Oh, so what's the difficult part?"

"Remembering, when you go home. That is the difficult part."

"Nonsense. There's no way I'd forget at home." But with those words, my heart sank. "Oh, Lord, Mould, I've just realised: I can't go. I've no petrol."

"No need for concern, Sir. We keep supplies in reserve, and I took the liberty of filling your tank. I have also brought the vehicle round since the courtyard is so slushy."

"My goodness, Mould, you think of everything. I wish I could take you home with me."

I caught the trace of a smile. "Your coat, Sir?"

"Ah, yes, please. I'll need that – the car's freezing."

He soon had me togged up for the trip. "May I help you with your suitcase?" he said as he gave me my scarf.

"No, no, absolutely no need. Light as a feather, but I could do with some directions. How do I get to the main road?"

"No problem, Sir. Just keep going."

"Really? As easy as that? There's a pea souper out there."

"No need to worry. It'll clear as you go."

"Is that so? Right-ho, I wouldn't dare doubt you." I paused. "Well ..." I said, "I suppose that's it. Better be off," and made for the front door.

The bolts were already drawn back. The butler lifted the latch and pulled. Outside, the Hillman was waiting at the bottom of the steps, and in no time I had the suitcase loaded. I got aboard and wound down the window. "Good-bye, Mould. Thank you for looking after me."

"You're welcome, Sir," he replied from the doorway.

I pressed the ignition button. The engine sprang to life, and with a wave of the hand I was on my way home.

❧

The End
&
The Beginning

❧